Microsoft SQL Azure: Enterprise Application Development

Build enterprise-ready applications and projects with SQL Azure

Jayaram Krishnaswamy

BIRMINGHAM - MUMBAI

Microsoft SQL Azure: Enterprise Application Development

First published: December 2010

Production Reference: 1031210

Published by Packt Publishing Ltd.

32 Lincoln Road

Olton

Birmingham, B27 6PA, UK.

ISBN 978-1-849680-80-6

www.packtpub.com

Cover Image by David Guettirrez (bilbaorocker@yahoo.co.uk)

Credits

Author
Jayaram Krishnaswamy

Reviewers
Maarten Balliauw

Siddharth Mehta

Acquisition Editor
Kerry George

Development Editor
Swapna Verlekar

Technical Editors
Arun Nadar

Bianca Sequeira

Copy Editor
Laxmi Subramanian

Indexer
Rekha Nair

Editorial Team Leader
Aditya Belpathak

Project Team Leader
Ashwin Shetty

Project Coordinator
Zainab Bagasrawala

Proofreaders
Jacqueline McGhee

Linda Morris

Graphics
Geetanjali Sawant

Production Coordinator
Alwin Roy

Cover Work
Alwin Roy

About the Author

Jayaram Krishnaswamy studied at the Indian Institute of Science in Bangalore, India, and at the Madras University in India and taught at the Indian Institute of Technology in Madras. He went to Japan on a Japanese Ministry of Education Research scholarship to complete his PhD in Electrical Engineering from Nagoya University. He was a Postdoctoral Fellow at Sydney University in Australia, a Government of India, Senior Scientific Officer at the Indian Institute of Science in Bangalore, and the Indian Institute of Technology at Kanpur. He was a visiting scientist at the Eindhoven Institute of Technology in Netherlands, a visiting professor of Physics at the Federal University in Brazil, an Associate Research Scientist at a government laboratory in Sao Jose dos Campos in Sao Paulo, Brazil, a visiting scientist at the National Research Council in Ottawa, Canada, before coming to USA in 1985. He has also taught and worked at the Colorado State University in Fort Collins and North Carolina State University in Raleigh, North Carolina. He worked with Northrop Grumman Corporation on a number of projects related to high energy electron accelerators/Free Electron Lasers. These projects were undertaken at the Brookhaven National Laboratory in Long Island, New York and in the Physics Department at Princeton University, New Jersey. He has over 80 publications in refereed and non-refereed publications and eight issued patents. He is fluent in Japanese and Portuguese and lives in Plainsboro, New Jersey, USA. He is also an affiliate of the IEEE Computer Society and a member of the American Physical Society.

He has been working in IT related fields since 1997. He was once a Microsoft Certified Trainer in Networking and a Siebel Certified Developer. He has worked with several IT related companies, such as the Butler International in their Siebel practice; with several IBM subcontractors and smaller companies. Presently, he is active in writing technical articles in the IT field to many online sites, such as CodeProject.com, APSFree.com, DevShed.com, DevArticles.com, OfficeUsers.org, ASPAlliance.com, Egghead Café, SSWUG.org, Packt Article Network, databasedev. co.uk, cimaware.com, and many others. Between 2006 and 2010 he wrote more than 400 articles mostly related to database and web-related technologies covering Microsoft, Oracle, Sybase, ColdFusion, Sun, and other vendor products.

He has also written two Microsoft Business Intelligence related books for Packt Publishing. He regularly writes to his four blogs on Blogger; `http://hodentek.blogspot.com`. `http://hodentekHelp.blogspot.com`, `http://hodentekMSSS.blogspot.com`, and `http://hodentekMobile.blogspot.com`. He recently received Microsoft's *Microsoft Community Contributor* award for 2011.

Acknowledgement

I would like to thank Packt Publishing for giving me this opportunity to write a book, for a third time, and their continuing encouragement. Kerry George, the Senior Acquisition Editor for enterprise books — my early contact for this book — was most helpful and without her guidance and meticulous editing, this book would not have been possible. I am most grateful for her advice, which she gave generously at every step of the way.

I would like to thank Zainab Bagasrawala, the Project Coordinator for having monitored the flow of correspondence successfully and for her timely reminders. I also would like to thank Swapna Verlekar the Development Editor of this book for her valuable input and pointers, which has added great value to the book. I would also like to record the help of others who helped at various stages of this book including Arun Nadar with the prefinal edits, Bianca Sequeira for more edits, both of whom worked on the Appendix collecting and testing all the links in the book, and Maitreya Bhakal, in addition to many others at Packt Publishing. I also would like to thank Priya Mukherji, the Project Manager at Packt Publishing for guiding me through the contract process, the very first step in writing this book. I thank my son for reading through the initial chapter and making suggestions and picking out errors.

I sincerely thank the reviewers Siddharth Mehta and Maarten Baillauw, Microsoft MVP who meticulously went through the book and provided very valuable advice. They both have added great value to the book. Their pointed questions and well directed advice has made portions of this book more readable and clearer, and I am most thankful to them.

I would like to thank my parents who would have shared my joy. I thank my brothers and sisters, and the whole-hearted support of our Subbagiri family. I cannot sufficiently thank my wife Michiko Fukumoto, my son Krishna Jayaram, and his wife Jannet Jayaram for their continuous encouragement.

Last but not the least, I would like to thank Microsoft Corporation for making evaluation software available and allowing me to participate in their various events, live as well as on the web, including the boot camp. I am most indebted to the MSDN forums specially related to Windows Azure and SQL Azure and their moderators and mentors from whom I have received unstinted support. I also would like to thank Neudesic for allowing me to participate in their boot camp as well as the numerous third-party vendors whose evaluation software has added value to the book

About the Reviewers

Maarten Balliauw has a Bachelor's degree in Software Engineering and has about eight years of experience in software development. He started his career while he was still studying, when he founded a company doing web development in PHP and ASP.NET. After graduation, he sold his shares and joined one of the largest ICT companies in Belgium, RealDolmen, where he continued web application development in ASP.NET and application lifecycle management in Visual Studio Team System. He is a Microsoft Certified Technology Specialist in ASP.NET and Most Valuable Professional (MVP) ASP.NET, and works with the latest Microsoft technologies such as LINQ and ASP.NET 3.5, and has published many articles in both PHP and .NET literature such as MSDN magazine Belgium and PHP architect. Maarten is a frequent speaker at various national and international events.

Blog: http://blog.maartenballiauw.be

E-mail: maarten@maartenballiauw.be

Twitter: http://twitter.com/maartenballiauw

Maarten wrote the book *ASP.NET MVC 1.0 Quickly* with Packt Publishing.

Siddharth Mehta is a Business Intelligence professional, and presently works in Mumbai for Capgemini India Pvt. Ltd. (BIM Business Unit) in the capacity of a Senior Consultant. He generally serves as a Technical/Design Lead and works majorly on data warehousing projects involving Microsoft BI. He has a key interest and insight in developing solutions using cloud-based business intelligence design, and he has been working with SQL Azure right from the time of its evolution.

He started his career in 2002 with Visual Basic and SQL Server and since then he has been majorly working with SQL Server, Business Intelligence-related technologies, and Microsoft .NET. He has worked globally (India, US, Singapore, and London) on various domains for his employers to serve multinational corporations like CitiBank, Walt Disney Pictures and Television, Allegis Group, Transport for London, and others.

Siddharth is also a BI author, and has authored various articles on community sites such as MSSQLTips.com, SQLServerCentral.com, SQL-Server-Performance.com, and others. He also authored a whitepaper for MSDN, titled *Bulk Report generation using SSIS and SSRS 2008 R2*. He has been awarded Capgemini India Envoy Award for the financial year 2010 for his contributions to the technical community by his authoring. He shares his insight on technical subjects through his blog: http://siddhumehta.blogspot.com.

My biggest thanks to my parents — Divya and Kaushik and my brother Rahul for their immense support while I was busy reviewing this book.

www.PacktPub.com

Support files, eBooks, discount offers and more

You might want to visit www.PacktPub.com for support files and downloads related to your book.

Did you know that Packt offers eBook versions of every book published, with PDF and ePub files available? You can upgrade to the eBook version at www.PacktPub.com and as a print book customer, you are entitled to a discount on the eBook copy. Get in touch with us at service@packtpub.com for more details.

At www.PacktPub.com, you can also read a collection of free technical articles, sign up for a range of free newsletters and receive exclusive discounts and offers on Packt books and eBooks.

http://PacktLib.PacktPub.com

Do you need instant solutions to your IT questions? PacktLib is Packt's online digital book library. Here, you can access, read and search across Packt's entire library of books.

Why Subscribe?

- Fully searchable across every book published by Packt
- Copy and paste, print and bookmark content
- On demand and accessible via web browser

Free Access for Packt account holders

If you have an account with Packt at www.PacktPub.com, you can use this to access PacktLib today and view nine entirely free books. Simply use your login credentials for immediate access.

Table of Contents

Preface

The arrival of Cloud Services has been a defining moment for enterprises, small businesses, and the public sector. The landscape is changing from moment to moment. Although Microsoft entered this arena a little late, it made up for lost time by making an immense effort by building its mega data centers around the world. In handling this new business strategy, Microsoft hoisted its entire software powerhouse, honed and built over the years, on to the cloud one after another and is continuing to do so.

When I agreed to write this book, I was thinking that this will be yet another book on SQL Server, and when I finished filling so many pages I was satisfied that there indeed was a need. Writing this book started in the first CTP period and posed many challenges, as the Azure platform components including SQL Azure was undergoing rapid changes. You would not fail to notice the impact of some of these changing scenes in the book.

Microsoft SQL Azure: Enterprise Application Development is an outcome of my many years of familiarity with Microsoft data-related products and my recent passionate monitoring of this emerging platform. This book not only covers the various aspects of SQL Azure and SQL Server 2008 R2, but also covers the web application development.

A software's success depends on the tools available to work with it and in this respect SQL Azure already has a large *répertoire* of tools including those from third parties. This book provides a comprehensive list of tools with usage examples. Creating and migrating data are aspects that are inherent for any application as the businesses grow, transform, and scale out. This aspect has been described by including the various strategies.

On the application side, businesses may opt to keep their data as well as their applications on any location they are comfortable with, and with the Cloud as yet another location, the choices have increased, although some choices are more restrictive than others. The book deals with applications and data on different locations and how to handle them. The examples use a reduced data set and are simple but the concept is clear and quite straightforward to extend. Business Intelligence has emerged as a must-have feature of businesses. Some of the aspects of business intelligence as related to SQL Azure are treated in this book using Microsoft's business intelligence stack, the SQL Server Integration Services (SSIS), and the SQL Server Reporting Services (SSRS). Also non-Microsoft languages are not left out in the book as languages such as Java and PHP have garnered worldwide interest and usage. The advent of the mobile platform, which is sure to make a shift in the way businesses are handled, and the reality that they may have to work in a disconnected mode, brings new challenges to businesses — the ability to synchronize data becomes extremely important. Microsoft has provided a robust strategy to make this possible by its synchronization software, which synchronizes data across diverse platforms from handheld to cloud spanning the oceans. The book has examples of how this is carried out using the synchronization technology.

The book covers from the CTP period, including references to the developments taking place up to October 2010, and the projects in incubation. During this period, much has happened and as a consequence some of the links in the book might have moved or broken, some of the program versions might have seen an upgrade; but the core of what is treated in this book should be of considerable value to the reader. Our technical editors bring added value by collecting all the links in the book in a central place to assist the reader looking at a hardcopy.

What is left out was a reference to the recent PDC and readers are encouraged to hear the near future developments in SQL Azure by listening to David Robinson's video on 'What's New in Microsoft SQL Azure?' here: `http://europe.msteched.com/Topic/List`. In closing, the author takes the entire responsibility for errors and omissions and he may be contacted at `jkrishnaswamy@comcast.net`.

What this book covers

Chapter 1, Cloud Computing and Microsoft Azure Services Platform answers important questions such as: Why a business would like to move its business applications and data to the cloud?, What is meant by cloud computing?, and so on. Some significant cloud computing implementations are described including Microsoft Azure.

Chapter 2, SQL Azure Services explains the differences between SQL Server 2008 and SQL Azure. Accessing the SQL Azure Portal, administering a relational database, and creating and modifying objects are described with screenshots and step-by-step guidance to work with many of the tasks, in detail.

Chapter 3, Working with SQL Azure Databases from Visual Studio 2008 describes the architectural details of SQL Azure. It explains the Microsoft data access strategy. You can follow the examples of accessing SQL Azure using Client APIs such as ADO. NET, ODBC, and OLEDB, as well as Server APIs. The secure methods of accessing SQL Azure using these APIs are described in detail.

Chapter 4, SQL Azure Tools provides a comprehensive description of most of the SQL Azure tools. This includes Microsoft Tools, third-party tools, as well as the open source tool, OpenOffice.

Chapter 5, Populating SQL Azure Databases covers transferring data in and out of SQL Azure, to in and out of on-site SQL Servers. This chapter and *Chapter 4* describes about a dozen methods of populating SQL Azure databases using Bulk Copy Program (BCP) to scripting; from migration wizard to data-tier components, and so on.

Chapter 6, SSIS and SSRS Applications using SQL Azure describes how SSIS and SSRS can be used together with SQL Azure, even though these programs are not ported to the cloud as yet. However, in the near future SSRS will be hosted on Windows Azure Platform.

Merging SQL Azure data with on-site data, moving a MySQL database to SQL Azure, creating a report using the SQL Azure database, and ad hoc reporting on SQL Azure data with Report Builder 3, are some of the topics described in this chapter.

Chapter 7, Working with Windows Azure Hosting describes how to host a data-centric application on Windows Azure. This chapter also describes how the SQL Azure database may be used to authenticate users using forms authentication.

Chapter 8, Database Applications on Windows Azure Platform Accessing SQL Server Databases describes with examples, different kinds of data-centric projects that can be hosted on Windows Azure. Ground to Cloud, Cloud to Cloud, and Cloud to ground applications are described with complete examples.

Chapter 9, Synchronizing SQL Azure describes Synchronizing SQL Azure with the SQL Server using the Microsoft SQL Azure Data Sync Tool. Also described are practical examples of synchronizing with SQL Server Compact 3.5 and using SQL Server Data Sync Services.

Chapter 10, Recent Developments describes all the 2010 updates, some with examples. Some of the recent developments include OData services, PowerPivot, Sql Azure security, WebMatrix, accessing SQL Azure with non-Microsoft languages, and many more.

What you need for this book

- Visual Studio 2008 SP1
- Visual Studio 2010 Express
- SQL Server 2008 R2
- SQL Server Express
- Windows Azure Tools
- Windows Azure AppFabric
- Account for using Windows Azure Services
- IIS 7

Who this book is for

If you are a .NET developer, an architect, or a DBA who wants to develop enterprise applications and projects and extend your on-site skills with SQL Azure, then this book is for you.

This book does not assume any experience in Windows Azure or SQL Azure, nor is a high level of competency in SQL Server or the .NET Framework and associated technology required. However, a basic understanding of Visual Studio, C#, VB, SQL Servers, XML, web, and WCF is required. If you decide to work with SQL Azure, then this book will provide you with the most up-to-date and practical information.

Conventions

In this book, you will find a number of styles of text that distinguish between different kinds of information. Here are some examples of these styles, and an explanation of their meaning.

Code words in text are shown as follows: "The server-related views: `sys.sql_logins` and `sys.databases` can be used to review logins and databases."

A block of code is set as follows:

```
Initial Catalog=Bluesky
```

```
Data Source=tcp:Your Server Name.database.windows.net
User ID=Your Project Name @Your Server Name
Password=Your Password;
Trusted_Connection=False
Encrypt=True
```

When we wish to draw your attention to a particular part of a code block, the relevant lines or items are set in bold:

```
Provider = SQLNCLI10.1;
Server = tcp:Your Server Name.database.windows.net;
Database = Bluesky;
UID= Your Project Name @ Your Server Name;
Password = Your Password;
```

Any command-line input or output is written as follows:

```
C:\Windows\Microsoft.NET\Framework\v2.0.50727>aspnet_regsql /?
```

New terms and **important words** are shown in bold. Words that you see on the screen, in menus or dialog boxes for example, appear in the text like this: "Click on the **Next** button".

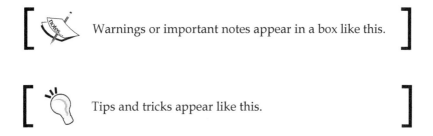

Warnings or important notes appear in a box like this.

Tips and tricks appear like this.

Reader feedback

Feedback from our readers is always welcome. Let us know what you think about this book—what you liked or may have disliked. Reader feedback is important for us to develop titles that you really get the most out of.

To send us general feedback, simply send an e-mail to feedback@packtpub.com, and mention the book title via the subject of your message.

If there is a book that you need and would like to see us publish, please send us a note in the **SUGGEST A TITLE** form on www.packtpub.com or e-mail suggest@packtpub.com.

If there is a topic that you have expertise in and you are interested in either writing or contributing to a book, see our author guide on www.packtpub.com/authors.

Customer support

Now that you are the proud owner of a Packt book, we have a number of things to help you to get the most from your purchase.

> **Downloading the example code for this book**
>
> You can download the example code files for all Packt books you have purchased from your account at http://www.PacktPub.com. If you purchased this book elsewhere, you can visit http://www.PacktPub.com/support and register to have the files e-mailed directly to you.

Errata

Although we have taken every care to ensure the accuracy of our content, mistakes do happen. If you find a mistake in one of our books—maybe a mistake in the text or the code—we would be grateful if you would report this to us. By doing so, you can save other readers from frustration and help us improve subsequent versions of this book. If you find any errata, please report them by visiting http://www.packtpub.com/support, selecting your book, clicking on the **errata submission form** link, and entering the details of your errata. Once your errata are verified, your submission will be accepted and the errata will be uploaded on our website, or added to any list of existing errata, under the Errata section of that title. Any existing errata can be viewed by selecting your title from http://www.packtpub.com/support.

Piracy

Piracy of copyright material on the Internet is an ongoing problem across all media. At Packt, we take the protection of our copyright and licenses very seriously. If you come across any illegal copies of our works, in any form, on the Internet, please provide us with the location address or website name immediately so that we can pursue a remedy.

Please contact us at copyright@packtpub.com with a link to the suspected pirated material.

We appreciate your help in protecting our authors, and our ability to bring you valuable content.

Questions

You can contact us at questions@packtpub.com if you are having a problem with any aspect of the book, and we will do our best to address it.

1

Cloud Computing and Microsoft Azure Services Platform

This book is about one of the components of the Windows Azure Platform that provides support for a relational database in the Cloud. However, as it is a component of a more comprehensive, larger system it is essential to understand how it is positioned *in relation to* the Windows Azure Platform. In addition to introducing the larger picture, the book also describes how Windows Azure cloud applications access and leverage relational data; how the business intelligence applications interact with the cloud-hosted relational data; how the relational database provides support for authenticating web clients; how the cloud and ground-based relational databases can be accessed from ground (on-site) as well as cloud applications, and many others.

The book, therefore, begins with an introduction to cloud computing as it is generally spoken about by reviewing the most popular cloud offerings and more specifically introduces the main components of Windows Azure Platform. Also included in this chapter is a section that you will need to go through before you access the Windows Azure Platform services.

In this chapter, we will look at the motivation for cloud computing. We will discuss the following:

- What is cloud computing?
- Why a business would like to move its business applications and data to the cloud
- Types of cloud services

- The hybrid cloud
- How cloud computing is implemented with examples of some major cloud computing vendors
- Windows Azure

What is cloud computing?

Cloud computing is still evolving and perhaps one of the more enduring, all embracing, definition of cloud computing may be defined according to the NIST (`http://csrc.nist.gov/nice/states/maryland/posters/cloud-computing.pdf`) as follows:

> *"Cloud computing is a model for enabling convenient, on-demand network access to a shared pool of configurable computing resources that can be rapidly provisioned and released with minimal management effort or service provider interaction."*

The resources, as it is implied here, would include not only the hardware but also the software that cloud computing would use.

The industry watchdog Gartner (`http://www.gartner.com/it/page.jsp?id=1035013`) on the other hand defines cloud computing as follows:

> *"Cloud computing is a style of computing where scalable and elastic IT-enabled capabilities are delivered as a service to external customers using Internet technologies."*

Why a business would like to move its business applications and data to the cloud

Economic and business considerations have persuaded businesses to move to the next level of productivity with economically valuable features such as extensibility, agility, elasticity, and security. Availability of such a resource removes the constraints from maintaining an in-house infrastructure (Hardware, Software, and IT manpower) and, therefore, brings in great business value. It also enables businesses with meager resources to concentrate their effort in developing their business rather than getting concerned about the resources.

The "Cloud" vendors aggregate all their resources at data centers, which they can maintain and make them available to businesses on a subscription basis. Recognizing early on, the importance of this cloud-based business paradigm, companies such as Amazon.com (`http://aws.amazon.com/`); Google (`http://www.google.com/apps/intl/en/business/index.html`); SalesForce.com (`http://www.salesforce.com/`) and a few others jumped into this business model and implemented applications offered from the cloud. Although all of them were 'Cloud' offerings, they meant different things as seen in their implementation. The single feature that is basic to all implementations in the cloud is the highly flexible, highly agile, highly virtualized (Servers, storage, and many more), and automated hardware capable of being created on the fly with a high degree of redundancy accessible by a very fast network.

As seen recently, businesses have started liking the flexibility of cloud services related to optimum resource utilization with virtually no overheads; with minimum support personnel and, therefore, smaller payroll expenses; smaller real estate commitment, and the ability to rescind in case of an emergent economic or financial crisis. One of the factors that still deter businesses to go all out for cloud computing perhaps, is security concerns.

Types of cloud services

There are several types of cloud implementations and they sharply differ from on-premises services in that the resources are shared by more than one party or business. Some of the most popular and widely known services are of the following types:

Infrastructure as a Service (IaaS)

This is strictly using the infrastructure where you access storage and virtual servers in the cloud. The storage and servers are of the industry standard, which you can add or remove depending on your requirements (your load characteristics).

Platform as a Service (PaaS)

Here, Platform on the cloud is where you execute the application. You use the platform specific programming API. The provider completely supports the maintenance of programs, diagnostic and monitoring, and so on—a one stop service for all web-based applications.

Software as a Service (SaaS)

In this case, users don't own the software but rent it. Users also don't concern themselves with the maintenance of the program or the servers on which it is hosted.

Some examples of SaaS are the Sales Force automation, financial services, content management, and collaboration. However, content management is also supported on vendors who are typically IaaS and PaaS providers.

The hybrid cloud

In the hybrid, it is not entirely cloud that is hosting the applications, a part of hardware and software also exists on premises. There are various implementations of this and it is customizable.

While Security and Privacy are some of the concerns, the round-the-clock availability and performance are the most attractive features. Looking into the near future, cloud appliances will make their debut, which offers a packaged 'mini-cloud' to enterprises to host cloud applications to address some of the security and privacy-related concerns. With the cloud appliance the complete infrastructure is under lock and key and owned by the enterprise without the security concerns of a cloud service.

How does Microsoft Azure Cloud offering measure up? From what you will read further on, you will notice that Microsoft Windows Azure not only provides the agile infrastructure at its globally dispersed data centers and its Windows Azure Platform OS but it also provides a scalable relational database. Azure AppFabric provides support for security and privacy as well as hybrid applications. Microsoft is also moving forward with Windows Azure Appliances (review this link: `http://www.microsoft.com/windowsazure/appliance/`) for private Windows Azure Cloud systems that run on user data centers. The Windows Azure platform is, therefore, all of IaaS, PaaS, and SaaS bundled into an integrated offering.

How cloud computing is implemented with examples of some major cloud computing vendors

The implementations described here are not the only ones. Lots of major events (both public and private) are happening bringing more and more players including the US Government (Read about **Apps.gov** here: `http://www.informationweek.com/blog/main/archives/2009/11/uncle_sams_2442.html;jsessionid=UIWZYUIKFN J1LQE1GHPSKHWATMY32JVN?queryText=app.gov`), to the field as this line is written. The implementations described here are highlighted just to indicate how different the cloud offerings could be, and show the paths they have pursued.

Amazon Web Services

Amazon Web Services through its Amazon Elastic Compute Cloud (EC2) offered customers dynamically scaled computer infrastructure for running their application programs, thus offering *infrastructure as a service*. The term elastic came about by the ease with which the user can create, launch, and terminate the active virtual server instances used in running the programs. To be elastic there was built-in redundancy in the resources and automated scaling, which tracked the load.

Also, to cater to wide-scale adoption, there were a number of sizes the users could choose; from small instances to High-CPU extra-large instances. The applications could run on a computing platform that the customer can choose from, which can be accessed by a web service (one of many Amazon Web Services). Although, EC2 supported Linux operating system in the beginning, it rapidly added other platforms such as Open Solaris and Solaris Express Community Edition and even Windows. By adding Windows OS (2003 and 2008 Servers) it provided full support for all Microsoft applications (ASP.NET, AJAX, Silverlight, and so on) to be hosted on EC2 with data originating in SQL Server Express and SQL Server 2008 server (`http://aws.amazon.com/windows/`) instances. EC2 by itself had only temporary storage for data but later added Simple Storage Service (S3) and Elastic Block storage (EBS) for persisting data (`http://news.cnet.com/8301-10784_3-9917948-7.html`).

The 'Elasticity' of this cloud computing was further enhanced by Elastic IP, Elastic-load balancing, and a reliable monitoring service in the form of Amazon Cloud Watch. Most recently, Amazon added a *relational database as a service* (`http://aws.amazon.com/rds/`) by adding MySQL to its roster of web service offerings, accessible by simple API calls, which could work with EC2.

SalesForce.com

Force.com (`Salesforce.com`) has a secure, reliable, and fast cloud infrastructure spanning two continents with more than 60,000 businesses running a myriad of applications. This was a model of *Software as a Service*. Whereas, the keyword to describe Amazon Web Services was 'elastic', the keyword here is 'real-time'.

SalesForce.com has a multitenant architecture with tenants sharing a single copy of the program customized to their specific needs. It has an ISO 27001 security certification, which is trusted by financial and health services; reliable data centers with backup and disaster recovery plans; high scalability, real-time query optimizer, real-time status information, and real-time upgrades. The sharing model allows companies on Salesforce to communicate and share data with each other leveraging the multitenant, single core architecture. Reliability is increased with a redundant network bone.

Furthermore, Force.com (SalesForce) allows integration of almost anything with anything that includes most vendor products such as Google, Oracle, Twitter, Microsoft, and many more to mention just a few. Although it is possible to build custom applications, there is also the AppExchange, which provides hundreds of pre-built business components that can be used without reinventing the wheel. Force.com (SalesForce) also provides components for bridging with other clouds such as Amazon Web Services, Google AppEngine, and others.

For development purposes a sandbox environment is available, which can be created with a single-click. It boasts of programmable UI's, programmable logic, website development, real-time analytics, and so on. Video demos can be viewed here: `http://www.salesforce.com/platform/cloud-platform/database.jsp`.

Google

Google's App Engine (`http://code.google.com/appengine/`) Platform leverages Google's infrastructure to run Google's web *applications as a Service*. The configuration allows public as well as authenticated access to these resources. The tagline is "easy to build, easy to maintain, easy to scale". The Google App Engine's infrastructure handles all of the storage, distribution, replication, load balancing, and a few more. All of these activities are accessible by a simple API. The platform supports a powerful query engine as well as transactional processing support, key elements for commerce. The programming languages supported are python and java runtime but any language that uses a JVM-based interpreter or compiler (JavaScript, Ruby) can be used.

The storage of data is not in a relational database and therefore, SQL is not used but a Google Specific Query Language (GQL) is (`http://code.google.com/appengine/docs/python/datastore/gqlreference.html`). The nice thing about the Google model is you can get started for free with some 500MB of storage with enough bandwidth to serve a couple of million page views a month (as advertised). Even using the paid service is on pay-per-use basis. It also has an authenticating and e-mailing service as well as providing a local developmental environment.

Microsoft

Microsoft entered this area relatively late but directed a lot of its effort to branch out into this important business area very quickly and thus Microsoft Azure was born. The Microsoft Azure platform in Microsoft Data Centers spans three continents North America, Europe, and East Asia. Microsoft Azure not only makes available this humongous infrastructure but also provides its signature software products; Windows Servers; SQL Server; and components of .NET Framework. It is, therefore, both *infrastructure and software as service*. It is, in fact, heading towards offering its entire *framework as service*. Framework as a service would offer not only the extensibility of the platform for years to come but also leverages the regular enhancements made to the framework on which the Windows Azure is based. On the downside one gets locked into proprietary service.

The Azure platform is resting on three pillars, the Windows Azure Services, the SQL Azure Services, and Azure AppFabric. The Azure platform not only caters to cloud-based applications but also to applications that run on premises. Services that run part in the cloud and part on-premises are called hybrid services and the Azure Platform lends itself easily to create such services. The Azure platform is structured to be developer-friendly, and can be leveraged by desktop, web, and mobile devices using many of the programming languages such as PHP, Ruby, and so on in addition to Microsoft's VB, C#, and F#. As the software programs that work with the Azure platform are not limited to those that are Microsoft-Specific, the adaptability is much more general. As the accessibility uses Open Internet standards, clients can be on any platform. The main concerns that are being looked into are related to security and privacy as for any of the cloud offerings, however there are many ways the Windows Azure platform is made secure using encrypted transport, firewalls, and so on. Identity verification and user access based on Security Assertion Markup Language (SAML) tokens mitigate some of these concerns. However, for the hardcore control freaks Microsoft is offering the Windows Azure Appliance where security is now the user's concern.

More in-depth discussion of security is described in the following video, which is a must if you want to understand how Windows Azure security looks under the hood (http://technet.microsoft.com/en-us/edge/security-talk-windows-azure-security-a-peek-under-the-hood.aspx?query=1).

Review the case study of a late 2009 implemented business solution using Microsoft Azure components at: http://www.microsoft.com/casestudies/Case_Study_Detail.aspx?CaseStudyID=4000005882.

Also review this note about small business profiting by moving to cloud, http://howto.techworld.com/sme/3211586/how-to-move-your-small-business-to-the-cloud/.

On a practical footing, the Azure Platform, its hardware and software are physically located in the various Microsoft data centers: http://news.cnet.com/8301-10805_3-10277976-75.html.

Even as the various cloud paradigms (IaaS, PaaS, and SaaS) were developing, cloud computing has evolved to produce more varied patterns. Private clouds have emerged to satisfy the special requirements of certain industries (http://cloudstoragestrategy.com/2009/03/bechtel-harnesses-the-cloud-a-case-study-in-service-delivery.html) and even Microsoft will be launching its Windows Azure Appliance to address that possible growth area.

The following table shows at a glance some of the differences between the cloud offerings by these vendors:

Feature	Amazon	Google	Microsoft	SalesForce(Force.com)
Name	AWS	GAE (Google AppEngine)	Windows Azure	salesforce.com
Genre	Infrastructure as Service (EC2) IaaS	Application as Service AaaS	Platform as Service PaaS *Future ITaaS	Software as Service SaaS

Feature	Amazon	Google	Microsoft	SalesForce(Force. com)
Status of business	Strong on traffic patterns and metrics Recently added some free services for limited periods	Small to enterprise, also some free services with limited access to resources	Presently developers and small businesses	Over 60000 users (at the beginning of this writing) health care and Financial
Target	Those who are yearning for hardware resources and manage their software including programming	Free to start and pay as you go. Small to big businesses such as eBay.	Small Business but appears Enterprise end is waiting at door step	Enterprise as well as Small Business
Motivation	Derive revenue from its (AMZN) Capacity and more	Enhance revenue from Ads. Push Ads revenue idea to App Builders	Move Office, SharePoint, and .NET Framework	
Database support	MySQL Amazon SimpleDB Amazon Relational Database Services SQL Server 2008 SQL Express	Non-relational distributed data storage with query engine and transaction support Gmail query language	SQL Azure relational data storage and Storage Service for non-relational data. Tools to migrate MySQL and MS Access are presently available and Fox Pro may be added in the future.	Force.com object-based database using APEX language.
Development Environment	Free to choose, Eclipse Platform, .NET	Full featured web-based AppEngine simulated environment on developers' computer	Windows Azure simulated sandbox environment on developers' computer with almost 90 percent of full features using Visual Studio	Single-click Sandbox for development using Eclipse IDE

Feature	Amazon	Google	Microsoft	SalesForce(Force. com)
Programming Language Support	Ruby, Python, or Java (jar)	Java, Python, and any language supported by JVM	.NET languages (VB,C#,F#), Ruby, Java, PHP, and Perl	Most of the programming languages
Platform	Linux/UNIX, SUSE Linux, Windows Server, or Amazon VPC.	Not very much known about hardware	Windows Server 2008	APEX code, VisualForce using traditional MVC paradigm.

- ITaaS combines IaaS, PaaS, and SaaS, review this link: `http://www. cloudcentered.com/microsoft-confirms-again-that-azure-will-have`

Windows Azure

In the following sections, a summary of the Windows Azure Platform details are described. The hardware system at the Microsoft Data Centers provides the physical support for all the programs and activities, and the software architecture is built on this resource.

Azure platform details

The Azure platform is a collection of services shown in the following image that operate in the cloud and orchestrate to provide businesses with an integrated set of programs that improve and enhance their business. The following image shows the three components of the Windows Azure Platform:

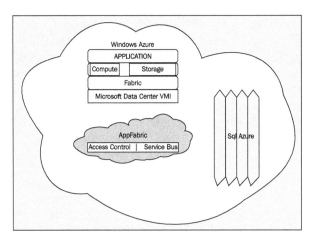

Businesses develop their application on their site in a simulated cloud environment, which may be compared with how you develop web applications on the development web server and then deploy it over an internet connection. End users access these applications on the cloud using familiar internet protocols such as SOAP, HTTP, REST, and more. Prior to February 2010, when the Windows Azure Platform was open to the public, the operating system changed over from CTP to Guest Operating System 1.0. Since then many updates to the operating system have been made as shown in the following table taken from Microsoft documentation at this URL `http://msdn.microsoft.com/en-us/library/ee924680.aspx`.

Guest OS	Release date
Windows Azure Guest OS 1.6 (Release 201008-01)	September 1, 2010
Windows Azure Guest OS 1.5 (Release 201006-01)	July 20, 2010
Windows Azure Guest OS 1.4 (Release 201005-01)	June 17, 2010
Windows Azure Guest OS 1.3 (Release 201004-01)	April 30, 2010
Windows Azure Guest OS 1.2 (Release 201003-01)	April 5, 2010
Windows Azure Guest OS 1.1 (Release 201001-01)	January 30, 2010
Windows Azure Guest OS 1.0 (Release 200912-01)	December 7, 2009

However, in order to develop for the cloud you also need the appropriate software development kit (SDK). Not every release of OS has an associated SDK. The SDKs released as of this writing and the appropriate OS for which the SDK can be used is shown in this table from the same documentation. Windows Azure SDKs provide the software support for running the development fabric (a mini version with most features of the application running on the cloud platform) on the local (on-site) machine and the development server.

Windows Azure SDK version	Compatible Windows Azure operating system releases
Windows Azure SDK version 1.2 (June 2010)	Guest OS 1.3 or newer
Windows Azure SDK version 1.1 (February 2010)	Guest OS 1.1 or newer
Windows Azure SDK version 1.0 (November 2009)	Guest OS 1.0 or newer

The Azure platform is accessible from programs in the cloud as well as from on-premises applications. In this sense, it works seamlessly between what the businesses have on their premises and those they have implemented, or propose to implement, in the cloud. In order to maximize the ROI and commensurate with their security needs, the businesses may move their data and applications, whole, or in part to the cloud. The present trend appears to be that the businesses move their less serious data initially when they buy into the cloud platform; and as they get more comfortable and gain confidence with the platform, move their applications and data to the cloud.

While security and reliability are of utmost concern to most businesses the most alluring features of "Cloud Computing" is the ease and rapidity with which a business on the internet can be installed. These concerns (outages, hacking, malware, and data loss) are making businesses refrain from large scale adoption according to several polls. Another preoccupation of business is to do with how customer data is stored. When the business removes data from its cloud application for whatever reason, what surety do they have that all of their data is completely removed without a trace? In order to satisfy the round the clock availability, the data is replicated to many locations in the data center, sometimes even to geographically separated locations. For small businesses however it appears to be an excellent fit where economic returns are tangible.

While all security concerns have not been addressed to the satisfaction of the users several major measures are implemented in the form of forms authentication for both Azure Table Storage and SQL Azure and enabling SSL with a self-signed certificate on Windows Azure. Also Microsoft has implemented comprehensive security measures for all physical security-related issues at its data centers.

The Platform hardware is housed in the various Microsoft Global Hosting Data Centers (see for example:http://www.datacenterknowledge.com/archives/category/microsoft/, also http://www.computerworld.com/s/article/9118190/Ozzie_details_Azure_Microsoft_s_cloud_version_of_Windows) with two in USA and one each in East Asia and Europe. The data centers are large installations (tens to hundreds of thousands of square foot area) with containerized hardware comprising of more than 2000 servers and other needed network interfaces. The infrastructure consists of Virtual Machines running Windows Servers 2008 provided by a Microsoft modified Hyper-V-based hypervisor. When a developer desires to host an application, the VMs get provisioned. User code gets into these VMs and users interact with the VMs using the internet. An excellent reference to some of the hardware details are found in this reference: http://whitepapers.techrepublic.com.com/thankyou.aspx?&tag=content;leftCol&docid=972383&view=972383&load=1&regSrc=wp&authId=ynwzchQWj6So7PJTwBg6rhE0o0VIkE8N2rj+2Ss6Rdz47retSuySS1C+kCljTZba.

Platform components

As previously mentioned, the Microsoft Azure platform URL accessible through its portal, using Windows Live Login, consists of the three components, which will be discussed later in this chapter. The details of accessing the portal are described later in the chapter.

In the next section, an overview of each of the three components is described. For the purposes of this book, the Windows Azure Service, which consists of the Compute and Storage items and the AppFabric are only tangential, as the emphasis of this book is on SQL Azure. However, these components will be addressed in the later chapters with some more detail so far as they are used for creating web-facing applications using SQL Azure, or on-premises SQL Servers.

Windows Azure

As described previously, Microsoft Data Centers contain the clusters of Windows Server 2008 (64 bit), which are virtualized to provide the Virtual Machine Images (Cloud Virtual Machines), which in turn hosts the User Code and Runtime APIs. These are accessed through the portal using the Service Management Service (a REST-based Service). In addition to compute VM clusters, the data center also hosts Storage Clusters for the storage service. These are also accessible through Representational State Transfer (REST), a new client-server software architecture built on transfer of resource representations. The developers using Visual Studio 2008 SP1 and Visual Studio 2010, presently in Beta 2 (VS 2010 will be available during 2010), and the Windows Azure SDKs as mentioned previously need Windows Azure Visual Tools: `http://www.microsoft.com/downloads/details.aspx?familyid=6967FF37-813E-47C7-B987-889124B43ABD&displaylang=en`. The servers hosting SQL Azure Services are separate from the ones used for the Compute and Storage Services.

Compute: Windows Azure Hosting Service

The Windows Azure Service, as you will be seeing later in Exercise 1.2, consists of components called roles enclosed within a service boundary built with managed code. This is where your executable program is hosted using this role-based model.

By design, it is mandated that the service should have at least one role. There are two kinds of roles; the Web Role, supported by IIS7 and ASP.NET, is well suited for web-applications defining a single HTTP/HTTPS endpoint for external clients and a Worker Role for running background programs. The storage service, the other component, can be accessed by the worker role to feed data to the web role. An application hosted on Windows Azure can have more than one role of each kind and a service hosted on Windows Azure can run multiple instances of these roles. The Azure Platform can replicate these across multiple virtual machine images. From an external location the service is reachable by a single Virtual IP Address (VIP) for load-balanced traffic to multiple end points.

The web role to worker role communication takes place through internal endpoints over TCP and HTTP shown schematically in the following figure:

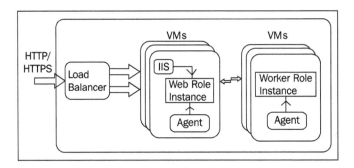

While the previous figure shows the constituent parts of the compute service, the application is developed using Visual Studio at the user's premises. Visual Studio is the main programming IDE used. The SDKs provide the necessary hook ups to the Cloud Simulation and a number of different kinds of application templates (ASP. NET Web Application, WCF Service, Web Service, and more). The tools are needed for the application to be run in the development fabric (the program that simulates the Cloud environment locally on the premises) with the support of a locally installed IIS 7 server.

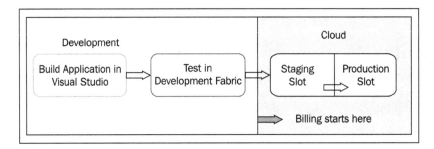

Typically, applications are developed in Visual Studio and tested in the simulated development environment followed by deployment. In the development process the development fabric comes into play and this is where 'debugging' of the application can be done effectively. The user will also have access to development user interface and a development local storage. The deployment can be a two-step process with an initial deployment to a **Staging Slot** (a client-specific staging URL) followed by a Public or web-facing URL, the **Production Slot**. After deployment, logging the messages is the only way available for developers to track the application.

The billing for the Windows Azure-hosted service starts whenever an application is hosted irrespective of whether it is in Production or Staging, irrespective of whether it is stopped or active. If you don't want to be billed you delete the application. In order to delete you must first stop it. In fact the Windows Azure Portal posts a warning to this effect.

Windows Azure storage

You need to get a storage account to work with Windows Azure Storage. Cloud-hosted applications use client data stored in Storage Accounts, and/or relational data in the SQL Azure. The Storage Account accessed by the Storage Service API, which as mentioned previously, is REST-based. You manipulate data in the Storage Service using POST, PUT, and DELETE requests and retrieve using GET. SQL. Azure data, on the other hand, is accessed by both applications as well as on-premises SQL Servers using T-SQL and ADO.NET. Users can access this Azure Storage Service from within an application running in Windows Azure, or directly from the internet by sending HTTP/HTTPS (version 1.0 for some operations and HTTP/HTTPS 1.1) requests and processing the returned responses.

Users should make sure of the storage service version they will be using by looking it up here: `http://msdn.microsoft.com/en-us/library/dd894041.aspx`. Just as in the case of hosted services, a development storage service is provided for local testing to simulate cloud storage service using local SQL Express servers (default 2005 or 2008 versions) or any local instance of SQL Server.

The following figure shows the components of the Windows Azure Storage. The Windows Azure Drive was added on Feb 1, 2009 which writes to Page blobs. The Windows Azure Drive makes it easier to migrate applications to the cloud as it appears as another durable disk drive. For applications that use file I/0 the disk availability provides a high degree of flexibility using the standard Windows NTFS APIs.

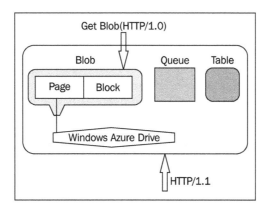

The Storage Account you hold is the top element in the namespace, which is accessed with authentication. The REST API exposes the storage account as a resource consisting of:

- BLOBS—Stores Text and Binary data
  - Block blobs for streaming
  - Page Blobs for random read/write operations organized in containers

- Queues—Stores unlimited 8KB sized messages
  - Messages accessible to storage account holder
  - Messages added to the end of the queue and retrieved from the front of the queue

- Tables—Provides structured tables (not relational)
  - Store data as a collection of entities (similar to rows) with a primary key and a set of properties unlike relational databases, which are schema bound
  - Every entity has PartitionKey and RowKey properties handled by the developer and a Timestamp property provided by the server
  - REST API is ADO.NET Data Services Compliant
  - Any number of tables with uniquely identifiable names can be created

- Windows Azure Drive—NTFS Virtual Hard Drive volumes for applications
  - Random read/write to Page Blob up to Page Blob limit of 1 TB
  - Supported by Windows Azure OS version 1.1 or later. Data to drives uploaded/downloaded through Page Blob

SQL Azure

SQL Azure is a relational database built leveraging SQL Server Technology in its latest embodiment—the SQL Server 2008 R2 (version 10.5). SQL Azure services offer a platform for hosting SQL Azure databases in the Windows Azure platform. Users can build web-facing database applications using SQL Azure as the 'cloud end'. In mid-February 2010, SQL Azure was updated with SU1.

Being built on SQL Server technologies and the agile, extensible, scalable data center infrastructure, SQL Azure provides a highly scalable, highly available, multi-tenant database service in the cloud. The ease with which you can create a database is truly amazing as the provisioning is extremely fast as we see later in the book.

The provisioning and management offered by this cloud service abstracts away an important part of how the databases are traditionally installed and managed. In fact many businesses do not need to employ IT professionals who work on the physical (hardware) side of database installation and management. This will be one of the selling points where the ROI is highly perceptible. As the databases are replicated in the cloud with a high degree of redundancy, users need not concern themselves regarding replication issues to the extent they were concerned traditionally. Also with the SQL Server being a mature technology there is a very little learning path to move user data to the cloud. The very familiar T-SQL is supported and the databases created in the cloud can be accessed through familiar tools such as Microsoft SQL Server Management Studio, SQLCMD, and so on.

The SQL Azure service architecture follows the schematic shown in the following figure:

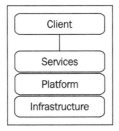

The hardware is installed in the Microsoft Data Centers. SQL Server instances are installed on these machines, which provide the SQL Server and SQL Server Management Services. The SQL Azure hardware is separate from hardware used for Azure Compute and Storage but is shared across all clients. The SQL Azure fabric controller works in the platform layer. The SQL Azure Fabric is a part of the computing system that handles automatic failover, load balancing, and automatic replication between the servers in the data centers. It is, therefore, tightly integrated with the data center infrastructure such as servers, network, and storage. The services layer does most of the provisioning, billing and metering and connection routing. The Services layer is accessed by the Client through the portal using TDS (Tabular Data Stream). Tabular data stream is also accessible through the familiar ODBC and ADO.NET data services. SQL Server applications and tools can access the services layer using TDS but customer applications written in any of the familiar languages such as PHP, Java, and .NET languages can access through ODBC and ADO.NET and through HTTP/REST. These are the same languages that access on-premises SQL Servers; therefore, it makes it very easy to work with SQL Azure.

At present, in addition to SQL Azure, the SQL Azure Data Sync application—based on Microsoft Sync Framework 2.0—provides a useful tool to synchronize SQL Azure data with on-the-premises SQL Server, thus enabling remote access to data on the cloud to mobile clients connecting through remote sites.

Although SQL Server Integration Services, the SQL Server Reporting Services, are not on the cloud, these applications available in the local servers can be used with the cloud-based SQL Azure databases. It is envisaged that these Business Intelligence (BI) applications will also be available in a future version of Microsoft Azure Platform.

Azure AppFabric

The AppFabric addresses the needs of securely accessing widely distributed resources. What used to be called .NET Services in the earlier versions of Windows Azure is now called AppFabric. As you will see later in this chapter, you can access the AppFabric from the Windows Azure Portal (`http://windows.azure.com`) after logging in with your Windows Live ID. It is a service just like the Windows Azure discussed previously.

The AppFabric consists of the Service Bus and Access control. These provide building blocks to .NET Applications to function reliably in the Microsoft Windows Azure platform. The necessity arises because one needs authentication and access to widely distributed resources that programs need, which reside behind machine firewalls and network firewalls. Furthermore, the stateless nature of web applications together with the changeable nature of the hosting environment makes for a loosely connected system requiring a way to manage connections. AppFabric provides these very important functionalities, which are needed for taking applications to the cloud:

- Bidirectional application connectivity through firewalls
- Claims-based access control

The Service Bus "relays" messages from clients to applications running on the premises sidestepping obstacles such as firewalls, NATs, and other objects as shown in the next figure. In this respect, it may be compared to a "relay phone" in the USA, which acts as a relaying point to connect your phone to a phone in another country, for example, a procedure used by Skype. Many Internet chat services work on the same principle of relayed connectivity.

The "Service" opens a bidirectional connection to the "Relay" by an outbound connection and a "Relay Address". The client (Application) connects to this address through an outbound connection. This way the Client can connect to the Service bypassing the barriers. The client application need not know where the service resides. The Service Bus provides a network infrastructure for interconnecting applications using a variety of messaging patterns.

The Service Bus supports the following forms of communication:

- One way messaging
- Request-Response
- Publish-Subscribe (multicast)
- Asynchronous

The security provided by the barriers is in no way compromised. Additionally, the Service Bus can also negotiate for direct connection between applications under some circumstances as in the following image:

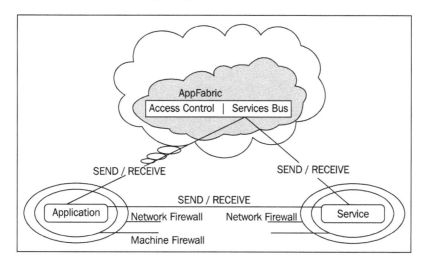

The Service Bus works with Access Control through claims and a trust relationship. Both the client and the service must provide credentials to the Access Control to obtain a security token. Access Control provides a generic way to implement the authentication and authorization (using claims) program separate from applications. This relieves the developers from writing custom authentication and authorization routines and rules. The Access Control provides a claims transformation program that can leverage federated identity (delegated identity) providers facilitating enterprise clients to use their authentication in Active Directory. It is envisaged that other Identity Providers, such as Facebook connect, Google Accounts, and Windows Live ID will be available in the future.

Both of these services are accessible through open protocols and standards such as SOAP, REST, ATOM, and ATOMPUB, which allows more flexible program integration.

The AppFabric SDK, which may be downloaded from here: (`http://www.microsoft.com/downloads/details.aspx?FamilyID=0bd0b14f-d112-4f11-94bf-90b489622edd&displaylang=en`; Version 1.0 in Beta 1, November 2009) provides a great deal of help in understanding and working with these services by way of codes and samples. Windows Communication Foundation WCF is the primary programming model for working with the Service Bus. The SDK simplifies the task of integrating these services into your .NET Applications on the premises by introducing new concepts like **WCF Relay Bindings**. Similar SDKs are also available for Java and Ruby developers.

Most recently, Microsoft has released (`http://blogs.msdn.com/b/windowsazureappfabric/archive/2010/09/19/windows-azure-appfabric-sdk-september-release-available-for-download.aspx`) Windows Azure AppFabric SDK (Version V 1.0) for both x32 and x64 bit computers. If you want to use this September release follow this link:

`http://www.microsoft.com/downloads/en/details.aspx?FamilyID=39856a03-1490-4283-908f-c8bf0bfad8a5&displaylang=en`.

However, note that the name of the installer has now changed to `WindowsAzureAppFabricSDK-x86.msi`.

System requirements

These requirements are for the tools and SDKs used by developers (clients) to create, host, and modify their applications and services on the Windows Azure Platform.

- Windows Azure Tools for Microsoft Visual Studio and SDK.

  You may need to register to get the tools with your Windows Live ID.

  Open the MSDN Developer Center link shown here: `http://msdn.microsoft.com/en-us/evalcenter/ee460823.aspx`.

  Read the information on this page.

  Presently there are two versions of the tools to go with Windows Azure OS.

- Version 1.0 prior to Feb 1, 2010

  Versions 1.0 download URL: `http://www.microsoft.com/downloads/details.aspx?FamilyID=6967ff37-813e-47c7-b987-889124b43abd&displaylang=en`.

- Version 1.1 Feb 1, 2010 release

  Versions 1.1 download URL: `http://www.microsoft.com/downloads/details.aspx?FamilyID=5664019e-6860-4c33-9843-4eb40b297ab6&displaylang=en`.

- Version 1.2 June 2010 release

  Versions 1.2 download URL: `http://www.microsoft.com/down-loads/en/details.aspx?familyid=2274A0A8-5D37-4EAC-B50A-E197DC340F6F&displaylang=en`.

  Many new enhancements were added including support for .NET 4.0, VS2010 RTM, and other diagnostic tools for applications running on the cloud.

 The Windows Azure provides for backward compatibility with Version 1.0 by specifying the same in the configuration files.

Only one version of the tool is to be installed on a computer.

  Supported Operating Systems:
- Windows 7 (Hotfixes for Visual Studio stability and Fast CGI support not required)
- Windows Server 2008
- Windows Server 2008 R2 (Hotfixes for Visual Studio stability and Fast CGI support not required)
- Windows Vista SP1
- Windows Vista SP2

  IIS version
- IIS 7.0 [with ASP.NET and WCF HTTP Activation and optionally CGI]
- Use guidance here: `http://learn.iis.net/page.aspx/28/install-iis-7-on-windows-vista-and-windows-7/` to install IIS 7.0

  Development IDEs
- Microsoft Visual Studio 2008 SP1
- Microsoft Visual Studio 2010 Beta 2 — Native debugging Hotfix not required
- Microsoft Visual Web Developer 2008 Express Edition SP1

  SQL Servers
- SQL Server 2005 Express Edition
- SQL Server 2008 R2 or later
- Hardware and software required
- Getting started with Azure Platform and accessing services

In addition, the hands-on exercise in this chapter will teach you how to acquire the needed materials and permissions to work with this platform.

Hardware and software required

For working with the practical elements in this book, the following hardware and software components were used:

- Aspire 4810TZ notebook computer

Intel Pentium SU2700/1.3 GHZ, 3GB DDR3 SDRAM-1066MHz, 24x(CD)/8x(DVD), 14in TFT Active Matrix, Ethernet/Wireless LAN, 3 x Hi-Speed USB Interfaces with Vista Home Premium:

- Windows 7 Ultimate (installed after removing Vista Home Premium)
- Wired and Wireless LAN
- SQL Server 2008 R2 Nov-CTP Enterprise (Evaluation)
- Visual Studio 2008, SP1
- Visual Studio 2010 Beta 2

Getting started with Azure Platform and accessing services

In order to work with this book it will be necessary to have an account for using the Windows Azure Platform. This is not a free service starting from February 1, 2010. During January 2010, this was a free service for evaluation but since February 1 it is a service you can subscribe to and a number of different subscription plans are available. Presently, you need to purchase a subscription to use this service. Exercise 1.1 describes the steps you need to take for purchasing the subscription. Exercise 1.2 describes the steps for accessing the services purchased by accessing the Azure Portal. In particular, a hosting service will be created. The actual hosting will be described in *Chapter 7, Working with Windows Azure Hosting*. The access to SQL Azure (*Chapter 2, SQL Azure Services*) and AppFabric (*Chapter 8, Database Applications on Windows Azure Platform Accessing SQL Server Databases*) from the portal will be described later.

Exercise 1.1: Purchasing a subscription on Windows Azure Platform

There are various subscription options available for purchase and each business has to make a choice suitable for its needs. For the initial parts of this book the choice made is described here. There are three parts to this process shown as follows:

Signing up for a Windows Live ID

- Purchasing a subscription
- Activating the Service

Signing up for a Windows Live ID

The following assumes a new sign up. If you already have a login for Windows Live ID this step is not necessary.

1. Go to the following URL: `http://home.live`.
2. Click on **Sign up** to open the URL: `https://signup.live.com/signup.aspx?id=251248&ru=http%3a%2f%2fhome.live.com%2f%3fnew%3dtrue&cp=2&mkt=en-US&rollrs=12&lic=1` as follows.

3. Fill in the required details. You may have to check and see if it is available. If your first choice is not successful you can try again until you get an ID. You have to provide demographic information and provide a strong password. You also need to agree to the service agreement by clicking the **I Accept** button (not shown in the previous screenshot).

4. If everything is OK a Windows Live ID account will be created. You may review the account information from one of the links on this page. You can sign out of the account on this page clicking **Sign out** at top right.

Purchasing a subscription

To purchase a subscription, go to the following URL and choose an offer that is suitable for you: `http://www.microsoft.com/windowsazure/offers/`. The various options are shown in the following screenshot (follow previous URL to see the complete page):

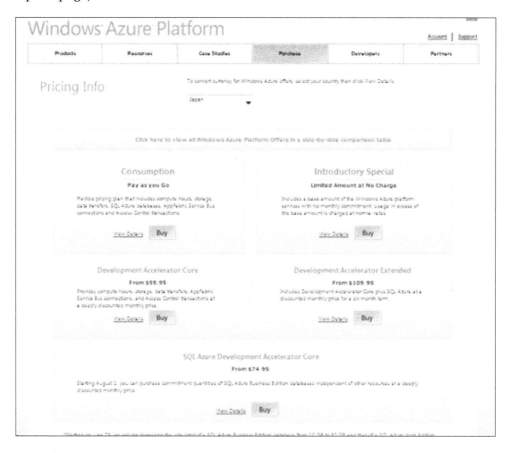

1. For this book, the first option was chosen.

2. Click on the **Buy** button. You will be taken to the Microsoft Online Services page (URL: `https://login.live.com/login.srf?wa=wsignin1.0&rpsnv=11&ct=1283982570&rver=5.5.4177.0&wp=SAPI&wreply=https:%2F%2Fmocp.microsoftonline.com%2Fsite%2Fbuy%2FMS-AZR-0001P&lc=1033&id=255559`) where it is assumed you have already created a windows Live ID login.

3. Enter your password and click **OK**. This will take you to the **My Profile** page of your account, as shown, where you need to provide a few more pieces of information about your physical address and telephone number.

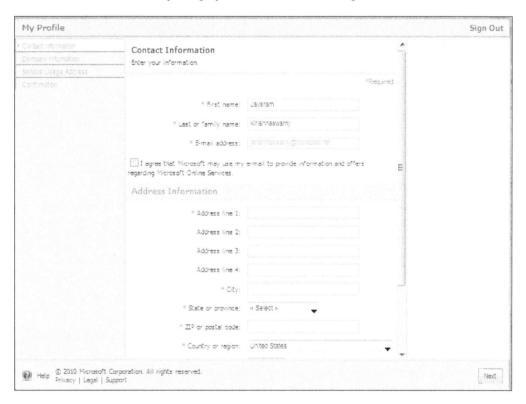

4. Click on the **Next** button. This will bring you to the Company Information page where you need to fill in a few more required items.

5. Click **Next**. This will take you back to the Service Usage Address page of **My Profile**.

6. Click **Finish**. This will take you to the Confirmation page of **My Profile**.

7. Now click **Close** on this URL link. This will take you to the Microsoft Online Services' Customer Portal where you can review the services, subscriptions, and so on as shown here: `https://mocp.microsoftonline.com/Site/ShoppingCartPage.aspx`.

8. Check the Customer acknowledgement regarding the agreement. Keep a copy for your files.

9. Click **Checkout >**. This will take you to the Billing Information wizard's **Payment Options** Page. Herein, you can use a Credit Card (New) or provide a purchase order number.

10. Click **Next** on this page. Provide the Credit card information here.

11. Click **Next**. You are once again taken to the Microsoft Online Subscription Agreement page where you again need to agree to the terms. You also provide the full customer name and a title.

12. Click the **I Accept button**. This will bring you to the **Review and Confirm Order** page of **Billing Information**.

13. Click **Confirm**. This brings up the Confirmation page with a confirmation number, which you can file for your records.

14. Click on **Proceed to activation**.

Activating the service

The previous action will take you to the service activation page. You need to provide a subscription name. This name will be used for the subscription as well as to provide a name for the first project with the Windows Azure Platform. The Service name is mapped to the billing information. Here is an example from **Service Activation** with the subscription name: **mysorian**.

1. Click **Next**. This will take you to the **Service Administrator** page, which will show the Windows Live ID and contact information of the Administrator.

2. Click **Next**. This will take you to the summary page as shown in the following screenshot. Note the Azure portals that will be provisioned for the **mysorian** subscription.

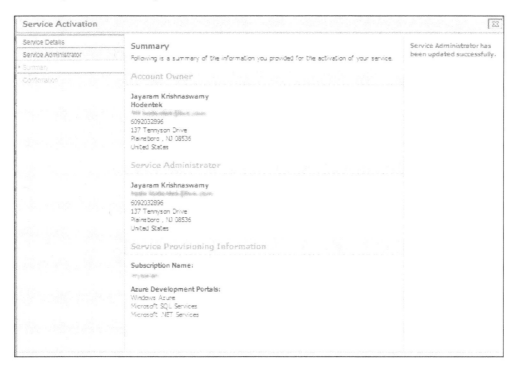

3. Click **Finish**. This brings you to the Confirmation page.

4. Click **Close**. The Online Services page comes up showing the status as **Activation in Progress**.

Now you are subscribed. You should check up your subscription status at the following URL: `https://mocp.microsoftonline.com/Site/Manage.aspx`.

Exercise 1.2: Accessing Windows Azure Portal

Now, we will access the Windows Azure Portal. Herein, although you can set up your project for all the three components of the Platform, you will only set up your Windows Azure Hosting Service as follows:

- Verifying status of account and browsing to Windows Azure Portal
- Creating an account and reviewing the portal
- Creating a Windows Azure Service

In the next chapter, you will be setting up the SQL Azure Services from the same portal.

Verifying status of account and browsing to Windows Azure Portal

To verify the status of your account, you will need to complete the following steps:

1. Browse to the following URL: `https://mocp.microsoftonline.com/Site/Manage.aspx`.

   You will notice that the status has changed to **Service Active**. Herein, you can edit both the Service as well as the Billing details as follows:

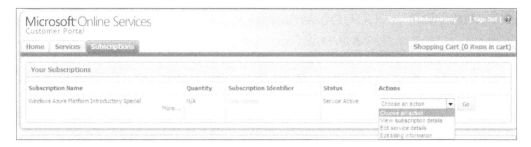

2. Browse to the following Windows Azure portal: `http://windows.azure.com` to display the New Account page as follows.

This page shows the components of the Windows Azure Platform, Windows Azure, SQL Azure, AppFabric, and Marketplace. From this page you may access the Billing information; review your projects as well as sign out of live.com. Notice that the developer portal account is tied to Windows Live ID. Read the privacy statement, which provides useful information regarding the services provided as well as where to get help if needed (Windows Azure Platform Support: `http://www.microsoft.com/windowsazure/support/`). Marketplace is not discussed in this book but it is a direct contender to one of the services offered by SalesForce.com.

Creating an account and reviewing the portal

To create an account and review the portal, you will need to do the following:

1. Click **I Agree**. You get a congratulatory message to the effect that your account has been created.

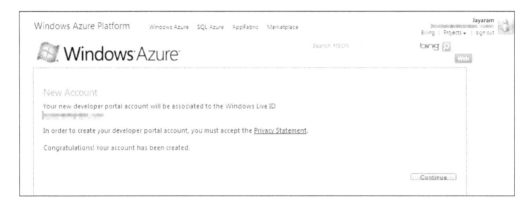

2. Click **Continue**. Voila, your portal is ready with the Project Name that you provided during setting up the service account as shown. You are in the Windows Azure Page of your services portal. The three components will all be associated with the same **Project Name** as all of them are **Enabled**.

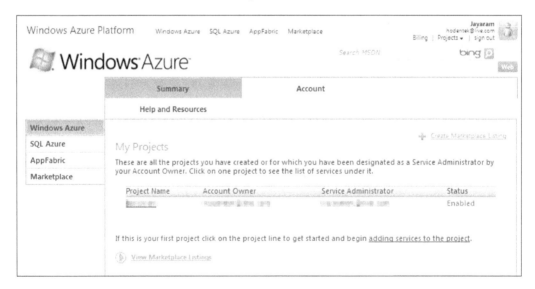

Creating a Windows Azure Service

You can add services to your project as described here.

1. Click on the hyperlink under **Project Name** to open the Windows Azure Project page as follows.

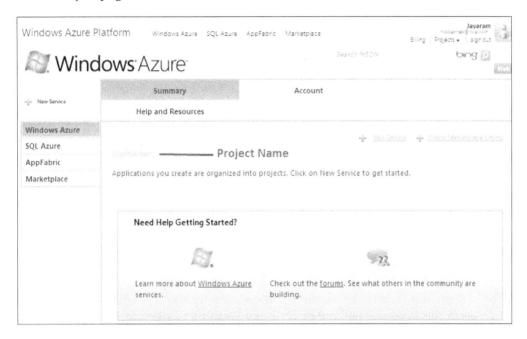

Here, you can create a **New Service** as well as a Marketplace Listing. For the purposes of this book you need not create a Marketplace Listing. However, you will be hosting applications in the Windows Azure cloud platform and, therefore, you will be creating a **New Service**. When you create a **New Service**, provisioning of various resources will be made for your project. This is also the place where you can find more information on Windows Azure as well as access the various forums where you can pose questions and hopefully find answers.

2. Click **+New Service** at either one of the locations shown on the previous screenshot. This will display the following page:

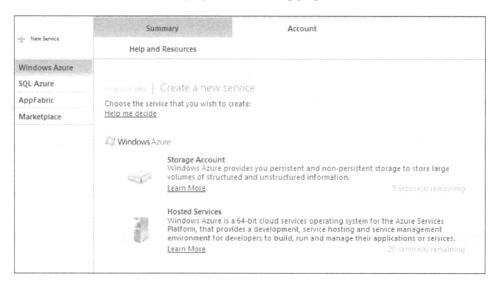

There are two accounts that you can set up here, a **Storage Account** and an account for the **Hosted Services**. You can see that you can set up 5 **Storage Accounts** and 20 **Hosted Services** accounts. You must remember that these are all billable and use caution while setting up the accounts. For the purposes of this book we will not be setting up a **Storage Account**.

3. Click **Hosted Services**. This opens the Project's **Create a Service** page where you provide a Service Label and a Service description, which will be used only on developer portal as follows:

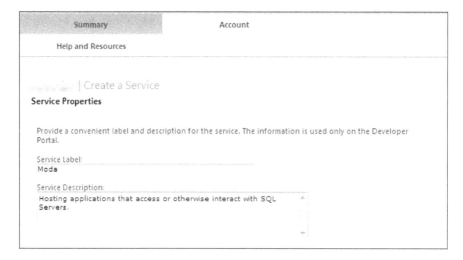

4. Click **Next.** This takes you to the **Hosted Service** page. Herein, you will need to provide a name for the publicly accessible name for the service (you may need to ascertain the availability) as well as the Hosted **Service Affinity Group**. For the purposes of this book, this is not of any great concern. However, if you are using **Storage** or any other **bandwidth sensitive** items, you may want to keep your data and application in the same region. Here, **mysorian** has been used for the Service URL and **Anywhere US** for the Affinity Group.

5. Click **Create**. The details of the **Hosted Service** created will be displayed as follows.

When you create a project that you want to host on Windows Azure, this is where you will come to deploy. Applications hosted on **Production** are live and publicly accessible. In practice, you may want to test and verify the application on a **Staging** server. Windows Azure has this provision.

6. Click on the Vertical bar on the right with an arrow pointing left in the previous screenshot to display the following:

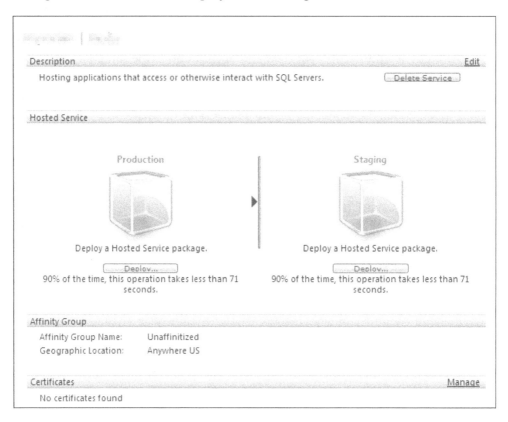

You first deploy to **Staging**, which is not public and after you are satisfied you can bring it over to **Production**. When you deploy the application to **Staging** a new control will be spawned, which will allow you to transfer the application to **Production**. You can also manage certificates that you upload and by default there are no certificates. Whether you deploy your application to **Staging** or **Production** you will be charged and the amount charged will depend on the plan you choose.

7. Sign out of the portal. We will host a number of applications in *Chapters 7, Working with Windows Azure Hosting* and *Chapter 8, Database applications on Windows Azure Platform accessing SQL Server databases*. We will set up the SQL Azure Service in the next chapter.

Summary

The advantages of taking a business to the "Cloud Platform" were discussed highlighting the ease with which a complex business can be established in the cloud, without incurring the startup cost in terms of infrastructure and human resources. After defining what cloud computing is, the different forms of Cloud Computing Platforms were discussed with reference to some existing major vendors. The major components that make up the Windows Azure Platform, the Windows Azure Compute/Storage Services, the SQL Azure, and the AppFabric were discussed in some detail. Also discussed were the hardware and software requirements as well as the Windows Azure Operating System versions, SDKs, and Tools. Working through the two examples will help you get started in understanding the Windows Azure Platform. The two examples in this chapter, show you how to subscribe to this service and review the various services offered. Guidance to activate the service was also described as well as the deployment options in the cloud.

In the next chapter, SQL Azure services will be described in detail with a number of examples providing you with the ability to work with this relational database in the cloud effectively.

2
SQL Azure Services

In this chapter, you will learn about what SQL Azure Services are, and how different the SQL Azure Server is from a local, on-site SQL Server 2008. This chapter deals with the following:

- Overview of SQL Azure Services
- Accessing SQL Azure Services from the portal
- Creating a user database and setting up a firewall
- Connecting to SQL Azure from SQL Server Management Studio
- Working with SQL Azure from SQL Server Management Studio
- Basic administration of the database objects
- Basic monitoring of the database

The practical elements of this chapter are presented following a step-by-step approach. The focus is on helping the administration of the server/databases in SQL Azure Services. In order to work with the practical elements, some familiarity with the use of SQL Server Management Studio is assumed. The recommended version of SQL Server Management Studio is the one that gets installed with SQL Server 2008 R2 November CTP (Presently SQL Server 2008 R2).

Overview of SQL Azure Services

SQL Azure is a database service in the cloud on Microsoft's Windows Azure platform well-suited for web facing database applications as well as a relational database in the cloud.

SQL Azure Services was briefly introduced in *Chapter 1, Cloud Computing and Microsoft Azure Services Platform*. The present version mostly deals with the component analogous to a database engine in a local, on-site SQL Server. Future enhancements will host the other services such as Integration Services, Reporting Services, Service Broker, and any other yet-to-be defined services. Although these services are not hosted in the cloud, they can leverage data on SQL Azure to provide support. SQL Server Integration Services can be used to a great advantage with SQL Azure for data movement, and highly interactive boardroom quality reports can be generated using SQL Azure as a backend server (*Chapter 6, SSIS and SSRS Applications Using SQL Azure*).

Infrastructure features

SQL Azure is designed for peak workloads by failover clustering, load balancing, replication, and scaling out, which are all automatically managed at the data center. SQL Azure's infrastructure architecture is fashioned to implement all of these features.

High availability is made possible by replicating multiple redundant copies to multiple physical servers thus, ensuring the business process can continue without interruption. At least three replicas are created; a replica can replace an active copy facing any kind of fault condition so that service is assured. At present, the replicated copies are all on the same data center, but in the future, geo-replication of data may become available so that performance for global enterprises may be improved. Hardware failures are addressed by automatic failover.

Enterprise data centers addressed the scaling out data storage needs, but incurred administrative overheads in maintaining the on-site SQL Servers. SQL Azure offers the same or even better functionality without incurring administrative costs.

How different is SQL Azure from SQL Server?

SQL Azure (version 10.25) may be viewed as a subset of an on-site SQL Server 2008 (version 10.5) both exposing **Tabular Data Stream (TDS)** for data access using T-SQL. As a subset, SQL Azure supports only some of the features of SQL Server and the T-SQL feature set. However, more of T-SQL features are being added in the continuous upgrades from SU1 to SU5. Since it is hosted on computers in the Microsoft Data Centers, its administration—in some aspects—is different from that of an on-site SQL Server.

SQL Azure is administered as a service, unlike on-site servers. The SQL Azure server is not a SQL Server instance and is therefore administered as a logical server rather than as a physical server. The database objects such as tables, views, users, and so on are administered by SQL Azure database administrator but the physical side of it is administered by Microsoft on its data centers. This abstraction of infrastructure away from the user confers most of its availability, elasticity, price, and extensibility features. To get started with SQL Azure, you must provision a SQL Azure Server on Windows Azure platform as explained in the *After accessing the portal* subsection, later in the chapter.

SQL Azure provisioning

Provisioning a SQL Azure Server at the portal is done by a mere click of the mouse and will be ready in a few minutes. You may provision the storage that you need, and when the need changes, you can add or remove storage. This is an extremely attractive feature especially for those whose needs start with low storage requirements and grow with time. It is also attractive to those who may experience increased load at certain times only.

SQL Azure databases lie within the operational boundary of the customer-defined SQL Azure Server; it is a container of logical groupings of databases enclosed in a security firewall fence. While the databases are accessible to the user, the files that store the relational data are not; they are managed by the SQL Azure services.

A single SQL Azure Server that you get when you subscribe, can house a large number (150) of databases, presently limited to the 1 GB and 10 GB types within the scope of the licensing arrangement.

- What if you provision for 1 GB and you exceed this limit?

  Then either you provision a server with a 10 GB database or get one more 1 GB database. This means that there is a bit of due diligence you need to do before you start your project.

- What if the data exceeds 10 GB?

The recommendation is to partition the data into smaller databases. You may have to redesign your queries to address the changed schema as cross-database queries are not supported. The rationale for using smaller databases and partitioning, lies in its agility to quickly recover from failures (high availability/fault tolerance) with the ability to replicate faster while addressing the issue of covering a majority of users (small business and web facing). However, responding to the requests of the users, Microsoft may provide 50 GB databases in the future (the new update in June 2010 to SQL Azure Services will allow 50 GB databases).

- How many numbers of SQL Azure Servers can you have?

You can have any number of SQL Azure Servers (that you can afford) and place them in any geolocation you choose. It is strictly one server for one subscription. Presently there are six geolocated data centers that can be chosen. The number of data centers is likely to grow. Best practices dictate that you keep your data nearest to where you use it most, so that performance is optimized. The SQL Azure databases, being relational in nature, can be programmed using T-SQL skills that are used in working with on-site SQL Servers. It must be remembered though, that the SQL Azure Servers are not physical servers but are virtual objects. Hiding their physical whereabouts but providing adequate hooks to them, helps you to focus more on the design and less on being concerned with files, folders, and hardware problems. While the server-related information is shielded from the user, the databases themselves are containers of objects similar to what one finds in on-site SQL Servers such as tables, views, stored procedures, and so on. These database objects are accessible to logged on users who have permission.

After accessing the portal

To get started with SQL Azure Services, you will need to get a Windows Azure platform account, which gives access to the three services presently offered. The first step is to get a Windows Live ID and then establish an account at Microsoft's Customer Portal as described in *Chapter 1, Cloud Computing and Microsoft Azure Services Platform*. If you have completed the examples in *Chapter 1*, you will have an account on the platform by this time. In this chapter, you will be provisioning a SQL Azure Server after accessing the SQL Azure Portal.

Server-level administration

Once you are in the portal, you will be able to create your server for which you can provide a username and password. You will also be able to drop the server and change the password. You can also designate in which of the data centers you want your server to be located. With the credentials created in the portal, you will become the server-level principal; the equivalent of **sa** of your server. In the portal, you can also create databases and firewall fences that will only allow users from the location(s) you specify here. The user databases that you create here are in addition to the **master** database that is created by SQL Azure Services; a repository of information about other databases. The **master** database also keeps track of logins and their permissions. You could get this information by querying the **master** for `sys.sql_logins` and `sys.database` views.

If you are planning to create applications, you may also copy the connection strings that you would need for your applications, which are available in the portal. You would be typically using the Visual Studio IDE to create applications. However, SQL Azure can be used standalone without having to use the Windows Azure service. Indeed some users may just move their data to SQL Azure for archive.

Once you have provisioned a server, you are ready to create other objects that are needed besides creating the databases. At the portal, you can create a database and set up a firewall fence, but you will need another tool to create other objects in the database.

Setting up firewall rules

Users accessing SQL Azure Server in the Cloud need to go through two kinds of barriers. Firstly, you need to go through your computer's firewall and then go in through the firewall that protects your SQL Azure Server. The firewall rules that you set up in the portal allow only users from the location you set up for the rule, because the firewall rules only look at the originating IP address.

By default, there are no firewall rules to start with and no one gets admitted. Firewall rules are first configured in the portal. If your computer is behind a **Network Address Translation (NAT)** then your IP address will be different from what you see in your configuration settings. However, the user interface in the portal for creating a firewall discovers and displays the correct IP address most of the time.

A workaround is suggested here for those cases in which your firewall UI incorrectly displays your IP Address: `http://hodentek.blogspot.com/2010/01/firewall-ip-address-setting-in-sql.html`.

Firewalls can also be managed from a tool such as SSMS using extended stored procedures in SQL Azure. They can be managed programmatically as well from Visual Studio.

In order for you to connect to SQL Azure, you also need to open your computer's firewall, so that an outgoing TCP connection is allowed through port 1433 by creating an exception. You can configure this in your computer's Control Panel. If you have set up some security program, such as Norton Security, you need to open this port for outgoing TCP connections in the Norton Security Suite's UI.

In addition, your on-site programs accessing SQL Azure Server and your hosted applications on Windows Azure may also need access to SQL Azure (*Chapter 8, Database Applications on Windows Azure Platform Accessing SQL Server Databases*). For this scenario, you should check the checkbox **Allow Microsoft Services access to this server** in the firewall settings page.

The firewall rule only checks for an originating IP address but you need to be authenticated to access SQL Azure. Your administrator, in this case the server-level principal, will have to set you up as a user and provide you with appropriate credentials.

Administering at the database level

SQL Azure database administration is best done from SSMS. You connect to the Database Engine in SSMS, which displays a user interface where you enter the credentials that you established in the portal. You also have other options to connect to SQL Azure (*Chapter 3, Working with SQL Azure Databases from Visual Studio 2010* and *Chapter 4, SQL Azure Tools*). In SSMS, you have the option to connect to either of the databases, the system-created **master** or the database(s) that you create in the portal. The Object Explorer displays the server with all objects that are contained in the chosen database. What is displayed in the Object Explorer is contextual and the use of the USE statement to change the database context does not work. Make sure you understand this, whether you are working with Object Explorer or query windows. The server-level administrator is the 'top' administrator and he or she can create other users and assign them to different roles just like in the on-site SQL Server. The one thing that an administrator cannot do is undertake any activity that would require access to the hardware or the file system.

Role of SQL Azure database administrator

The SQL Azure database administrator administers and manages schema generation, statistics management, index tuning, query optimization, as well as security (users, logins, roles, and so on). Since the physical file system cannot be accessed by the user, tasks such as backing up and restoring databases are not possible. Looking at questions and concerns raised by users in forums, this appears to be one of the less appealing features of SQL Azure that has often resulted in remarks that 'it is not enterprise ready'. Users want to keep a copy of the data, and if it is a very large database, the advantages of not having servers on the site disappear as you do need a server on-site to back up the data. One suggested recommendation by Microsoft is to use SQL Server Integration Services and bulk copying of data using the SQLCMD utility.

SQL Azure databases

These databases are no different from those of on-site SQL Server 2008 except that the user database node may not have all the nodes of a typical user database that you find in the on-site server. The nodes **Database Diagrams**, **Service Broker**, and **Storage** will be absent as these are not supported. In the case of the system database node, only the **master** will be present. The **master** in SQL Azure is a database that contains all information about the other databases.

You can only access the SQL Server with **SQL Server Authentication**, whereas you have an additional option, **Windows Authentication** in the case of an on-site SQL Server. All the allowed DDL, DML operations can be programmed using templates available in SSMS. Some of the more common ones, as well as access to the template explorer, which provides a more complete list, are detailed later in the chapter.

User administration and logins

Security is a very important aspect of database administration and it is all the more important in the case of the multi-tenant model used in hosting SQL Azure to control access.

The server-level administrator created in the portal is the top level administrator of SQL Azure Server. While he/she can create other databases in the portal, he/she will have to create other database objects including users and their login, using the SSMS.

Server-level administration

The **master** database is used to perform server-level administration, as the **master** database keeps records of all logins and of the logins that have permission to create a database. You must first establish a connection to the **master** database while creating a *New Query* to carry out tasks to CREATE, ALTER, or DROP LOGINS or DATABASES. The server-related views: sys.sql_logins and sys.databases can be used to review logins and databases. Whenever you want to change the context of a database, you have to login to the database using the **Options** in the SSMSs UI, **Connect to Server**.

Creating a database using T-SQL is extremely simple as there are no file references to be specified and certain other features that are not implemented. The following syntax is for creating a database in an on-site SQL Server instance:

```
CREATE DATABASE database_name
    [ON
        [ PRIMARY ] [ <filespec> [ ,...n ]
        [ , <filegroup> [ ,...n ] ]
    [ LOG ON { <filespec> [ ,...n ] } ]
    ]
    [ COLLATE collation_name ]
    [ WITH <external_access_option> ]
]
[;]

To attach a database
CREATE DATABASE database_name
    ON <filespec> [ ,...n ]
    FOR { ATTACH [ WITH <service_broker_option> ]
        | ATTACH_REBUILD_LOG }
[;]


<filespec> ::=
{
(
    NAME = logical_file_name ,
        FILENAME = { 'os_file_name' | 'filestream_path' }
        [ , SIZE = size [ KB | MB | GB | TB ] ]
        [ , MAXSIZE = { max_size [ KB | MB | GB | TB ] | UNLIMITED } ]
        [ , FILEGROWTH = growth_increment [ KB | MB | GB | TB | % ] ]
) [ ,...n ]
}
<filegroup> ::=
{
FILEGROUP filegroup_name [ CONTAINS FILESTREAM ] [ DEFAULT ]
```

```
      <filespec> [ ,...n ]
}
<external_access_option> ::=
{
  [ DB_CHAINING { ON | OFF } ]
  [ , TRUSTWORTHY { ON | OFF } ]
}
<service_broker_option> ::=
{
    ENABLE_BROKER
  | NEW_BROKER
  | ERROR_BROKER_CONVERSATIONS
}
Create a database snapshot
CREATE DATABASE database_snapshot_name
    ON
        (
        NAME = logical_file_name,
        FILENAME = 'os_file_name'
        ) [ ,...n ]
    AS SNAPSHOT OF source_database_name
[;]
```

Look how simple the following syntax is for creating a database in SQL Azure:

```
CREATE DATABASE database_name
        [(MAXSIZE = {1 | 10} GB )]
[;]
```

However, certain default values are set for the databases, which can be reviewed by issuing the query after creating the database:

```
SELECT * from sys.databases
```

Managing logins

After logging in as a server-level administrator to **master**, you can manage logins using CREATE LOGIN, ALTER LOGIN, and DROP LOGIN statements. You can create a password by executing the following statement for example, while connected to **master**:

```
CREATE LOGIN xfiles WITH PASSWORD = '@#$jAyRa1'
```

You need to create a password before you proceed further. During authentication, you will normally be using **Login Name** and **Password**, but due to the fact that some tools implement TDS differently, you may have to append the `servername` part of the fully qualified server name `<servername>.<database name>.<windows>.<net>` to the `Username` like in `login_name@<servername>`. Note that both `<login_name>` and `<login_name>@<servername>` are valid in the **Connect to Server** UI of SSMS.

Connecting to SQL Azure using new login

After creating a new login as described here, you must confer database-level permissions to the new login to get connected to SQL Azure. You can do so by creating users for the database with the login.

Logins with server-level permissions

The roles `loginmanager` and `dbmanager` are two security-related roles in SQL Azure to which users may be assigned, that allows them to create logins or create databases. Only the server-level principal (created in the portal) or users with `loginmanager` role can create logins. The `dbmanager` role is similar to the `dbcreator` role and users in this role can create databases using the CREATE DATABASE statement while connected to the **master** database.

These role assignments are made using the stored procedure `sp_addrolemember` as shown here for users, `user1` and `user2`. These users are created while connected to **master** using, for example:

```
CREATE USER User1 FROM LOGIN 'login1';
CREATE USER User2 FROM LOGIN 'login1';
EXEC sp_addrolemember 'dbmanager', 'User1';
EXEC sp_addrolemember 'loginmanager', 'User2';
```

Migrating databases to SQL Azure

As most web applications are data-centric, SQL Azure's databases need to be populated with data before the applications can access the data. More often, if you are trying to push all of your data to SQL Azure, you need tools. You have several options, such as using scripts, migration wizard, bulk copy (`bcp.exe`), SQL Server Integration Services, and so on. More recently (April 19, 2010 update) Data-tier applications were implemented for SQL Azure providing yet another option for migrating databases using both SSMS as well as Visual Studio. We will look at these in *Chapter 5, Populating SQL Azure Databases*.

Monitoring SQL Azure databases

SQL Azure partially supports six categories of **Dynamic Management Views (DMV)** that help diagnose performance problems caused by:

- Blocked or long-running queries
- Resource-related bottlenecks
- Poor queries

The following are the dynamic management views that you can query (see `http://www.sys-con.com/node/1291144`):

- `sys.dm_exec_connections`
- `sys.dm_exec_requests`
- `sys.dm_exec_sessions`
- `sys.dm_tran_database_transactions`
- `sys.dm_tran_active_transactions`
- `sys.dm_db_partition_stats`

A user must have a View Database State permission granted to him in order to view these DMVs. A later section shows how this may be carried out, for a user of a database, with two examples of the previous views.

Data synchronization and SQL Azure

Microsoft Sync Framework is leveraged to provide synchronization between on-site applications with SQL Azure. The notion of a data hub in the cloud allows on-site clients to synchronize with each other using the data hub. Synchronization will be described in *Chapter 9, Synchronizing SQL Azure*.

Application access to SQL Azure

Ground-based client applications access the SQL Azure Services (databases) on the cloud using standard client libraries such as ODBC, ADO.NET (using TDS protocol), PHP, and so on. What this means, is that all of these technologies are familiar to application developers and do not require learning new developmental techniques, a feature Microsoft calls **Developer Agility**. In addition to Microsoft technologies, open source programming languages can also be used to develop Azure applications. We will look at the details of how client libraries access SQL Azure in the next chapter. Web applications accessing SQL Azure will be described in *Chapter 8, Database Applications on Windows Azure Platform Accessing SQL Server Databases*.

The third component described in *Chapter 1, Cloud Computing and Microsoft Azure Services Platform* that is soon to be commercialized, the AppFabric, would support Windows Azure platform to integrate with on-site application despite the security fences that isolate the on-site application. This would make it more appealing for enterprise applications. This will be considered in *Chapter 8*.

Troubleshooting

There may be any number of reasons why interacting with SQL Azure may not always be successful. For example, there may just be a possibility that the service level agreement that assures 99.99 percent may not actually be possible, there may be a problem of time-out that is set for executing a command, and so on. In these cases, troubleshooting to find out what might have happened becomes important. Herein, we will see some of the cases that prevent interacting with SQL Azure and the ways and means of troubleshooting the causes.

- Login failure is one of the common problems that one faces in connecting to SQL Azure. In order to successfully login:
  - You need to make sure that you are using the correct SSMS.
  - Make sure you are using **SQL Server Authentication** in the **Connect to Server** dialog box.
  - You must make sure your login name and password (type in exactly as you were given by your administrator) are correct. Password is case sensitive. Sometimes you may need to append server name to login name.
  - If you cannot **browse** the databases, you can type in the name and try.

  If your login is not successful, either there is a problem in the login or the database is not available.

  If you are a server-level administrator you can reset the password in the portal. For other users the `administrator` or `loginmanager` can correct the logins.

- Service unavailable or does not exist.

  If you have already provisioned a server, check the following link: `http://www.microsoft.com/windowsazure/support/status/servicedashboard.aspx`, to make sure SQL Azure Services are running without problem at the data center.

Use the same techniques that you would use in the case of SQL Server 2008 with network commands like `Ping`, `Tracert`, and so on. Use the fully qualified name of the SQL Azure Server you have provisioned while using these utilities.

- You assume you are connected, but maybe you are disconnected.

  You may be in a disconnected state for a number of reasons, such as:
  - When a connection is idle for an extended period of time
  - When a connection consumes an excessive amount of resources or holds onto a transaction for an extended period of time
  - If the server is too busy

  Try reconnecting again. Note that SQL Azure error messages are a subset of SQL error messages.

T-SQL support in SQL Azure

Transact-SQL is used to administer SQL Azure. You can create and manage objects as you will see later in this chapter. CRUD (`create`, `read`, `update`, `delete`) operations on the table are supported. Applications can insert, retrieve, modify, and delete data by interacting with SQL Azure using T-SQL statements.

As a subset of SQL Server 2008, SQL Azure supports only a subset of T-SQL that you find in SQL Server 2008.

The supported and partially supported features from Microsoft documentation are reproduced here for easy reference.

The support for Transact-SQL reference in SQL Azure can be described in three main categories:

- Transact-SQL language elements that are supported as is
- Transact-SQL language elements that are not supported
- Transact-SQL language elements that provide a subset of the arguments and options in their corresponding Transact-SQL elements in SQL Server 2008

The following Transact-SQL features are supported or partially supported by SQL Azure:

- Constants
- Constraints
- Cursors
- Index management and rebuilding indexes
- Local temporary tables
- Reserved keywords
- Stored procedures
- Statistics management
- Transactions
- Triggers
- Tables, joins, and table variables
- Transact-SQL language elements
- Create/drop databases
- Create/alter/drop tables
- Create/alter/drop users and logins
- User-defined functions
- Views

The following Transact-SQL features are **not supported** by SQL Azure:

- Common Language Runtime (CLR)
- Database file placement
- Database mirroring
- Distributed queries
- Distributed transactions
- Filegroup management
- Global temporary tables
- Spatial data and indexes
- SQL Server configuration options
- SQL Server Service Broker
- System tables
- Trace flags

T-SQL grammar details are found here: http://msdn.microsoft.com/en-us/library/ee336281.aspx.

Accessing SQL Azure Services from the portal

In *Chapter 1, Cloud Computing and Microsoft Azure Services Platform*, the procedure to access the Windows Azure Services was described, which allowed you to host applications on the Windows Azure platform. In a similar manner, you can also access the SQL Azure Services that allow you to create databases and firewall rules. Firewall rules provide the security blanket for your cloud-based resources. This allows you and only you, or users designated by you, from IP addresses specified by you, to access your cloud-based SQL Azure database from an external location.

First time access to SQL Azure from the portal

By completing the following steps, you will be able to access SQL Azure Services from the portal:

1. Browse to the following URL: `http://windows.azure.com`.

2. The **Windows Live ID** sign in page opens up as shown in the following screenshot. It is assumed that you have already created a Live ID. In case you have multiple Live IDs, make sure you use the Live ID account that you used while buying the subscription. This is because the Windows Azure Portal's projects or services are only accessible to subscribed users.

3. Insert your password and click on **OK**.

4. The Windows Azure Portal opens with **Windows Azure** in the left navigation menu. Click on **SQL Azure** to open the user interface for SQL Azure Services as shown in the next screenshot. The **Project Name, Account Administrator**, and the **Service Administrator** names are displayed (pixelated). These were chosen while creating the subscription as we saw in the previous chapter. Both **Account Administrator** and **Service Administrator** have the same entries, as that of the **Live ID username**. Note that you can also directly come to this page by accessing the URL: `http://sql.azure.com`.

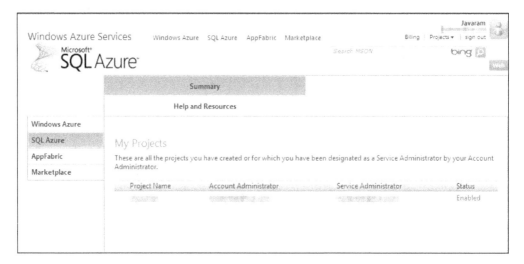

5. Next, click on the **Project Name** (assuming that the **Status** is **Enabled**). The **Terms of Use** page gets displayed. (Only a relevant portion of the portal is shown in the following screenshot.)

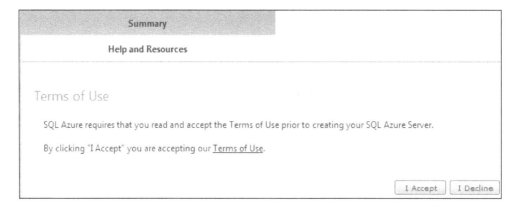

6. You have to agree to the terms before you proceed then click the **I Accept** button.

Creating a SQL Azure Server

For a given subscription, you can create only one SQL Azure Server. If you need more servers, you may need to purchase additional subscriptions. However, you can create multiple databases in one SQL Azure Server.

Herein, you can create the Server Administrator Credentials. As for locations, in addition to **North Central US**, three other options are available: South Central US, North Europe, and South East Asia (two more were added recently). More will be available in the future. Choose the same geographical location for both data and application so that you get a better performance. This may also have an impact on what you pay for the service. Choose the geographical location from the drop-down list displayed by clicking the drop-down handle for **Location**.

1. Click on the **I Accept** button.

2. This opens the **Create Server** page where you will be able to create the SQL Azure Server in the cloud.

3. Next, you will need to fill in the details providing an **Administrator Username** and an **Administrator Password**. Retype the password and choose a location for your server from the drop-down menu.

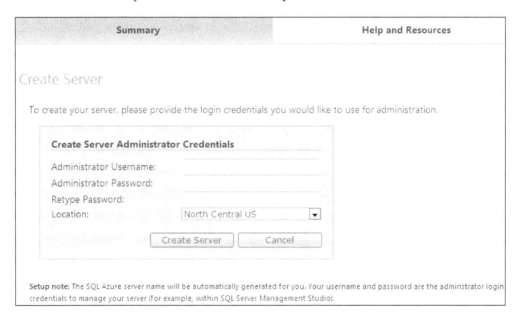

4. The password you use should have all the required items as in the following list. Also make sure that the password field does not have any three consecutive characters in the username, as shown in the following screenshot:

A password must be at least 8 characters long and contain at least three of the four following classes:

- Latin uppercase letter (A-Z)
- Latin lowercase letter (a-z)
- Base 10 digit (0-9)
- Non-alphanumeric characters such as: exclamation point (!), dollar sign ($), number sign (#), or percent (%)

For more information, please visit the MSDN documentation.

Password cannot contain any three consecutive characters in the username.

 Note that the Administrator's (server-level principal) account is a master account used for server administration and it (the name and password) should not be exposed in connection strings or otherwise.

5. Click on the **Create Server** button. Sometimes an unexpected error could occur and you should save the screen to troubleshoot, as shown in the next screenshot, so that you can take up the issue with the help desk.

Summary	Help and Resources

An unexpected error has occurred. Please go back and retry your operation.

Please use activity id '42b34d1e-5531-4e74-8768-72a98b5e8d99' when contacting customer support.

6. If the details are fully accepted, you should see the following display in the browser:

7. Notice that a server was created with the details, as shown in the previous screenshot (all author-specific details are shown pixelated). The **Server Name** is provided (a random choice) by the provisioning system. The **Administrator Username** and the **Server Location** were chosen by the subscriber (you) to the service. The fully qualified name of the server in this case is: **XXXXXXXXX.database.windows.net** - <servername.database. windows.net>.This is the name you will be using while connecting to SQL Azure from most applications. Also notice that the **Server Information** panel allows you to **Reset Password** as well as to **Drop Server**.

    In addition, while provisioning the server, the system creates the **master** database of 1 GB.

8. In the bottom pane's first tabbed page, you see the **master** as well as any other databases that you may create. Notice that there are buttons, which will enable you to create a database as well as to delete databases you created. Since the information about the databases you create is recorded in the **master**, you will not delete this database.

    In the **Databases** tab you can **Test Connectivity** as well as get the **Connection Strings;** the textual information you need for connecting to SQL Azure from applications.

Setting up a firewall

As security is one of the most important aspects, a firewall, that allows users only from those locations whose IP ranges are registered in the portal needs to be set up and configured. The following steps show how this may be carried out at the portal by the administrator of the account:

1. Click on the tab **Firewall Settings** to display the following screenshot:

2. Just like the firewall on computers as well as networks, SQL Azure is also protected by a firewall fence. The user will specify the firewall by providing a name (**Rule Name**) and indicating the IP addresses (below **IP Address Range**) from where the user will connect to SQL Azure while accessing it externally. This means that the databases (includes **master** as well) that the user created can be accessed from those locations only. The firewall settings may consist of a single IP address or a range of IP addresses. There must be at least one firewall rule configured in order to access SQL Azure.

3. The interface also allows creating multiple rules. These will be created using the **Add Rule**, **Edit Rule**, and **Delete Rule** buttons. Also, if the **Allow Microsoft Services access to this server** is not checked, SQL Azure access from applications running in the Windows Azure hosting site will not be possible. This also needs to be checked if you want to test connectivity to a database in the server using the **Test Connectivity** button described earlier. When this is checked a system configured firewall rule; Microsoft Services with the range 0.0.0.0 to 0.0.0.0 gets added.

4. Assuming that you have not set up the firewall, if you try to access the SQL Azure Server from the SSMS on your computer you will get a **Cannot connect to XXXXXX.database.windows.net** error message, as shown in the following screenshot:

5. Although you can run the `sp_set_firewall_rule` stored procedure from the master database, you need to access the master database, which requires a firewall setting on SQL Azure. This is best done in the portal.

Creating a user database and setting up a firewall

Now, you will create a user database in SQL Azure and set up firewall rules so that you can access SQL Azure from your ground-based, on-site location. While creating a user database makes use of the SQL Azure portal, these can be done from your ground-based SSMS, or other utilities that support T-SQL. Database and firewall rules can also be programmatically created from Visual Studio 2008 SP1 or Visual Studio 2010 (Beta 2 as well as RC).

Creating a user database in the portal

As seen, when we accessed SQL Azure Services from the portal, the **master** database is created during the provisioning process in the portal and user databases can also be created in the portal.

SQL Azure presently provides creating two *Types* of databases, a web type of 1 GB and a business type of 10 GB. Each provisioned SQL Azure Server can have a total of 150 databases including the **master**.

 The February 17, 2010 update of SQL Azure SU1 (February 2010) now allows upgrading or downgrading the Types between Web and Business. This feature was not available in the previous version of SQL Azure.

Following are the steps to create a database in the portal:

1. Click on the **Databases** tab in the SQL Azure Server. Click on **Create Database**.

2. This pops up a small opaque dialog, as shown in the following screenshot, that allows you to create a **1 GB** or **10 GB** database, which requires a name. You may provide a name of your choice. You may also cancel this operation if you like.

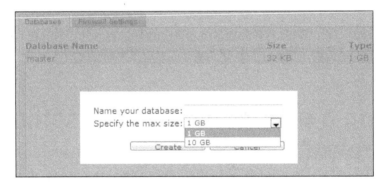

3. Type in a name and click **Create** after picking the database type from the drop-down.

4. Herein, a **1 GB** database with the name **Bluesky** was chosen. Sometimes when you click create, you may get an error message telling you to try again. When successful, you will see that the **1 GB**, **Bluesky** database is added to your list of databases, which was initially empty, as shown in the next screenshot. At this point, you can create other databases of either type from here.

5. When you need to access a SQL Azure database programmatically from an application, you need **Connection Strings** to establish a connection. These strings can be displayed by using the **Connection Strings** button at the bottom of the previous screen.

6. Click on **Bluesky** to highlight it and click on **Connection Strings**.

7. This displays the following opaque screen. There are two ways in which you can connect, using **ODBC** or **ADO.NET**. Review this carefully and notice that for SQL Azure, a SQL Server Login is required with a User ID and a Password as specified in these strings. All author-specific items are shown pixelated.

8. You can easily drop a database as well by just clicking **Drop Database** after highlighting the database.

You can alter the database size (up and down) by using the following statement, which you can run only in SSMS:

```
ALTER DATABASE database_name
{
    MODIFY (MAXSIZE = {1 | 10} GB)
}
[;]
```

More recently, after the release of SQL Server 2008 R2, SQL Azure databases can also be renamed.

If you realize at any time that you need a larger database than the one you are using you can use the previous statement, but during the change you cannot access the databases.

Setting up firewall rules

If you were to access the **Bluesky** database from your SSMS now, you would not be able to connect to the server and you would get an error message as shown earlier. This is because no firewall rules have been set up. We will now set up an IP address from which SQL Azure can be accessed. It may be noted that creating a user database is not a necessary condition for setting up a firewall fence. It can be done soon after provisioning the server by completing the following steps:

1. Click the **Firewall Settings** tab. Click the **Add Rule** button to open an opaque window.

2. You will notice that the window already has an IP address (**Your IP address: 68.83.182.13**). This IP address happens to be the IPv4 address of the author's service provider. Although the screen seems to require a range, you can set up a rule by just typing the same IP address in the **IP Range** boxes and a **Name** (of your choice), as shown in the following screenshot:

3. Although this should take effect in five minutes, longer durations have been experienced.

4. Then, click on **Submit.** The IP setting tabbed page gets updated, as shown in the following screenshot. With this setting, you will be able to connect to the SQL Azure Server from your SSMS, or other similar utility.

5. Although just one rule was added, you can add any number of rules each with a name and a range. The following screenshot shows a number of IP addresses set up for a server on SQL Azure (December 2009 version), this feature remains unchanged in this version of SQL Azure. You can make the SQL Azure accessible from any IP address by using a very wide range. However, you must use caution to restrict the range to those you would use. Placing a check mark for the checkbox **Allow Microsoft Services access to this server** resulted in the rule **MicrosoftServices** with the range **0.0.0.0 - 0.0.0.0**.

Rule Name	IP Address Range
ComcastJan2010	68.83.182.13 - 68.83.182.13
HomeNet	192.168.1.100 - 192.168.1.105
IP Example 1	10.0.0.0 - 10.0.0.255
MicrosoftServices	0.0.0.0 - 0.0.0.0
oneIP	69.253.170.127 - 69.253.170.127
TakaHana	210.128.65.70 - 210.128.65.70
TestFirewall	69.253.170.127 - 69.253.171.127

 Presently only 128 firewalls may be set up in SQL Azure.

6. The rule **TakaHana** in the previous screenshot was added to enable access from a location in Japan. Note that some ISPs reveal only the link-local IPv6 addresses (as happened in the case of the location in Japan) and not an IPv4 address. However, the **Firewall Settings** UI is only configured for IPv4, and for link-local addresses; it may come up with a wrong IP address, as shown here with my notes:

> This is what I copied from the SSMS error message and I added this to the firewall rule.
>
> **Add Firewall Rule**
>
> Name: TakaHana
> IP Range: 210.128.65.70
>   to
>   210.128.65.70
>
> Your IP address: 210.149.120.71
>
>   [Submit] [Cancel]
>
> **Note:** Firewall rules may take up to 5 minutes before they come into effect.

In this case, the easiest way to get the corresponding IPv4 is to obtain it by connecting to SQL Azure from SSMS as explained here: `http://hodentek.blogspot.com/2010/01/firewall-ip-address-setting-in-sql.html` and not rely on what the **Firewall Settings** UI displays.

Also note that it is just as easy to edit or delete a rule using the buttons at the bottom of this screen. When you try editing the rule you will see that you can only change the IP address range and not the name.

After setting up a database and an IP address you will be able to connect to SQL Azure from your local machine using SSMS as described next.

 Since Windows Azure applications and SQL Azure databases can be located in different data centers, the firewall rules may have to take this into consideration by manually adding the IP addresses of the data centers to the firewall rules.

IP ranges of Microsoft Azure data centers

The following are the IP ranges of the various data centers:

- United States (North/Central): 65.52.0.0/21, 65.52.8.0/21, 65.52.16.0/21, 65.52.24.0/21, 207.46.203.64/27, 207.46.203.96/27, 207.46.205.0/24

- Europe (North): 94.245.88.0/21, 94.245.104.0/21, 65.52.64.0/21, 65.52.72.0/21, 94.245.114.0/27, 94.245.114.32/27, 94.245.122.0/24

- Asia (Southeast): 111.221.80.0/21, 111.221.88.0/21, 207.46.59.64/27, 207.46.59.96/27

Connecting to SQL Azure from SQL Server Management Studio

The SQL Azure Portal can manage servers, databases, and firewall settings as seen earlier. However, if you want to work with the databases and/or create objects you need an external utility. SQL Server Management Studio R2 provides the ability to work with databases by providing T-SQL support. There are other tools to connect to SQL Azure. SQL Azure supports only a limited set of features that SQL Server 2008 is capable of as described earlier in this chapter and all these features can be used in SSMS once you are connected to SQL Azure Server.

Connecting to SQL Azure from SSMS

Connecting to SQL Azure from SSMS is like connecting to any of the local SQL servers. To do this, you will need to perform the following steps:

1. Open the SSMS (the version used here is the one that came with SQL Server 2008 R2 November CTP installation) from its shortcut in **Start** in the Windows 7 desktop.

2. The **Connect to Server** dialog box will pop up wherein you need to insert the required information. The **Server name** and **Login** fields are author authentication information, shown pixelated. The **Server name** was automatically provided by Windows Azure while provisioning and the **Login** and **Password** of the administrator were provided by the user.

Make sure that the authentication is using **SQL Server Authentication**, as shown in the following screenshot:

3. Next, click on **Options>>**. This opens the **Connection Properties** tabbed page of the **Connect to Server** window, as shown in the next screenshot.

4. Click on the drop-down handle for the database, which displays the two options, shown in the following screenshot:

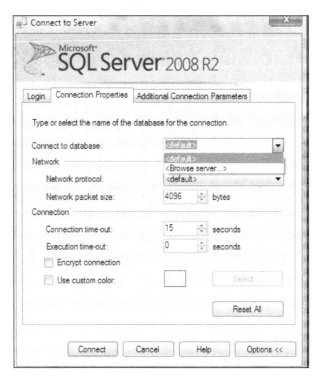

5. Click the **<Browse Server...>** menu item.

6. You will get the **Browse for Databases** window, as shown in the following screenshot. Click on **Yes**.

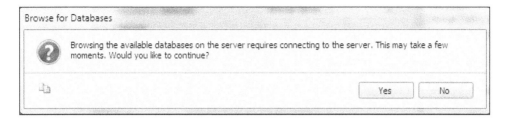

7. If you installed SQL Server 2008 R2 November CTP (or SQL Server 2008 R2) and did not access SQL Azure, then you will not be able to browse to the server in some instances. In this case, type in the server name and the password and click on **Connect**. You should then get connected to the SQL Azure Server.

8. The **Connect to Server** window will be displayed, as shown in the following screenshot, with the nodes expanded:

9. There are two databases on this server. The system database **master** is created by the SQL Azure provisioning system, and the **Bluesky** was user created.

10. Click on **master** or **Bluesky** to enable the **OK** button, and then click on **OK**.

11. The **Connect to server** window then gets updated with this information.

12. Click on **Connect**. Now, you will be able to see the databases on the server, as shown in the following screenshot. The nodes in the two databases are expanded. While in the user-created database there are four default users, the **master** database has one more user, the **Server Administrator**.

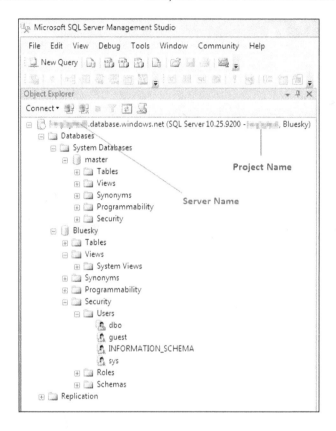

Once you are in SSMS with your SQL Azure Server displayed, as shown in the previous screenshot, you can work with the server as you would with any other SQL Server. You need to remember though, that SQL Azure statements/queries are executed in the cloud even though you may see the queries and query results in SSMS. Also, remember that not all features of SQL Server 2008 are supported in the cloud. Refer to the discussion in the earlier part of this chapter regarding features that are supported.

What we have seen till now are steps for ideal conditions of connection. In practice, you may encounter a variety of messages such as the ones shown here:

- Sometimes the SQL Azure may not respond immediately, in which case you may get the following message:

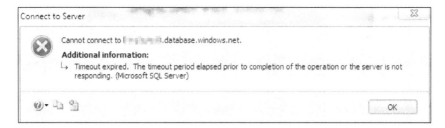

- Sometimes you may have established a connection, which remained for a considerable time without being used, resulting in the following message, and you may have to try to reconnect.

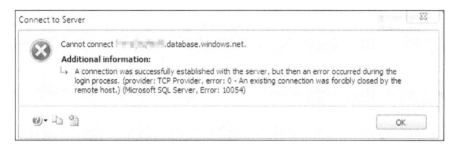

- The firewall should be established when you configure it in the server and it may take about five minutes to get established. This is the first administrative task in SQL Azure. If you were to try to connect to the server using SSMS without setting up the firewall you may get the next message. As observed, in practice there are times when the process may take more than five minutes. In all these cases, the recommendation is to try again until you establish a connection. As long as the firewalls are in place and you are connecting to the server from an allowed site, you should be able to connect to the SQL Azure Server.

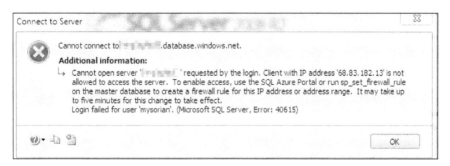

Note that for the username you have the following two options and both of them are valid:

    a.   `<login_name>`

    b.   `<login_name>@<servername>`

Working with SQL Azure from SQL Server Management Studio

When you are connected to the SQL Azure Server from SSMS, you can work with the server objects as you would with local servers except that SQL Azure supports (presently) only a subset of the features supported by SQL Server 2008 R2 (November CTP). We will now review a number of features that are supported fully or partially.

Creating queries

Querying databases is one of the important tasks that you would do on a regular basis and the process of querying SQL Azure is no different from querying other databases except for some changes in the commands, as follows:

1. Click on **Connect | Database Engine...** toolbar item in SSMS to open the **Connect to Server** dialog.

2. Enter the credentials as before and click the **Connect** button.

3. This opens up the Object Explorer displaying the SQL Azure Server objects. As we saw earlier, there are two databases, **master** and **Bluesky**.

4. Click the **New Query** toolbar item, as shown in the following screenshot, to open the query window pane. Some of the SQL Azure-related items are annotated but masked.

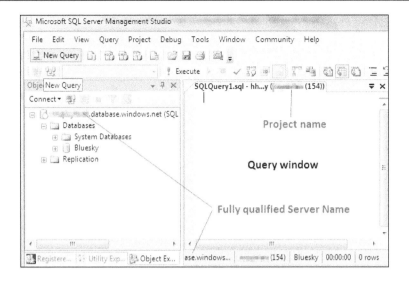

5. Note that you can also create a new query after dismissing the **Connect to Server** dialog as well. But the **Connect to Server** comes up again. After entering the credentials as detailed previously, the query window gets displayed (but the object browser will be empty) for the **connection you specified**. In the tabbed page of the query, you can review a number of options, as shown in the following screenshot:

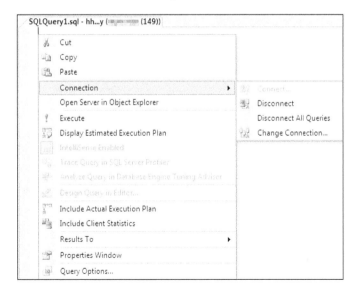

General queries

Herein, we test a few general queries to find the version of SQL Server, the number and details of databases, and the current time, and so on. In order to do this, you will need to perform the following steps:

1. Enter the query, as shown in the following screenshot and click on **Execute**.

2. The version of SQL Server on which the query is executed will be displayed. The version is 10.25 (SQL Server 2008 R2 is 10.5).

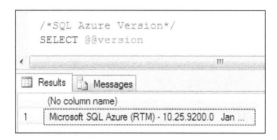

3. Enter the query shown in the following screenshot and click on **Execute**. The query returns the details of the databases on the SQL Azure Server.

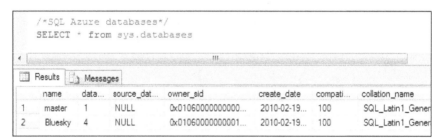

4. Presently the **Bluesky** database is empty, but make sure you review all the returned columns for the database as a number of property values are returned such as **collation_name**, ANSI nulls, and so on.

5. Enter the query shown in the next screenshot and click on **Execute**. The query returns a whole list of objects in SQL Azure.

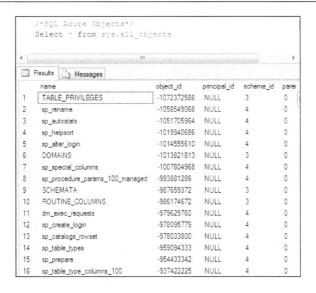

6. Make sure you review the **master** database as it contains a wealth of information on SQL Azure.

Querying date and time

Here, we look at the date and time set for the SQL Azure portal by querying for Current time, UTC time, and so on. In order to do this, you will need to perform the following steps:

1. Enter the query as shown in the next screenshot and click on **Execute**. The returned row shows the date and time of the physical location of SQL and not the time where it was accessed from. SQL Azure's current time is set the same as UTC time to provide a predictable behavior with any of the other datacenter systems (`http://social.msdn.microsoft.com/Forums/en-US/ssdsgetstarted/thread/dead9cb4-b2a9-4996-9015-7660fa3d310d`).

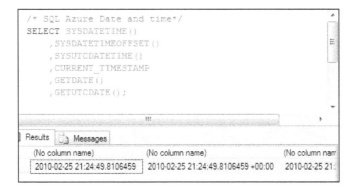

Create and display firewall rules

Earlier we saw how a firewall rule was set in the SQL Azure portal. This can also be carried out in SSMS. In order to create a firewall rule, you must be connected to the **master** while executing the query. First, we will display the existing rule and later we will create a new rule.

1. Enter the following statement and click on **Execute**.

2. The firewall details in SQL Azure portal gets displayed, as shown in the following screenshot:

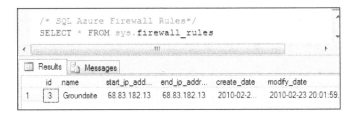

3. Creating and deleting a firewall is achieved by executing the two System Extended Stored procedures, `sys.sp_set_firewall_rule` and `sys.sp_delete_firewall_rule`.

4. Enter and execute `sys.sp_set_firewall_rule`, as shown in the following screenshot. Make sure that you declare the variables, as in the following screenshot:

```
Declare @name nvarchar(128),
        @start_ip_address varchar(50),
        @end_ip_addesss varchar(50)
set @name =N'TestFireWall'
set @start_ip_address= N'192.168.1.10'
set    @end_ip_addesss= N'192.168.1.100'
exec sys.sp_set_firewall_rule @name,  @start_ip_address,@end_ip_addesss
```

Messages

(1 row(s) affected)

5. If you need to copy and paste, you may use the following code:

```
Declare @name nvarchar(128),
        @start_ip_address varchar(50),
        @end_ip_addesss varchar(50)
set @name =N'TestFireWall'
set @start_ip_address= N'192.168.1.10'
set    @end_ip_addesss= N'192.168.1.100'
exec sys.sp_set_firewall_rule @name,  @start_ip_address,@end_ip_
addesss
```

6. Login to the SQL Azure portal with your Windows Live ID and review the firewall rules of your server.

7. You will see that the **TestFireWall** rule has been added to your **Firewall Settings**, as shown in the following screenshot:

8. In a similar manner, you can delete a Firewall rule using `sys.sp_delete_firewall_rule` when you are connected to **master.**

9. Execute the extended stored procedure, as shown in the following listing. The following code shows the usage of `sys.sp_delete_firewall_rule`:

```
Declare @name nvarchar(128)
set @name = N'TestFirewall'
exec sys.sp_delete_firewall_rule @name
```

You may need to refresh the portal page (`http://sql.azure.com`) for the changes to become effective on the portal's display.

Find database usage and bandwidth usage

SQL Azure provides views of database usage and bandwidth usage that you may need to have for budgeting and monitoring usage. Make sure you are in the **master** database while running these queries.

1. Enter the next query to find database usage and click **Execute**.

2. The details of database usage are returned and get displayed. There is just one user database of the type **Web**, which was created previously.

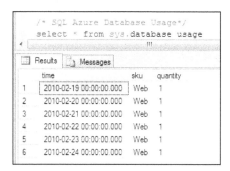

3. Enter the next query to find bandwidth usage and click on **Execute**. The bandwidth used by the database in data-intensive applications gets displayed. Since the database has not been used in any significant manner, there are no returned columns. You may revisit this query later (after working with web applications accessing data on SQL Azure) to get an idea of how much bandwidth usage costs. For applications in the cloud accessing SQL Azure there is no bandwidth usage cost, but for external applications there is a usage cost.

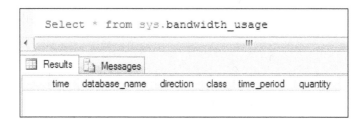

Basic administration of the database objects

While the administration of SQL Azure is similar to SQL Server 2008 R2, there are some differences as the strategy used for server management has changed. The security folder in the Object Explorer is your starting point for creating logins when you access SQL Server 2008. In SQL Azure, the server node in Object Explorer is mapped to several (one or more) physical computers at the datacenter(s). The object that is available for you in SQL Azure is the **master**. It is in the **master** that you create objects, which include databases, logins, and so on.

The securityadmin role in SQL Server 2008 R2 is replaced by the loginmanager (Administrative User) that you created in SQL Azure Portal (also known as the Security Principal) and he/she will be responsible for server level security for creating logins.

The dbmanager role in SQL Azure is akin to dbcreator role in an on-site SQL Server and this role can create a database when connected to the **master** and can drop a database created by any user. A user with dbmanager can also be assigned to the loginmanager role, which allows him/her to create logins as well. The SQL Azure roles are shown here. In general, you should give the permission based on the need, and exercise caution for the db_owner and dbmanager roles.

Creating logins, users, and roles

We will now create a login using the CREATE LOGIN command. You will then create a new user for the login you just created using the CREATE USER command. You will then give him the dbmanager role using a built-in stored procedure. Presently, you are connected to SSMS using your SQL Azure Server login (created in the portal).

1. Right-click on **master**, as shown in the following screenshot. This pops open a drop-down list, as shown in the following screenshot:

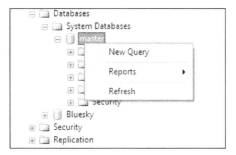

2. Click on **New Query** to open a query window.

3. Enter the command shown in the following screenshot and execute to create a login:

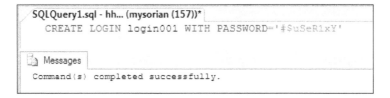

4. You may have to choose a password that is supported by the Windows password policy, otherwise you may get the following error:

```
Msg 15116, Level 16, State 1, Procedure sp_create_login, Line 1
Password validation failed. The password does not meet Windows
policy requirements because it is too short.
```

 For details about 'Strong Passwords', follow this link:
http://msdn.microsoft.com/en-us/library/ms161962.aspx.

Also, the previous command cannot be run in a batch. It should be the only statement in the query window.

You will have to work on this password choice. If you were to choose '1a2b3c4d5e' you will get the following message, but it is acceptable if you choose '$a2b3c4d5#':

```
Msg 15118, Level 16, State 1, Procedure sp_create_login, Line 1

Password validation failed. The password does not meet Windows policy
requirements because it is not complex enough.
```

In addition to CREATE LOGIN, you can also use ALTER LOGIN and DROP LOGIN commands.

For example, you can alter the login using the following command:

```
ALTER LOGIN login001 WITH PASSWORD = '#$1aBcD2'
```

Just creating a login with an acceptable password is not enough to log on to the server and you should have permissions to access database objects. If you do not have permissions, then you will get the following error message should you try connecting to the server.

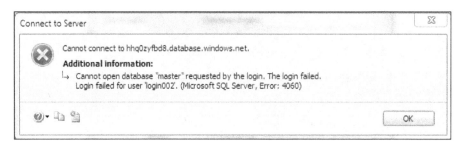

1. Enter the following and execute in the query window, as shown in the following screenshot:

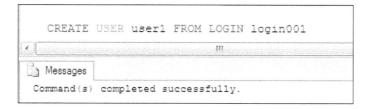

2. A new user, **user1** gets created for the login **login001** and the new user gets added to the **Users** node, as shown in the following screenshot. The CREATE USER statement should be the only command and cannot be used in a batch.

3. In order for the user to use the created login, they should be assigned a role, which determines what they can and cannot do. Roles are groupings into which users may be assigned. As mentioned previously, the dbmanager role is similar to the dbcreator role in the on-site SQL Server. We will bestow this role to **user1**.

4. Enter and execute the stored procedure in the query window, as shown in the following screenshot:

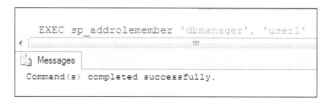

5. By scripting the **user1** in the **Object Explorer**, you would see that this action is equivalent to running the following query.

```
USE [master]
GO
/****** Object:  User [user1]     Script Date: 03/04/2010 15:34:39
******/
GO
CREATE USER [user1] FOR LOGIN [login001] WITH DEFAULT_SCHEMA=
[dbo]
GO
```

6. You can find all the logins by reviewing `sys.sys_logins`.

7. Execute the following query in the query window:

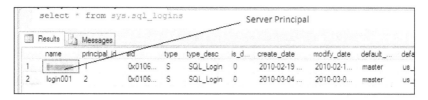

8. Another way to create a user is to use the Object Explorer while connected to the **master**.

9. Expand the **Security** node of the database for which you want to create a user and right-click the **Users** node and choose **New User...**. The template for creating a new user opens up in the query window as shown:

```
-- ===================================================
-- Create User as DBO template for SQL Azure Database
-- ===================================================
-- For login <login_name, sysname, login_name>, create a user in
the database
CREATE USER <user_name, sysname, user_name>
  FOR LOGIN <login_name, sysname, login_name>
  WITH DEFAULT_SCHEMA = <default_schema, sysname, dbo>
GO

-- Add user to the database owner role
EXEC sp_addrolemember N'db_owner', N'<user_name, sysname, user_
name>'
GO
```

Dropping a user can also be accomplished in the Object Browser quite easily.

1. Login to the SQL Azure Server with either the Security Principal's authentication or, the user who has the `loginmanager` permission. Right-click on the user you want to drop in the **Security** node of the database and choose **Delete**.

2. The **Delete Object** window gets displayed, as shown in the following screenshot:

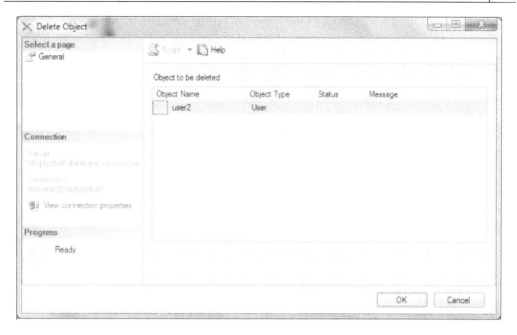

3. Highlight the user and then click on **OK**.

4. The chosen user will be dropped, which can be verified in the **Object Browser**.

Creating, altering, and dropping databases

Creating a database in the SQL Azure portal by the server administrator (Server-level principal) was described. In SSMS; databases may be created by the Administrator as well as those who have the appropriate role, such as the dbmanager.

You will need to login with credentials to create a database (Administrator or dbmanager) to **master** and execute the following statement:

```
CREATE DATABASE TestDB
```

TestDB will be created in SQL Azure.

> SQL Azure supports up to 150 databases in each SQL Azure server, including the **master** database. You can create up to 149 databases in each SQL Azure server.

You cannot rename the database (This has changed in the latest update to SQL Azure services). The workaround is to create a new database with the desired name and transfer data from the database that you want renamed.

In order to create a 10 GB database, you need to execute the following statement (Microsoft documentation):

```
CREATE DATABASE Test2 (MAXSIZE=10GB)
```

When you have a number of databases, you may want to go from one to the other. However, SQL Azure does not support the USE <database name> command. You can change over to another database by creating a new query and connecting to the desired database. If you need to confirm in what database you are currently working, you may run the following command:

```
Select db_name()
```

Also, it is just as easy to drop a database with the following command:

```
DROP DATABASE Test2
```

These objects immediately get updated in the portal.

After creating a database, you may also want to know the size of objects including the database you created, and for this you may use the system view as in the next statement. You may need to aggregate the reserved page count column using the following Select statement to get the size of the database:

```
select * from sys.dm_db_partition_stats
```

Creating tables and indexes

As relational data resides in tables, your relational data will reside in SQL Azure database tables (not to be confused with Tables in Windows Azure). Once you have created a database, you create a table(s) and index the table(s) appropriately.

1. Login and connect to the **Bluesky** database as described previously. Execute the following query in a query window:

   ```
   CREATE TABLE MyTable (
   ID int PRIMARY KEY CLUSTERED,
   FirstName varchar (20)
   )
   ```

   You can verify that a table **MyTable** gets created in the database **Bluesky**. In order to see this in the Object Browser you must be connected to this database.

Now you can insert values into the table. Note that unless you created the table with a clustered index as shown previously you may not be able to insert values. If a table is created without a clustered constraint, a clustered index must be created before an insert operation is allowed on the table.

2. Execute the following query to insert three rows in the table you created earlier.

```
INSERT INTO MyTable VALUES('1','John')
GO
INSERT INTO MyTable VALUES('2','Mary')
GO
INSERT INTO MyTable VALUES('3','Kristine')
GO
```

Now that you have populated the **MyTable** table you can see what it contains by running a `Select` query.

3. Execute the following query in the query window after making sure you are still connected to the **Bluesky** database.

```
Select * from MyTable
```

You would immediately see three rows returned in the results pane below the query window. Left-clicking the table does bring up a few options but it is nowhere near what you would get in the on-site SQL Server 2008 (`http://hodentek.blogspot.com/2009/11/sql-server-2008-r2-nov-ctp-installs.html`). This is because SQL Azure provides only a limited set of features.

Indexes are necessary for improved query performance. Creating an index in SQL Azure is no different from what you do in the on-site server.

4. Execute the following query to create an index on the **email** column:

```
CREATE INDEX IX_MyTable_email
ON MyTable(email)
```

This assumes that you have a column **email** in your table **MyTable** (please see the next section).

5. The newly created index can be found in the table's **Indexes** folder, as shown in the following screenshot:

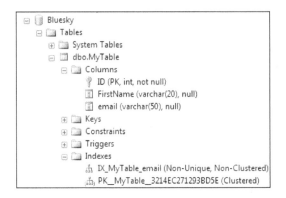

Add, remove columns, and constraints

You can also add and remove columns from a table. For adding a column that stores image data, you may want to alter the **MyTable** as follows:

```
ALTER TABLE MyTable
ADD Photo image;
```

Dropping a column is easy. Right-click on the column in the **Object Browser** and choose **Delete** in the drop-down menu. In the **Delete Object** window that gets displayed choose **OK**. This is very similar to the previous screenshot.

You have already seen the Primary Key constraint necessary while creating the table. You can also add a constraint to a column. The following two queries create a new column called **email** and add a default constraint to the e-mail column:

```
ALTER TABLE MyTable
ADD email varchar(50) ;

ALTER TABLE MyTable
ADD CONSTRAINT col_3_def
DEFAULT 'htek@mysorian.com' FOR email ;
```

In a similar manner, you can add check constraints as well. Review the following website for more details: http://www.w3schools.com/sql/sql_default.asp.

You can create tables to contain any of the data types that are supported by this version of SQL Azure. The next code listing shows a variety of data types defined for creating a hypothetical table called ACustomer:

```
CREATE TABLE ACustomer(
  [First_Name] [char](50) NULL,
  [Last_Name] [char](50) NULL,
  [Address] [varchar](50) NULL,
  [City] [char](50) NULL,
  [Country] [char](25) NULL,
  [Birth_Date] [date] NULL,
  [Salary] [money] NULL,
  [Photo] [image] NULL,
  [Russian_nickname] [ntext] NULL,
  [hobbies] [xml] NULL
)
```

And now if you run the following query you get all the details about the columns' content:

```
Select * from sys.columns
```

SQL Azure templates

Although only a few of the DDL and DML were described, a vast majority of them were not. However, SSMS has templates for what is supported in SQL Azure. The following steps show you how you may get to this template:

1. Open SSMS. Click **View** in the main menu and choose **Template Explorer** from the drop-down list.
2. This opens the **Template Explorer** in (far right) SSMS.
3. Expand the SQL Azure Templates node.

4. The SQL Azure Explorer node opens up, as shown in the following screenshot:

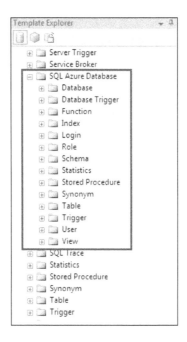

All items in these templates generally have **Create** and **Delete** nodes, which provide template code for carrying out the selected activity.

Basic monitoring of the database

Diagnosing SQL Server database-related performance problems whether they are related to databases, execution, or transaction, is best done using the related **Dynamic Management Views (DMV)**, a subset of those available in an on-site server. A user must have the permission to monitor or review these DMVs. Here, you will grant the permission to the user **DmvMonitor** who has a login001 to Bluesky.

1. Connect to SQL Azure with Server-level credentials.

2. Create a New Query to connect to Bluesky and execute the following statement:

```
/* login as Server-Level Principal and execute the
query while connected to 'Bluesky'*/
CREATE USER DmvMonitor FROM LOGIN login001
```

3. This creates the user `DmvMonitor` in `Bluesky`.

4. Grant **DmvMontior** the permission to view the DMV by executing the following statement:

   ```
   /*Grant permission to view DMV*/
   GRANT VIEW DATABASE STATE TO DmvMonitor;
   ```

5. Now that you have a user **DmvMonitor** with login `login001` in `Bluesky` database, you can run queries related to DMV.

6. Connect to the `Bluesky` database with the credentials (Username=`login001`, password=`#$1aBcD2`) and execute the query as follows:

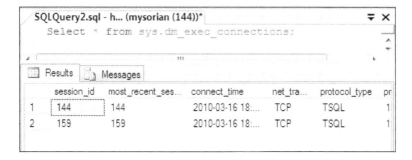

This view provides all the current connections to the Server. This view also provides the TDS protocol version used between the Client-Server as in the following query:

```
Select convert(varbinary(9),protocol_version)
from sys.dm_exec_connections
```

This will yield the following with both rows having the same value 0x730A0003 (see for example, `http://blogs.msdn.com/jenss/archive/2009/03/02/tds-protocol-versions-meet-client-stacks.aspx`). This hexadecimal value implies TDS version 7.3.

7. Now execute the query shown in the following screenshot and verify the results:

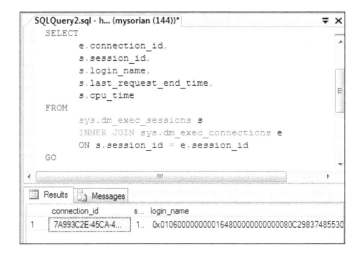

This previous query provides the session information about the current session.

Summary

In this chapter, we covered several aspects of SQL Azure Services beginning with provisioning of SQL Azure Server in the portal and later with related features such as setting up databases and firewalls; creating and administering SQL Azure databases; migration, summarizing synchronization, and monitoring of SQL Azure; troubleshooting and monitoring of databases.

Additionally, we focused on SQL Azure access using SQL Server Management, provisioning a server after accessing the portal for the first time; setting up firewall rules to allow on-site users access; creating user databases; running general to specific queries; creating users, logins and permissions; and monitoring SQL Azure usage, and so on.

In the next chapter, we will describe with examples, methods of accessing SQL Azure to create, modify, and manage database objects using both Client APIs and Server APIs. We will also describe the secure way of connecting to SQL Azure.

3
Working with SQL Azure Databases from Visual Studio 2008

SQL Azure Services fall under the umbrella of the **Windows Azure Platform**. Windows Azure Platform is one of the four online services that include The Windows Azure storage and compute, and Azure AppFabric offered by Microsoft. The other services are Bing, Live, and Microsoft Advertising.

In this chapter, we will be looking at how SQL Azure data may be accessed from the client premises by applications using well-known Microsoft technologies for data access. The emphasis will be more on administering the SQL Azure databases using the client and server APIs. We will also discuss the best practices of accessing data from the client. For the practical elements of this chapter, we will be mostly using Visual Studio 2008 SP1, and with some comments on using Visual Studio 2010. The following topics will be covered:

- SQL Azure architecture
- Microsoft data access technologies
- Easy way to connect to SQL Azure with Microsoft data access technologies
- Preferred way to connect to SQL Azure
- Connecting to SQL Azure using server APIs
- Creating database objects using ADO.NET

SQL Azure architecture

SQL Azure has a four-layered architecture, a **Client Layer** followed by a **Services Layer**, a **Platform Layer**, and finally the **Infrastructure Layer**. A schematic of the architecture is shown in the following diagram:

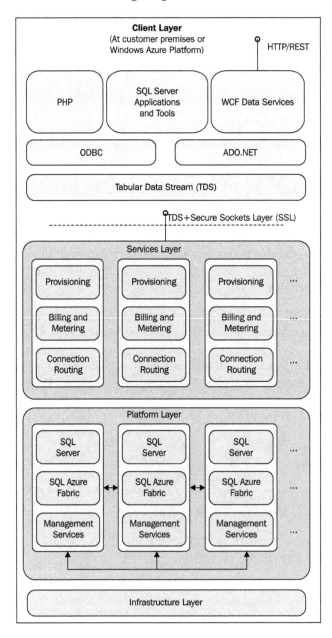

The **Infrastructure Layer** has all the associated hardware in the Microsoft Data Center as described in *Chapter 1, Cloud Computing and Microsoft Azure Services Platform*, managed automatically by the **SQL Azure Fabric**. The **Platform Layer**, which is above the **Infrastructure Layer**, has all the **SQL Server** clusters managed by the fabric as well as the **Management Services**. The **Services Layer** above the **Platform Layer** does all of the business logic, provisioning, connection routing, billing, and so on. The **Client Layer** above the **Platform Layer** can be at the client site or at the client's hosted site with all the applications that need access to SQL Azure.

Microsoft client technologies such as ODBC, ADO.NET, residing in the client site (or, in the Windows Azure Platform) converse with SQL Azure using TDS while WCF Data Services uses HTTP/REST. Applications such as PHP, SQL Server Applications and Tools, and WCF Data Services can work with ODBC and ADO. NET. Hence, TDS is the carrier of choice for information from SQL Server Tools, as well as the various applications.

The four-layered architecture shown in the previous diagram is based on the Microsoft documentation. As seen here, all applications access the **Services Layer** using **TDS+Secure Sockets Layer (SSL)** mediated by either **ODBC** or **ADO.NET**. The **Services Layer** routes the client requests to the **Platform Layer** where the **SQL Server** comes in, to process the client requests mediated by the **SQL Azure Fabric**.

The following diagram shows the **TDS Gateway Layering** in SQL Azure with some more details, copied, with permission, from a PowerPoint presentation by Jeff Currier to PDC 2009. This corresponds to the **Services Layer** of the previous image.

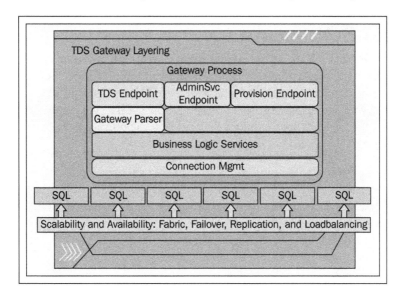

The Gateway layer enforces the authentication and authorization policy. This security enforcing layer isolates the application from the databases. The TDS Gateway takes care of a number of tasks, such as provisioning the endpoint, administering the AdminService, connection management, and so on. SQL Azure login requests arrive at the Gateway, which then accesses the Master and User DBs. Credentials to the User DB are matched to those on the Master and, after validation, a TDS session opens to forward requests to User DB. Make sure you watch the video presentation (Microsoft SQL Azure Database: Under the Hood) by Jeff Currier at the PDC here: `http://microsoftpdc.com/Sessions/SVC12`.

Application access to SQL Azure

Onsite client applications access the SQL Azure Services (databases) on the cloud using standard client libraries such as ODBC, ADO.NET (using TDS protocol), and so on. What this means, is that, all of these technologies are familiar to application developers and they are not required to learn new developmental techniques. In addition to Microsoft technologies, open source programming languages can also be used to develop Azure applications. We will look at the details of how client libraries access SQL Azure in this chapter. We will also learn how to manipulate database objects after accessing SQL Azure using T-SQL.

The client applications using TDS protocol arrive at the SQL Azure databases after passing through a load balancer, which forwards the TDS packets to the TDS Gateway layer, which then passes them on to the SQL Azure databases.

TDS and SQL Azure

Tabular Data Stream (TDS) was the technology originally created by Sybase to allow applications to access data stored in relational tables. Before SQL Azure came into existence, its predecessor **SQL Data Services (SDS)** was only able to access data using HTTP(s) or REST. Leveraging TDS, Microsoft skillfully morphed SDS into SQL Azure, so that the SQL Servers can be accessed in their native protocol and T-SQL code can be run in the cloud.

Presently, as shown in the following diagram based on the Microsoft documentation, data can be accessed by HTTP(s), as it is done by web facing applications (**Scenario B**) as well as using TDS from onsite applications and tools (**Scenario A**). Ultimately, however, it is **TDS + SSL** that finally reaches SQL Azure.

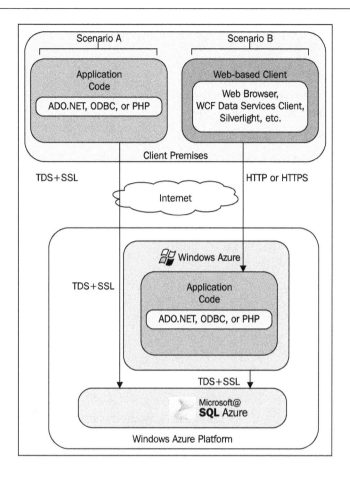

Microsoft data access technologies

There are two ways to interact with data using Visual Studio, either by designing an application using datasets and data adapters, or by performing direct operations on the data source, in this case the SQL Azure database. When and why you use one or the other depends on the situation you are trying to address. In situations where you are performing a database lookup, creating and modifying database structures, such as tables, views, stored procedures, or executing queries to get a single aggregate value, and so on, you directly interact with the database. This is because if you are creating or modifying database objects, you obviously cannot use datasets. On the other hand, if you are trying to access the data on the SQL Azure server from the web, you will be connecting using HTTP/HTTPS or REST-based technologies and will be using datasets and data adapters. The SQL Azure architecture accommodates both types of interaction. In this chapter, we will be looking at direct interaction with the database.

Using Visual Studio, you use data commands to work directly with the database. The steps to execute commands are as follows:

1. Create a connection.
2. Configure a command that uses the connection with a SQL statement or the name of a stored procedure.
3. Execute the command.
4. Retrieve the data that the command produces by a data reader.

Connecting to the database

In connecting to the SQL Azure database, you can use the following clients that are supported by Visual Studio 2008 by default:

- SqlConnection
- OdbcConnection
- OledbConnection
- EntityConnection

Data providers

When you use the assembly System.Data (C:\Windows\Microsoft.NET\ Framework\v2.0.50727\System.Data.dll), you can access the namespaces as shown in the following screenshot:

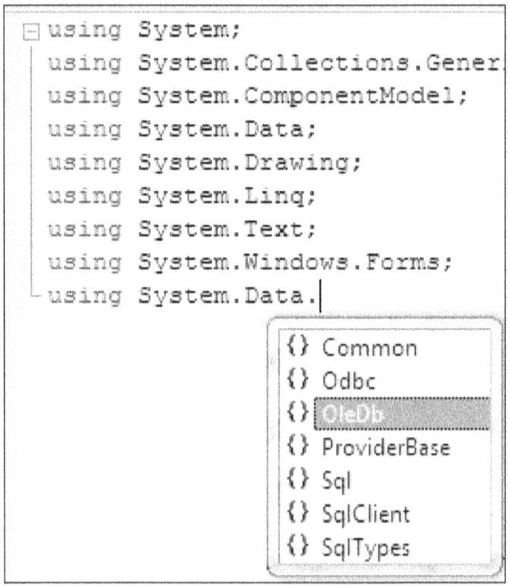

```
using System;
using System.Collections.Gener
using System.ComponentModel;
using System.Data;
using System.Drawing;
using System.Linq;
using System.Text;
using System.Windows.Forms;
using System.Data.|
                    {} Common
                    {} Odbc
                    {} OleDb
                    {} ProviderBase
                    {} Sql
                    {} SqlClient
                    {} SqlTypes
```

In order to access the `EntityConnection`, however, you should reference the `System.Data.EntityClient`.

 Presently, SQL Azure cannot be accessed using `EntityConnection` directly. We will look at this in *Chapter 8, Database Applications on Windows Azure Platform Accessing SQL Server Databases*.

The best way to understand the various namespaces/classes that help in connecting to the SQL Azure is to look at the namespaces/classes in the **Object Browser**.

The `SqlConnection` class member details are easily seen in the **Object Browser** when you search for `SqlConnection`.

Similarly, you search for `OdbcConnection` in the **Object Browser** to get all the related members.

Additionally, you can look up the details for `OledbConnection` and `EntityConnection` classes by referencing the corresponding namespaces. It is recommended that you review some of the members that create and manage database objects that we will be using later.

Connection string

In order to access the SQL Server you need to know the connection string. The connection string is a list of key/value pairs specific to each type of provider (SqlClient, ODBC, and OLEDB). If you know the connection string, you can directly specify it in the code, as shown here for **SqlConnection** without waiting for the intellisense to guide you, by typing it as an argument to **SqlConnection()**. Similar arguments may be made for the other providers.

```
SqlConnection myConn = new SqlConnection(
    ▲ 2 of 2 ▼  SqlConnection.SqlConnection (string connectionString)
    connectionString:
        The connection used to open the SQL Server database.
```

This is easily available in the Visual Studio IDE as an intellisense drop-down. Intellisense is a great help in being productive.

In the following screenshot, the connection string to the SQL Azure is provided but partially hidden in the view. The screenshot shows everything that is accessible to the `SqlConnection`:

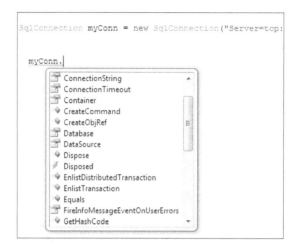

Following this, you will need to open the connection, which happens to be one of the methods of `SqlConnection`. The connection is necessary for you to create a command that you can execute.

Commands

The commands that we mainly use in SQL Azure are as follows:

- `SqlCommand`
- `OleDbCommand`
- `OdbcCommand`
- `EntityCommand`

Once the connection is established, you can create commands that can be run on the data source by setting up the code to create a command as follows:

```
SqlCommand cmd = new SqlCommand();
cmd.Connection = myConn;
cmd.CommandType= CommandType.
            StoredProcedure
            TableDirect
            Text
```

CommandType shown in the previous screenshot is another property associated with commands. You should exercise caution when this property is of type **Text**. This is where SQL injection attacks take place. A preferred type to deter injection attacks is **StoredProcedure** or a parameterized query.

What do the commands accomplish? SQL commands are issued to accomplish several tasks such as the following:

1. You can execute to return result sets that can be read with an associated reader such as:
    ◦ SqlDataReader
    ◦ OleDbDataReader
    ◦ OdbcDataReader
    ◦ EntityDataReader

   Search for everything that the `SqlDataReader` can do in the Object Explorer.

2. Execute **Data Definition Language (DDL)** commands to create, edit, and delete tables, stored procedures, and so on, provided you have permissions to do these operations.

3. Get database information by executing dynamic SQL commands to update, insert, and delete records.

4. Execute commands to return a single scalar value like an aggregate value.

5. Execute to return XML values and query the XML code.

In the following section, you will use connection builders to create tamper-free code that will prevent code injection by external means.

Using connection string builders

The previous section showed you how to use the connection strings to access the database. However, it is not good practice to send the strings in the form shown, as it can be tampered with. Connection strings must be carefully protected and secured. This is especially true when you are accessing them over the internet. One of the security considerations to prevent SQL injection attacks is to prevent externally injected script getting into the connection string. The injected script, while being syntactically correct, can introduce malicious code. If the connection string is obtained at runtime from user inputs, this is even more important.

While connecting to SQL Azure over the internet, make sure that the `ADO.NET` `Encrypt (=true)` and `TrustServerCertificate (=false)` connection properties are in place. This will ensure an encrypted connection and prevents the man-in-the-middle attacks (`http://msdn.microsoft.com/en-us/library/ff394108.aspx`).

In versions earlier to ADO.NET 3.5, compile-time checking of connection strings, formed by concatenating string values, did not occur, so at runtime, additional values of a malicious nature could be injected (for example, by adding a semi-colon followed by a key value pair). Review this article, for example: `http://www.codeproject.com/KB/database/Connection_Strings.aspx`.

Also, different providers supported a different syntax for connection string keywords (Password or PWD, and so on) making it difficult to string keywords manually and validate them. In ADO.NET 2.0, the new connection string builders for each .NET framework provider were introduced. The data providers, since then, included a connection string builder class, which would build a string for only acceptable key values for that provider. This acts as a filter for inserted code, allowing only those acceptable to the provider. You will find the details of these functions in `SqlConnectionStringBuilder`.

The different connection string builders trace their roots to the `DBConnectionstringBuilder` class. The .NET framework `Connection String Builder` class has the following connection string builders (EntityClient provider was added in Framework 3.5):

Provider	Connection String Builder
System.Data.SqlClient	SqlConnectionStringBuilder
System.Data.OleDb	OleDbConnectionStringBuilder
System.Data.Odbc	OleDbConnectionStringBuilder
System.Data.OracleClient	OracleConnectionStringBuilder
System.Data.EntityClient	EntityConnectionStringBuilder

In a manner similar to the connection strings, you can get a full appreciation of the properties that these classes support by looking them up in the Object Browser.

Using the connection builder is a recommended way of forming a connection string, not only for SQL Azure, but also for any place where a connection string is going to be used.

Accessing SQL Azure data using the Server Management Objects (SMO)

The Server Management Object model diagram available here: `http://msdn.microsoft.com/en-us/library/ms162209.aspx` reveals a rich feature set that this model offers to manage the SQL Server. SMO is based on **SQL Server Foundation Classes (SFC)**. This model is based on the SQL Server API and replaces the older **SQL-DMO (Distributed Management Objects)** and is very comprehensive with many new features announced for SQL Server 2008. With SQL Azure you can use SMO but only a subset of the features is supported. Features like snapshots, trace, replay SQL Server events, service broker, and so on are not supported.

The SMO model is built on a hierarchy of objects with the server at the very top. The rest of the objects are all instance class objects. Using this model you can program all aspects of the SQL Server. The objects are only loaded when specifically referenced.

To access a server you need to establish a connection first. This applies to using SMO as well. You create an instance of the server object and establish its connection to an instance of the SQL Server. In the present context, the connection we would like to establish is to the SQL Azure database. Following the creation of a server object, a `ServerConnection` object is created, a variable that can be used again and again. One difference with the Client APIs described earlier is that it is not necessary to call a Connect method. SMO will automatically connect when required and after the operation it is going to perform is finished, it releases the connection to the pool. It is also possible to call a Non-pooled Connection property of `ServerConnection` object.

If you are in doubt at any time using a method or property, make sure you access the SMO in the **Object Browser**.

In order to view this in the **Object Browser**, after adding the three references, right-click **Microsoft.SqlServer.Smo** and choose **View** in the **Object Browser**. The assembly node is then revealed in the Object Explorer. This is because, sometimes, even though the assembly is added to the project in the **Solution Explorer**, it does not get displayed in the **Object Browser**.

We will look at connecting to an SQL Azure database using SMO in this chapter with a practical example.

Accessing SQL Azure from Visual Studio 2010 Express

Visual Studio 2010 Express is a free program from the Visual Studio suite that can work with SQL Azure. The details of downloading this program are described here: `http://hodentek.blogspot.com/2010/06/get-these-web-development-tools-for.html`. You may download and install the program in a few easy steps starting from here: `http://www.microsoft.com/express/Web/`. After installing, you will have a shortcut in **Start** | **All Programs** from where you can launch the application. Visual Studio 2010 Express installs a Microsoft Visual Web Developer 2010 Express and a Microsoft Visual Studio 2010 Express for Windows Phone. You will be using the web developer.

- Launch the application as an administrator (**Run as administrator** option after a right-click).

- We will connect to SQL Azure from, for example, a web application.

- Click on **File** | **New Project** and create an **ASP.NET Web Application.**

- Change the default name from **WebApplication1** to one of your own, say **ConSQLAzure.**

- Click the menu item **Data** and click **Add New Data Source.**

- In the **New Data Source** window, click on the **Database** icon and click **Next>.**

- In the **Choose Your Data Connection** window, you may make a new connection using the **New Connection...** button.

- Click the **New Connection...** button to display the **Add Connection** window, as shown in the following screenshot:

 Note that there may already be a connection established. If it is to SQL Azure, you can go to the next step of the wizard by clicking **Next>**. Here, it is assumed you are making a new connection.

From here on the process is very similar to connecting to an SQL Server in Visual Studio, except you provide all information for your SQL Azure server.

The easy way to connect to SQL Azure using ADO.NET 3.5, ODBC, and OLE DB

You will now see how easy it is to connect to an SQL Azure database using Microsoft client programs such as ADO.NET, ODBC, and OLE DB. In connecting to the database, the single most important item is the connection string. The connection strings for SQL Azure are readily available at the portal as described in *Chapter 2, SQL Azure Services*. However, we may need to use appropriate arguments while constructing the connection string for OLE DB.

In the following steps a connection is opened and later closed for the Bluesky database, created in the first chapter with the ADO.NET 3.5, ODBC, and OLE DB.

- Run Visual Studio 2008 as an administrator from its shortcut in **Start | All Programs**.
- From **File | New Project...** (*CTRL + N*) |**Visual Basic**, choose from Visual Studio installed templates; a **Windows Forms Application** project in the default Framework option (3.5). Change the default name and click on **OK**. This adds a form **Form1.vb** and a **My Project** folder to the project (herein named TestConnect).
- Drag and drop three buttons on to the **Form1.vb**, as shown in the following screenshot:

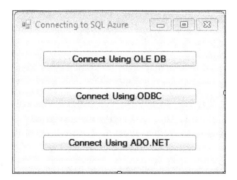

Using ADO.NET to connect to the SQL Azure database

The SqlClient is used for establishing an ADO.NET connection to the SQL Azure database as described previously.

In the following steps, you will be writing the code to one of the form's button click event that establishes a connection to the SQL Azure database.

1. To the click event of the button **Connect Using ADO.NET**, insert the code shown here:

```
Imports System.Data.SqlClient
'Imports System.Data.Odbc
'Imports System.Data.OleDb
Public Class Form1

    Private Sub Button1_Click(ByVal sender As System.Object, _
                              ByVal e As System.EventArgs) Handles
Button1.Click
        Dim conn As New SqlClient.SqlConnection
        conn.ConnectionString = "Server=tcp:Your SQL Azure Server
Name.database.windows.net;" & _
        "Database=Bluesky;User ID=Your User ID@ Your SQL Azure
Server Name;Password=Your Password;" & _
        "Trusted_Connection=False;Encrypt=True;"
        conn.Open()
If conn.State = ConnectionState.Open Then
            MessageBox.Show("Connection Opened")
        End If
        conn.Close()
        MessageBox.Show("Connection Closed")
    End Sub
End Class
```

The trick to insert the connection string easily without errors, is to copy and paste from the portal.

2. Open IE browser and log in to your Windows Live ID account. Open `http://Sql.Azure.com` in your IE Browser. The **Your User ID** in the portal is the same as the project name in the portal. Click on the **Database Name** you want to connect to in the portal after highlighting the project.

3. You should see the tabbed folder with the tabs **Databases** and **Firewall** settings.

4. Click on **Connection Strings** in the **Databases** tabbed page and click on **Copy to Clipboard**, the **ADO.NET connection string**.

5. Paste the code into the statement, `conn.ConnectionString=" "`.

6. Now replace **my password** with your password.

7. Build and run the form.

8. Verify that you can connect to the database.

Alternatively, you can also establish an ADO.NET connection to the database concatenating the following parameters:

```
Initial Catalog=Bluesky
Data Source=tcp:Your Server Name.database.windows.net
User ID=Your Project Name @Your Server Name
Password=Your Password;
Trusted_Connection=False
Encrypt=True
```

 Note that the USER ID can be either just the Project Name or Your Project Name @Your Server Name, but for ODBC and OLE DB just the Project Name for User ID is not supported.

Using ODBC to connect to the SQL Azure Database

This is no different from connecting to ADO.NET as shown in the previous steps except that, you must include the imports System.Data.ODBC in your code for the click event of the button **Connect Using ODBC**. Again, cutting and pasting from the portal is the easiest way.

From the portal, cut and paste the connection string for ODBC, as described in the previous steps, into the code for the click event of the button marked **Connect Using ODBC**, as shown here, and change the password:

```
'Imports System.Data.SqlClient
 Imports System.Data.Odbc
'Imports System.Data.OleDb

Public Class Form1
+ Private Sub Button1_Click ...(shown collapsed)
    Private Sub Button2_Click(ByVal sender As System.Object, _
                             ByVal e As System.EventArgs) Handles
Button2.Click
        Dim conn As New Odbc.OdbcConnection
        conn.ConnectionString = "Driver={SQL Server Native Client
10.0};" & _
        "Server=tcp:Your server Name.database.windows.
net;Database=Bluesky; " & _
        "Uid=Your Project Name@Your Server Name;Pwd=Your
Password;Encrypt=yes;"
        conn.Open()
If conn.State = ConnectionState.Open Then
            MessageBox.Show("Connection Opened")
        End If
        conn.Close()
```

```
        MessageBox.Show("Connection Closed")
    End Sub
End Class
```

Again, build the project and verify that you can connect to the database.

 Line break characters in Visual Basic must be inserted in Visual Studio 2008 but are optional in Visual Studio 2010.

Using OLE DB to connect to the SQL Azure database

Only ADO.NET and ODBC are supported on the SQL Azure platform. However, client connection to the SQL Azure database using OLE DB is possible. You need to construct the correct string that is supported by the OLE DB provider, SQLOLEDB. The connection string parameters are:

```
Provider = SQLNCLI10.1;
Server = tcp:Your Server Name.database.windows.net;
Database = Bluesky;
UID= Your Project Name @ Your Server Name;
Password = Your Password;
```

Enter the code to the click event of the button marked **Connect Using OLE DB**:

```
'Imports System.Data.SqlClient
'Imports System.Data.Odbc
Imports System.Data.OleDb
+ Private Sub Button1_Click ...(shown collapsed)
+ Private Sub Button2_Click ...(shown collapsed)
Private Sub Button3_Click(ByVal sender As System.Object, _
                          ByVal e As System.EventArgs) Handles
Button3.Click
        Dim conn As New OleDbConnection
        conn.ConnectionString = "Provider=SQLNCLI10.1;" & _
        "Server=tcp: Your server Name.database.windows.net;" & _
        "Database=Bluesky;" & _
        "UID= Your Project Name@Your Server Name;" & _
        "Password= Your Password;"
        Try

            conn.Open()
```

```
            If conn.State = ConnectionState.Open Then
                MessageBox.Show("Connection Opened")
            End If
            conn.Close()
            MessageBox.Show("Connection Closed")
        Catch ex As OleDb.OleDbException
            MessageBox.Show(ex.Message.ToString)
        Finally
        End Try
    End Sub
End Class
```

Again, verify that you can establish the connection by building the project and running the form.

In the previous code, a `Try...Catch` exception handling routine is added, which helps in trapping errors arising, while connecting to the database.

Using ADO.NET to connect to a SQL Azure database in C#

Although the code shown earlier is in VB, it could be easily written in C#, as shown here for one of the cases:

```
using System;
using System.Collections.Generic;
using System.ComponentModel;
using System.Data;
using System.Drawing;
using System.Linq;
using System.Text;
using System.Windows.Forms;
using System.Data.SqlClient;

namespace TestConCSharp
{
    public partial class Form1 : Form
    {
        public Form1()
        {
            InitializeComponent();
        }

        private void button1_Click(object sender, EventArgs e)
        {
```

```
            SqlConnection con = new SqlConnection();
            con.ConnectionString="Server=tcp:Your Server Name.
    database.windows.net;Database=Bluesky;User ID=Your Project Name@ Your
    Server Name;Password=Your Password;Trusted_Connection=False;Encrypt=T
    rue;";
            con.Open();
            if (
                    conn.State==ConnectionState.Open
                )
                    MessageBox.Show("Connection Opened");
                else
                    MessageBox.Show("Connection not open");
            con.Close();
            MessageBox.Show("Connection closed");
        }
      }
    }
```

Application using a SqlConnectionStringBuilder to connect to SQL Azure

As described previously, ConnectionString can be a point of entry for malicious attacks, which must be prevented. Of course, one could store the connection string either in an app.config file for Windows applications—as we shall see in a later exercise, or a web.config file in web applications. You will now learn the secure way to create a connection string using the class specifically created to handle this issue. It is not only secure and less error-prone, but also faster compared to one that can be custom built.

In each of the cases of malicious insertion of code, the program spits out the offending parameter.

In the following steps, you will be creating a Windows Forms Application, which accepts connection string-related information as input. For each of the correction parameters you will enter with injected code, you will review how the program reacts.

1. Run Visual Studio 2008 as an administrator from its shortcut in **Start** | **All Programs**.

2. From **File** | **New Project...** (*CTRL + N*) |**Visual Basic**, choose from Visual Studio installed templates; a Windows Forms Application project in the default Framework option (3.5). Change the default name and click on **OK**.

3. This adds a form `Form1.vb` and a `My Project` folder to the project (herein named `ConStringADONET`).

4. Drag and drop four textboxes, four labels, and a button on to the `Form1.vb`.

5. Change the text properties of the controls, as shown in the following screenshot:

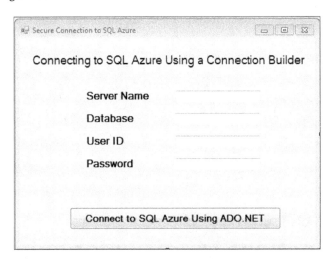

6. Double-click the form and in the displayed code page insert the following code, after deleting the displayed default code:

```vb
Imports System.Data.SqlClient
Imports System.Data.Common.DbConnectionStringBuilder
Public Class Form1

Private Sub Button1_Click(ByVal sender As System.Object, _
    ByVal e As System.EventArgs) Handles Button1.Click
        Dim conBldr As New SqlConnectionStringBuilder
          conBldr.DataSource = "tcp:" & Trim(TextBox4.Text) & _
          ".database.windows.net"
          conBldr.InitialCatalog = Trim(TextBox3.Text)
          conBldr.Encrypt = True
          conBldr.TrustServerCertificate = False
          conBldr.UserID = Trim(TextBox1.Text)
          conBldr.Password = Trim(TextBox2.Text)
          MessageBox.Show(conBldr.ConnectionString)
          Try
                Dim conn As New SqlConnection
                conn.ConnectionString = conBldr.ConnectionString
                conn.Open()
        If conn.State = ConnectionState.Open Then
```

```
                MessageBox.Show("Connection Opened")
            End If
            conn.Close()
            MessageBox.Show("Connection Closed")
        Catch ex As SqlException
            MessageBox.Show(ex.Message)
            MessageBox.Show(ex.ErrorCode)
        Finally
        End Try
    End Sub
End Class
```

The parent of the `SQLConnectionStringBuilder` is `System.Data.` `Common.DbConnectionStringBuilder` and is required to access `SqlConnectionStringBuilder`. This form is a typical UI to connect to the SQL Azure using the `Connection String Builder Class`. In the **Server Name** field (the one that you provisioned, here, a fictitious server is assumed) enter the highlighted portion of the SQL Azure server, namely **xhgytr9.database.windows.net**. For the field **USER ID** enter **<username>@xhgytr9**. Also enter the database name and the password.

As explained previously, the code will prevent malicious insertions into the connection string. The `Try...Catch...Finally...EndTry` block will trap errors that may be generated while making a connection.

If there are no errors (no malicious code injection), you should be able to connect successfully to the server with the following connection string in the message box:

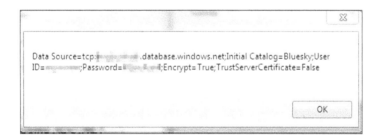

Testing the effectiveness of SqlConnectionStringBuilder

In order to test the efficacy of the UI against injection attacks, try entering a ";" (which happens to be a preferred method of SQL Injection) after any of the fields, the program throws an exception.

The following screenshot shows the connection string sent to the server when a ";" was added after the **Server Name** field before running the form. You can see that this is separated out as an extraneous string (underlined in red) from the connection string:

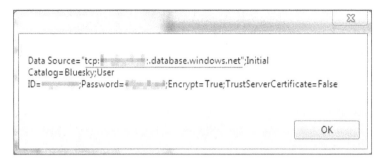

Now that the server is thrown out of the connection string, the program will throw an exception with an error code of **-2146232060**.

The following screenshot shows the connection string sent to the server when a ";" was added after the **Database** field before running the form:

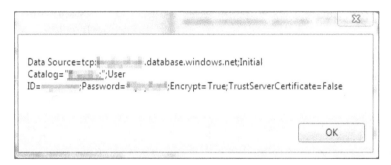

A **Cannot open database** exception will be thrown with an error code of **-2146232060**.

The following screenshot shows the connection string sent to the server when a ";" was added after the **USER ID** field before running the form:

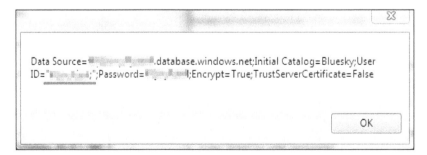

A **Login failed for user** exception will be thrown with an error code of **-2146232060**.

Finally, when you insert a ";" after the Password field, the connection string sent to the server is as follows:

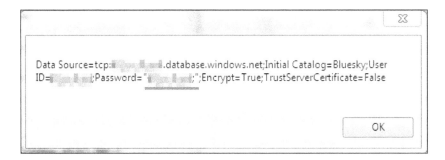

An exception gets thrown, as in the previous cases, with the same error code.

This shows that the `SqlConnectionStringBuilder` successfully thwarts any attempt to inject code into the connection string.

Demo using an SqlConnectionStringBuilder to connect to SQL Azure in C#

This demo is exactly the same as the previous one, but the code is in C#. We will be using the same user interface as in the previous case, but the code that is written is in C#.

1. Create a Windows Forms project in C# and add the same set of controls as in the VB project.

2. In the code for `Form1.cs`, add the following:

```
using System;
using System.Collections.Generic;
using System.ComponentModel;
using System.Data;
using System.Drawing;
using System.Linq;
using System.Text;
using System.Windows.Forms;
using System.Data.SqlClient;
using System.Data.Common;

namespace CSharpConBldr
{
```

```csharp
public partial class Form1 : Form
{
    public Form1()
    {
        InitializeComponent();
    }
    private void button2_Click(object sender, EventArgs e)
    {
        SqlConnectionStringBuilder mybldr = new
        SqlConnectionStringBuilder();
        mybldr.DataSource = "tcp:" + (TextBox4.Text).Trim() +
            ".database.windows.net".Trim();
        mybldr.InitialCatalog = (TextBox3.Text).Trim();
        mybldr.Encrypt = false;
        mybldr.TrustServerCertificate = false;
        mybldr.UserID = (TextBox1.Text).Trim();
        mybldr.Password = (TextBox2.Text).Trim();
        MessageBox.Show(mybldr.ConnectionString);

        try
        {
            SqlConnection conn = new SqlConnection();
            conn.ConnectionString = mybldr.ConnectionString;
            conn.Open();
            if (
                conn.State==ConnectionState.Open
                )
                MessageBox.Show("Connection Opened");
            else
                MessageBox.Show("Connection not open");
            conn.Close();
            MessageBox.Show("Connection Closed");
        }
        catch (SqlException ex)
        {
            MessageBox.Show(ex.Message);

        }
        finally
        {

        }
    }
}
```

The code is easy to understand, in terms of how it builds up the connection string, when you review the intellisense drop-down for the `mybldr` variable. Also note that the values to the variables are passed from the textboxes on the form.

As seen earlier, the connection string is the only item you need to change for ODBC and OLE DB connectivity.

Using SQL Server Management Objects (SMO) to connect to SQL Azure

For working with the SQL Server 2008, Microsoft has provided a collection of namespaces (SMO), which contain different classes, interfaces, and so on that help to programmatically manage the server. We will now use the elements of this namespace to access the SQL Azure server. This is a powerful tool, as it is based on the SQL Server API object model.

In the following steps, we will create a Windows Forms Application (even a console application can be used) and add references to the Server API that works with SMO and show how a connection can be established to SQL Azure.

1. Create a Windows Forms Application project (herein `SmoSqlAzure`) and to the default drag-and-drop a button.

2. Right-click on the **References** node and from the drop-down click on **Add Reference…**.

3. The **Add Reference** window gets displayed, as shown in the following screenshot:

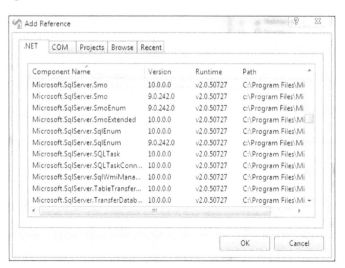

4. In the **Add Reference** window under **.NET** scroll down and add the following references:

```
Microsoft.SqlServer.ConnectionInfo
Microsoft.SqlServer.Management.sdk.Sfc
Microsoft.SqlServer.Management.Smo
```

5. The project folders in the **Solution Explorer** should appear, as shown, after the references are added.

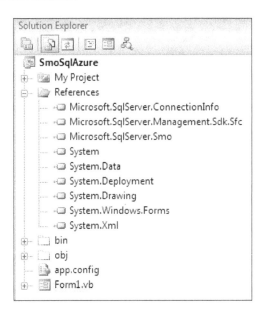

6. To the code page of Form1.vb, add the following code:

```
Imports Microsoft.SqlServer.Management.Smo
Public Class Form1

    Private Sub Button1_Click(ByVal sender As System.Object, _
            ByVal e As System.EventArgs) Handles Button1.Click
        'Provide SQL Azure connection Parameters as follows
        'Use the ConnectionContext of the server
        Dim srv As New Server("Your Server Name.database.windows.
net")
        srv.ConnectionContext.LoginSecure = False
        srv.ConnectionContext.Login = "Your ProjectName@Your
Server Name"
        srv.ConnectionContext.Password = Your Password"
        srv.ConnectionContext.DatabaseName = "Your Database Name"
        'create a strcutured exception block as shown
```

```
    Try
        srv.ConnectionContext.Connect()
    Catch ex1 As Exception
        MessageBox.Show(ex1.InnerException.ToString)
    Finally
        MessageBox.Show(srv.ConnectionContext.IsOpen)
    End Try
    If (srv.ConnectionContext.IsOpen) Then
        srv.ConnectionContext.Disconnect()
        MessageBox.Show(srv.ConnectionContext.IsOpen)
    End If
End Sub

End Class
```

The code shows some of the members of the SMO such as `ConnectionContext`, `IsOpen`, `Connect`, `Disconnect`, and so on.

SQL Server Management Objects (SMO) to connect to SQL Azure in C#

You can use the same procedure to create a project in C# and add references to the three namespaces as before. When you try to include `using Microsoft.Sqlserver.ConnectInfo` you may get a build error, even though you added it to the **References** node in the **Solution Explorer**. The build error you get is the following:

Error 1 The type or namespace name 'ConnectionInfo' does not exist in the namespace 'Microsoft.SqlServer' (are you missing an assembly reference?) C:\ Users\jay\Documents\Visual Studio 2008\Projects\SmoCSharpSqlAzure\ SmoCSharpSqlAzure\Form1.cs 11 27 SmoCSharpSqlAzure

Disregard it and use the code as follows:

```
using System;
using System.Collections.Generic;
using System.ComponentModel;
using System.Data;
using System.Drawing;
using System.Linq;
using System.Text;
using System.Windows.Forms;
using Microsoft.SqlServer.Management.Smo;
using Microsoft.SqlServer.Management.Sdk.Sfc;

namespace SmoCSharpSqlAzure
```

```
{
    public partial class Form1 : Form
    {
        public Form1()
        {
            InitializeComponent();
        }

        private void button1_Click(object sender, EventArgs e)
        {
            //Create a new server object and provide connection
parameters
            Server srv =
            new Server("Your Server Name.database.windows.net");
            srv.ConnectionContext.LoginSecure = false;
            srv.ConnectionContext.Login =
            "Your Project Name@Your Server Name";
            srv.ConnectionContext.Password =
            "Your Password";
            srv.ConnectionContext.DatabaseName = "Your Database Name";
            //create a structured exception block as shown
            MessageBox.Show(srv.ConnectionContext.ConnectionString);
            try{
                MessageBox.Show("OK");
                srv.ConnectionContext.Connect();
            if (srv.ConnectionContext.IsOpen)
            { MessageBox.Show("Connection Opened");}
                }
            catch (Exception ex1)
            {
                MessageBox.Show(ex1.Message);
                MessageBox.Show("Msg");
            }
            finally {
                srv.ConnectionContext.Disconnect();
                MessageBox.Show("Connection Closed");
            }
        }

    }
}
```

Creating database objects using ADO.NET

Here, you will now connect to the SQL Azure with your connection string stored in the application's settings file. You will also create and drop a database, create a table, and populate it, and so on. Although only the code for ADO.NET is demonstrated, ODBC and OLE DB may also be used.

Using connection string information in application settings

The very first thing, in this task, is to save the connection string information to the application settings. There are two databases in the SQL Azure server we have been working with, the master database and the database named Bluesky. In the next step, we will store the master database's connection string to the settings file.

1. Create a Windows Application project using the Windows Forms Application template and give it a name of your own (herein it is CreateDBObjects).

2. The program creates a project folder in the **Solution Explorer**, as shown in the following screenshot:

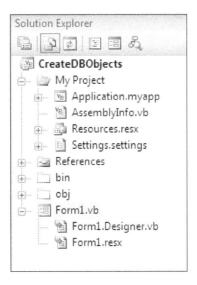

3. Add four buttons and a label and configure their visual appearance as follows:

The buttons are numbered from **1** to **4** and must be associated with the code that follows.

Inserting connection string information to the application settings file

In the following steps you will copy the connection string information from the SQL Azure portal and save it in the configuration file of your application.

1. Copy the connection string from the SQL Azure portal as you have done before (shown here details are masked).

   ```
   Server=xxxxxxxxxx.database.windows.net; Database=Bluesky;User
   ID=yyyyyy@xxxxxxx;Password=myPassword;Trusted_
   Connection=False;Encrypt=True;
   ```

2. From the **Projects** menu click open the projects properties page.

3. Click on the **Settings** tab in this window. This opens the **Settings** page of the application, as shown in the following screenshot:

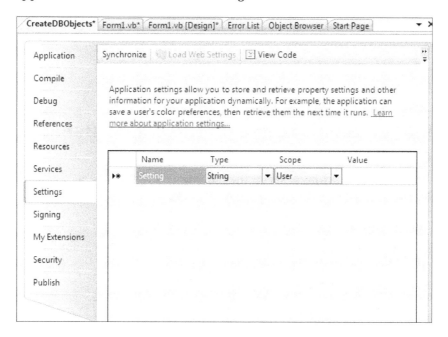

4. Set the following values for the four fields in the previous window:

   Name: Give a name (herein, it is `mdbs`).

   Type: String (no change).

   Scope: Application (choose from drop-down).

   Value: Enter the connection string of the master database you copied from the portal here. Make sure it is all in one line. If necessary, click on the value field, which opens a wider and a longer window.

5. Build the project. An **app.config** file gets added to the project.

6. Click on the **app.config** file.

7. The **app.config** file gets displayed as shown in the follwoing screenshot. Your connection string information will appear in the indicated position between **<value>** and **</value>**. Review the file and make sure there are no syntax errors, characters, such as "& _", which are common line continuation character strings in VB.NET, extra white spaces, and so on.

```
app.config  Form1.vb  Form1.vb [Design]  CreateDBObjects  Error List  Object Browser  Start Page
    <?xml version="1.0" encoding="utf-8" ?>
  <configuration>
      <configSections>...</configSections>
      <system.diagnostics>...</system.diagnostics>
      <applicationSettings>
          <CreateDBObjects.My.MySettings>
              <setting name="mdbs" serializeAs="String">
                  <value>      The    Connection  string  you  pasted will      appear      here </value>
              </setting>
          </CreateDBObjects.My.MySettings>
      </applicationSettings>
  </configuration>
```

Connect to the database on the server using the settings

In this code, you will be connecting to the database using the connection string you saved to the configuration file, in the previous section.

1. Click on the **app.config** file.

2. To the click event in the code page of `Form1.vb`, add the following code:

```
Imports System.Data.SqlClient
Public Class Form1

    Private Sub Button1_Click(ByVal sender As System.Object, ByVal
e As System.EventArgs) Handles Button1.Click
        GetConnected()
    End Sub
     Private Sub GetConnected()
        'Use the connection string in the settings page
        Dim constrg = New CreateDBObjects.My.MySettings
        Dim con As New SqlConnection
         'the current connection will use value in the 'settings
        con.ConnectionString = constrg.mdbs
        con.Open()
        If con.State = ConnectionState.Open Then
            MessageBox.Show("Connection is open now")
        End If
        con.Close()

    End Sub
```

3. Build the project and run the form.

4. Verify that you can connect to the SQL Azure server.

5. The database you will be connecting to will be the database in the connection string you supplied.

Create a test database and drop it

Now, you will create a database; verify that the database was created, drop the database, and verify you dropped the database before closing the connection. Why go to the trouble of creating and dropping? This is to keep the cost down for the demo. Any extra database you create is going to add to the charges.

In the following steps, you will be adding the code for creating a database, verifying it, and dropping the database before closing the connection.

To the click event of Button_2 add the following code:

```
Private Sub Button2_Click(ByVal sender As System.Object, _
        ByVal e As System.EventArgs) Handles Button2.Click
         'You are getting string info from settings
        Dim constrg = New CreateDBObj.My.MySettings
        Dim con As New SqlConnection
        con.ConnectionString = constrg.mdbs
        CreateTestDB(con)
    End Sub
    Private Sub CreateTestDB(ByVal MyConnection)
        Dim cmd As New SqlCommand
        cmd.Connection = MyConnection
        MyConnection.open()
        cmd.CommandType = CommandType.Text
        cmd.CommandText = "Create database ApiTest"
        cmd.ExecuteScalar()
        MessageBox.Show("Database created verify before you drop it")
        'You can verify this in the portal
        'run Select * from sys.databases in SSMS
        'you can add code to this procedure to check for database
ApiTest
        cmd.CommandText = ("Drop database ApiTest")
        cmd.ExecuteScalar()
        MessageBox.Show("Database is deleted verify before close
server")
        'Verify you successfully dropped the database
        MyConnection.close()
    End Sub
Dropping a table will not return any row and here using the
ExecuteScalar (does not return a set) method is the proper command to
use.
```

The following screenshot shows the new database created in the portal:

Database Name	Size	Type
ApiTest	0 B	1 GB
Bluesky	16 KB	1 GB
master	128 KB	1 GB

Tabs: Databases | Firewall Settings

Although this should work as previously coded, you may still get a transport error such as the following one. However, this does not always happen.

System.Data.SqlClient.SqlException was unhandled

  Class=20

  ErrorCode=-2146232060

  LineNumber=0

  Message="A transport-level error has occurred when receiving results from the server. (provider: TCP Provider, error: 0 - An existing connection was forcibly closed by the remote host.)"

  Number=10054

  Server="Your Server Name"

  Source=".Net SqlClient Data Provider"

  State=0

The best way to handle this is to try again, after a little while, as network errors of this kind can happen. You can read about this here: `http://social.msdn. microsoft.com/Forums/en-US/ssdsgetstarted/thread/0545004d-8fc4-405a-8fb8-a4f22f167d44?prof=required`.

The reason appears to be a mismatch between ADO.NET connection pool timeout and SQL Azure timeout differences. You can read about this here: `http://blog. ehuna.org/2010/01/how_to_stop_getting_exceptions.html`.

 In SU1 (first update after the February 2010 release), the SQL Azure timeout has been increased to 30 minutes.

One of the ways to handle this automatically is to catch a SqlClient Exception and if the error code is **-2146232060** try to connect again. But, this error code is emitted for other syntax errors as well and, therefore, you have to make sure there are no such errors.

Connect to the master database and get the Session ID

Every time you connect to the SQL Azure database from your application or SSMS, you will be opening a session through the gateway and it is associated with a Session ID. The next task does it programmatically. SessionID (or Session Tracing ID), together with server name and the approximate time will help to debug when calling Azure developer support.

1. To the click event of button **Connect to 'master' and get SessionID 3,** insert the following code:

```
Private Sub Button3_Click(ByVal sender As System.Object, ByVal e
As System.EventArgs) Handles Button3.Click
        Dim sessionId = Guid.Empty
        Dim constrg = New CreateDBObj.My.MySettings
        Dim con As New SqlConnection
        con.ConnectionString = constrg.mdbs
        Dim cmd As New SqlCommand
        cmd = con.CreateCommand
        cmd.CommandText = "SELECT CONVERT(NVARCHAR(36), CONTEXT_
INFO())"
        Dim contextInfo As String = CStr(cmd.ExecuteScalar)
        sessionId = New Guid(contextInfo)
        MessageBox.Show(sessionId.ToString)

    End Sub
```

Create a table if it does not exist and populate the table

Tables are integral to databases, as they store data in rows and columns. In SSMS, you can use the UI to create and populate the database using both graphical UI as well as script. In Visual Studio you can use the same script to create tables and populate them. You can create temporary tables as well as table variables in SQL Azure (please review these in the code bundle).

In the following steps, we will be creating a table after verifying that it does not already exist and then populate the table with some sample data:

1. Insert the connection string information in the app.config file. This was described earlier, but this time use the connection string for the Bluesky database on SQL Azure.

2. To the click event of **Create a table if it does not exist and populate it 4** button, insert the following code:

```
Private Sub Button4_Click(ByVal sender As System.Object, ByVal e
As System.EventArgs) Handles Button4.Click
        Dim conn As New SqlClient.SqlConnection
        conn.ConnectionString = bstrg
        conn.Open()
        Dim cmd As New SqlCommand
        'Create a SQL Command
        cmd = conn.CreateCommand
        'check and see if a table exists with the name
        cmd.CommandText = " if exists (select * from sys.tables
where sys.tables.name='myTbl')" & _
          "drop table myTbl"
        cmd.ExecuteScalar()
        MessageBox.Show("Check if table was dropped")
        'go verify in SSMS if it did get dropped
        'create the table, myTbl
        cmd.CommandText = "Create Table myTbl" & _
        "(id int Primary key clustered,fname varchar(20),age
Int,bday date)"
        cmd.ExecuteScalar()
        'insert values into table using the new feature in SQL
Servre 2008
        cmd.CommandText = "insert myTbl(id,fname,age,bday)" & _
        "values (1, 'Tom', 25, '1995'),(2,'Mary',30,'1990'),(3,'Har
ry',60,'1950')"
        cmd.ExecuteScalar()
        'select * from myTbl and display the results using a
SqlDataReader
        Dim cmd2 As New SqlCommand
        cmd2 = conn.CreateCommand
        cmd2.CommandText = "Select * from myTbl"
        Using rdr As SqlDataReader = cmd2.ExecuteReader()
            While rdr.Read()
                MessageBox.Show(rdr(0) & "," & rdr(1) & "," &
rdr(2))
            End While
        End Using
    End Sub
```

Creating database objects with SQL Server API

You will now use the SMO object model (SQL Server API) to connect to an SQL Azure database. Use SQL Server API to create a table in the database and add columns with chosen data types to the table and then create the table. While writing the code, wait for the intellisense to provide you with a drop-down list.

In the following steps, you will be creating database objects using the server API:

1. Create a Windows Application project using the Windows Forms Application template and give it a name of your own (herein, it is **SmoCreate**).

2. Right-click the project and choose **Add Reference**.

3. In the **Add Reference** window select and add the following references:

   ```
   Microsoft.SqlServer.ConnectionInfo
   Microsoft.SqlServer.Management.sdk.Sfc
   Microsoft.SqlServer.Management.Smo
   ```

4. Drag-and-drop a button on to the `Form1.vb`.

5. Add the following code to the code page of `Form1.vb`:

   ```
   Imports Microsoft.SqlServer.Management.Smo
   Public Class Form1

       Private Sub Button1_Click(ByVal sender As System.Object, _
               ByVal e As System.EventArgs) Handles Button1.Click
         'Provide SQL Azure connection Parameters as follows
         'Use the ConnectionContext of the server
         Dim srv As New Server("your server"
         srv.ConnectionContext.LoginSecure = False
         srv.ConnectionContext.Login = "your login"
         srv.ConnectionContext.Password = "your password"
         srv.ConnectionContext.DatabaseName = "your database,
         herein it is Bluesky"
         'create a strcutured exception block as shown
         MessageBox.Show(srv.ConnectionContext.ConnectionString)
         Try
             srv.ConnectionContext.Connect()
             MessageBox.Show(srv.ConnectionContext.IsOpen)
             Dim db As Database
             db = srv.Databases("Bluesky")
             Dim tbl As Table
             'Specify the parent database and the table name
   ```

```
                        'in the tables's constructor.
                        tbl = New Table(db, "MyHobbies")

                        'Add columns because the table must have at least
                        'one columns before it can be created.
                        Dim c1 As Column
                        'Specify the parent table, the column name and data
        'type in the Column's constructor. There are 4 'overloaded methods
                        c1 = New Column(tbl, "ID", DataType.Int)
                        tbl.Columns.Add(c1)
                        c1.Nullable = False
                        c1.Identity = True
                        c1.IdentityIncrement = 1
                        c1.IdentitySeed = 0
                        Dim c2 As Column
                        c2 = New Column(tbl, "Name", DataType.NVarChar(100))
                        c2.Nullable = False
                        tbl.Columns.Add(c2)
                        tbl.AnsiNullsStatus = True
                        'Create the table on the instance of SQL Server.
                        Dim c3 As Column
                        c3 = New Column(tbl, "Hobby ", DataType.VarChar(50))
                        tbl.Columns.Add(c3)
                        Dim c4 As Column = New         _
                        Column(tbl, "Date Started", DataType.SmallDateTime)
                        tbl.Columns.Add(c4)
                        tbl.Create()
                        'This next line would drop the table
                        'tbl.Drop
                        'The next two lines instantiates a trigger, etc
                        'Dim trg As Trigger
                        'trg = New Trigger(tbl, "MyHobbies")

                Catch ex1 As Exception
                        MessageBox.Show(ex1.InnerException.ToString)
                Finally
                        End Try
        End Sub
    End Class
```

6. Build the project and run the form. The program has been tested to function correctly.

7. You should get two messages. Verify that the connection string is correct.

8. Verify that a table is created in the database in SSMS, as shown in the following screenshot:

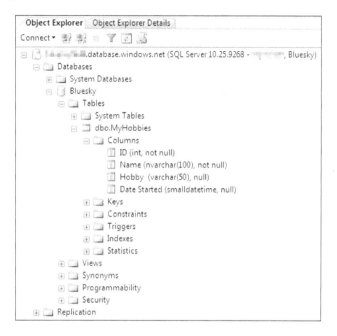

Summary

In this chapter, the SQL Azure architecture was briefly reviewed. Accessing SQL Azure to manipulate objects, therein using client technologies such as ADO.NET, ODBC, and OLE DB, was described with examples. Connecting to SQL Azure for data manipulation, using Server APIs with examples, was considered using Visual Studio 2008 SP1. Also considered was the best practice of using ConnectionBuilder to thwart SQL injection attacks in detail. Examples of using ADO.NET for creating database objects were detailed using both Client APIs as well as Server APIs. The method to connect to SQL Azure using the entity framework was not described here, but is described with a complete example in *Chapter 8, Database applications on Windows Azure Platform accessing SQL Server databases.*

In the next chapter, we will consider the different options we have for moving or migrating, schema and data to SQL Azure as well as from SQL Azure to onsite SQL Server databases.

4
SQL Azure Tools

The successful adoption of any software depends on the availability of a reliable and tested toolset. SQL Azure's success would also depend on this key requirement. Microsoft has largely contributed to the tools that can be leveraged working with SQL Azure, but a few third-party vendors and others have also created tools for SQL Azure.

This chapter describes some of the developments that have taken place in this area. Needless to say that some of the tools have already been covered in *Chapters 2, SQL Azure Services* and *Chapter 3, Working with SQL Azure Databases from Visual Studio 2008.*

In this chapter, we will discuss the following:

- Microsoft tools
- Third-party tools
- SQL Azure and OpenOffice

Microsoft tools

As we have seen earlier, SQL Azure is a subset of SQL Server 2008 R2 and, as such, the tools that are used with SQL Server can also be used with SQL Azure, albeit with only some of the features supported. The Microsoft tools can also be divided further between those that are accessed from the Visual Studio series of products and those that are not. However, it appears that with Visual Studio 2010, the SSMS may be largely redundant for most commonly used tasks.

Visual Studio related

From the very beginning, Visual Studio supported developing data-centric applications working together with the existing version of SQL Server, as well as MS Access databases, and databases from third parties. The various client APIs such as ODBC, OLEDB, and ADO.NET made this happen, not only for direct access to manipulate data on the server, but also for supporting web-facing applications to interact with the databases.

There are two versions, of particular interest to SQL Azure, that are specially highlighted as they allow for creating applications consuming data from the SQL Azure Server. Visual Studio 2008 SP1 and Visual Studio 2010 RC were released (April 12, 2010) recently for production. The new key features of the more recent update to SQL Azure are here: `http://hodentek.blogspot.com/2010/04/features-galore-for-sql-azure.html`. It may be noted that the SQL Azure portal provides the all-important connection strings that is crucial for connecting to SQL Azure using Visual Studio.

VS2008

Chapter 2, SQL Azure Services deals dealt with the details of working with SQL Azure and showed how to access and manipulate objects on SQL Azure databases directly using ODBC, OLE DB, and ADO.NET technologies. In *Chapter 8, Database Applications on Windows Azure Platform Accessing SQL Server Databases*, developing web facing applications using Visual Studio 2008 will be discussed.

Although you can access and work with SQL Azure using Visual Studio 2008, it does not support establishing a data connection to SQL Azure using the graphic user interface, like you can with an on-site application. This has been remedied in Visual Studio 2010.

VS2010

Visual Studio 2010 has a tighter integration with many more features than Visual Studio 2008 SP1. It is earmarked to make the cloud offering more attractive. Of particular interest to SQL Azure is the support it offers in making a connection to SQL Azure through its interactive graphic user interface and the recently introduced feature supporting Data-tier applications. A summary detail of the data tier applications are here: `http://hodentek.blogspot.com/2010/02/working-with-data-gotten-lot-easier.html`. The details of these applied to SQL Azure are described in a practical application in *Chapter 5, Populating SQL Azure Databases*.

SQL Azure explorer, a lightweight program described later in this chapter under third-party tools is an add-in for extending the capability of VS2010 to explore the objects on SQL Azure databases.

SQLBulkCopy for Data Transfer

In .NET 2.0, the SQLBulkCopy class in the `System.Data.SqlClient` namespace was introduced. This class makes it easy to move data from one server to another using Visual Studio. An example is described in the next chapter using Visual Studio 2010 RC, but a similar method can be adopted in Visual Studio 2008.**SQL Server Business Intelligence Development Studio (BIDS).**

The Business Intelligence Development Studio (BIDS) would fall under both SQL Server 2008 and Visual Studio. The tight integration of Visual Studio with SQL Server was instrumental in the development of BIDS. Starting off to a successful introduction in Visual Studio 2005 more enhancements were added in Visual Studio 2008, both to the Integration Services as well as Reporting Services, two of the main features of BIDS. BIDS is available as a part of the Visual Studio shell when you install the recommended version of SQL Server. Even if you do not have Visual Studio installed, you would get a part of Visual Studio that is needed for developing business intelligence-related integration services as well as reporting services applications.

SQL Server Integration Services

Microsoft SQL Server Integration Services (SSIS) is a comprehensive data integration service that superseded the Data Transformation Services. Through its connection managers it can establish connections to a variety of data sources that includes SQL Azure. Many of the data intensive tasks from onsite to SQL Azure can be carried out in SSIS. These will be considered in *Chapter 6, SSIS and SSRS Applications Using SQL Azure*.

SQL Server Reporting Services

SQL Server Reporting Services (SSRS) is a comprehensive reporting package that consists of a Report Server tightly integrated with SQL Server 2008 R2 and a web-based frontend, client software - the Report Manager. SSRS can spin-off reports from data stored on SQL Azure through its powerful data binding interface. Creating reports from data on SQL Azure will be described in *Chapter 6, SSIS and SSRS Applications Using SQL Azure*.

Entity Framework Provider

Like ODBC, OLE DB, and ADO.NET data providers Entity Framework also features an Entity Framework Provider (briefly described in *Chapter 2, SQL Azure Services*) although, it does not connect to SQL Azure like the others. Using Entity Framework Provider you can create data services for a SQL Azure database. .NET client applications can access these services. In order to work with Entity Framework Provider you need to install Windows Azure SDK (there are several versions of these), which provides appropriate templates.

Presently, the Entity Framework Provider cannot create the needed files for a database on SQL Azure. A workaround is adopted. This will be considered in *Chapter 7, Working with Windows Azure Hosting*.

SQL Server related

The tools described in this section can directly access SQL Server 2008 R2. The Export/ Import Wizard cannot only access SQL Servers but also products from other vendors to which a connection can be established. Scripting support, BCP, and SSRS are all effective when the database server is installed and are part of the SQL Server 2008 R2 installation. SQL Server Integration Services is tightly integrated with SQL Server 2008 R2, which can store packages created using SSIS. Data access technologies and self-service business integration technologies are developing rapidly, as this book is written, and will impact on cloud-based applications including solutions using SQL Azure.

SQL Server Management Studio

SQL Server Management Studio (SSMS) has been the work horse with the SQL Servers from the very beginning. SSMS also supports working with SQL Azure Server. SQL Server 2008 did not fully support SQL Azure, except it did enable connection to SQL Azure. This was improved in SQL Server 2008 R2 November-CTP and the versions to appear later.

As we have seen in *Chapter 2, SQL Azure Services*, you can connect to a SQL Azure Database either through the Data Engine interface or through a query window. We have seen both ways in *Chapter 2, SQL Azure Services*.

SSMS also provides the SQL Azure template, which includes most of the commands you will be using in SQL Azure.

Import/Export Wizard

The Import/Export Wizard has been present in SQL Servers even from earlier versions to create DTS packages of a simple nature. It could be started from the command line using DTSWiz.exe or DTSWizard.exe. In the same folder, you can access all dts-related files. You can double-click Import and Export Data (32-bit) in **Start | All Programs | Microsoft SQL Server 2008 R2**.

You may also run the DTSWizard.exe from a DOS prompt to launch the wizard.

The Import/Export wizard may be able to connect to SQL Azure using any of the following:

- ODBC DSN
- SQL Server Native Client 10.0
- .NET Data Source Provider for SqlServer

The Import/Export wizard can connect to the SQL Azure server using ODBC DSN. Although connection was possible, the export or import was not possible in the CTP version due to some unsupported stored procedure. This has been modified as we will see in the next chapter.

Import/Export works with the .NET Framework Data Provider, but requires some tweaking, and this is discussed in *Chapter 5, Populating SQL Azure Databases* on populating SQL Azure databases.

SyncFramework and SQL Azure

The ability to synchronize data between on-site data, data on SQL Azure, and data on handheld devices is an important consideration. The Microsoft Sync Framework and the power pack designed for SQL Azure supports this capability: (`http://hodentek.blogspot.com/2009/12/synchronizing-with-cloud-database.html`).

The following new components in the SyncFramework PowerPack for SQL Azure November CTP are designed to improve the user experience in synchronizing on-site data with SQL Azure:

- SqlAzureSyncProvider
- SQL Azure Offline Visual Studio Plug-in
- SQL Azure Data Sync Tool for SQL Server
- New SQL Azure Components
- Automated Provisioning

These components and the runtime components simplify synchronizing with the cloud while optimizing performance. The power pack also has a Visual Studio plugin that demonstrates offline capabilities to synchronize with a local SQL Server Compact.

The SyncFramework PowerPack for SQL Azure November CTP can be downloaded here: `http://www.microsoft.com/downloads/details.aspx?FamilyID=bce4ad61-5b76-4101-8311-e928e7250b9a&displaylang=en`.

In addition to the previous power pack you also need the Microsoft Sync Framework 2.0 SDK. You may download this software from here: `http://www.microsoft.com/downloads/details.aspx?FamilyID=89adbb1e-53ff-41b5-ba17-8e43a2e66254&displaylang=en`.

While the power pack provides elements specific to SQL Azure, the Sync Framework 2.0 SDK is a comprehensive platform that provides support for collaboration and offline scenarios for applications, services, and devices.

We will look at Synchronizing with on-site data with examples in *Chapter 9, Synchronizing SQL Azure*.

MySQL to SQL Azure Migration

The fact that MySQL and PHP are inseparable twins, and that MySQL has a large following, has persuaded Microsoft to provide support for both MySQL and PHP in its cloud offerings.

Microsoft SQL Server Migration Assistant 2008 for MySQL v1.0 CTP1 (SSMA 2008 for MySQL CTP1a.zip, 4 to 8 MB), which may be downloaded from here: (`http://www.microsoft.com/downloads/details.aspx?displaylang=en&FamilyID=0e6168b0-2d0c-4076-96c2-60bd25294a8e`) provides a toolkit to effortlessly migrate MySQL databases to SQL Azure. In this way, it provides a bridge for those who want to move their MySQL-based businesses to the cloud. The program can migrate, both schema and data.

SSMA 2008 for MySQL v1.0 CTP1 is designed to work with MySQL 4.1, 5.0, and 5.1, and all editions of SQL Server 2008 or SQL Azure.

The requirements are:

- Microsoft Windows Installer 3.1 or a later version.
- The Microsoft .NET Framework version 2.0 or a later version.
- The .NET Framework version 2.0 is available on the SQL Server 2008 product media. You can also obtain it from the .NET Framework Developer Center.
- MySQL Connector/ODBC v5.1.
- Access to and sufficient permissions on the computer that hosts the target instance of SQL Server 2008 or SQL Azure database.
- 1 GB RAM.

In the next chapter, an example of migrating MySQL Database objects to a SQL Azure database will be described. For updates follow: `http://blogs.msdn.com/b/ssma/archive/2010/08/12/microsoft-announces-sql-server-migration-assistant-for-mysql.aspx`.

Scripting support for SQL Azure

In addition to supporting T-SQL Commands through the SQL Server Object Explorer you can also do scripting, which allows you to write scripts against not only SQL Azure databases but also several other versions of SQL Server such as 2005 and 2008.

In order to create a script that you can run on SQL Azure, you will need to invoke the scripting option for the SQL Azure Database Engine and prepare the script for an object on the SQL Server 2008 R2. These can be configured in SSMS by going through **Tools | Options** in the main menu to open the **Options** window, as shown in the following image:

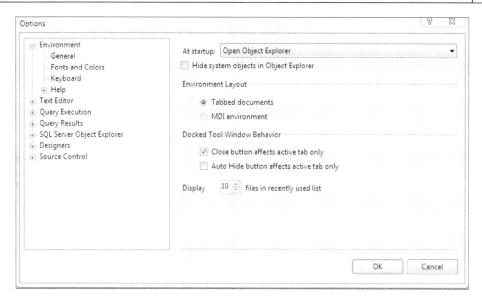

In **Options**, click open the menu item **SQL Server 'Object Explorer | Scripting** as shown in the following screenshot. Click on the **script for database engine type** and choose **SQL Azure Database**:

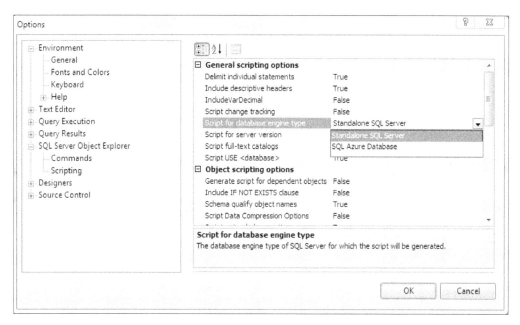

Click on **Script for server version** and from the drop-down list choose **SQL Server 2008 R2** as shown in the following screenshot:

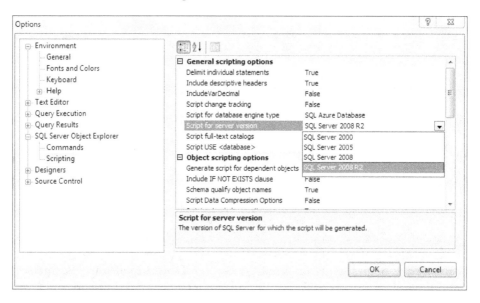

Using scripts to transfer a database is described in *Chapter 5, Populating SQL Azure Databases*.

SQLCMD

SQLCMD is a command-line utility that is shipped with the SQL Server. With SQLCMD you can carry out the following:

- Connect to SQL Azure database
- Enter and run T-SQL Statements
- Run script files and System procedures

The following are the two ways you can run SQLCMD:

- From a DOS prompt
- From SSMS

SQLCMD can be run from a DOS prompt or in the **Query** menu item **SQLCMD Mode** by choosing to create a **New Query** in SSMS as shown later in this section.

SQLCMD utility has many options and you can get help on using these options by executing the following statement from the command line C:\sqlcmd /? as shown in the following screenshot:

```
C:\Windows\system32\cmd.exe                                    ⬚  ◻  ▨

Microsoft Windows [Version 6.1.7600]
Copyright (c) 2009 Microsoft Corporation.  All rights reserved.

C:\Users\jay>sqlcmd /?
Microsoft (R) SQL Server Command Line Tool
Version 10.50.1352.12 NT INTEL X86
Copyright (c) Microsoft Corporation.  All rights reserved.

usage: Sqlcmd              [-U login id]           [-P password]
  [-S server]              [-H hostname]           [-E trusted connection]
  [-N Encrypt Connection][-C Trust Server Certificate]
  [-d use database name]   [-l login timeout]      [-t query timeout]
  [-h headers]             [-s colseparator]       [-w screen width]
  [-a packetsize]          [-e echo input]         [-I Enable Quoted Identifiers]
  [-c cmdend]              [-L[c] list servers[clean output]]
  [-q "cmdline query"]     [-Q "cmdline query" and exit]
  [-m errorlevel]          [-V severitylevel]      [-W remove trailing spaces]
  [-u unicode output]      [-r[0|1] msgs to stderr]
  [-i inputfile]           [-o outputfile]         [-z new password]
  [-f <codepage> | i:<codepage>[,o:<codepage>]] [-Z new password and exit]
  [-k[1|2] remove[replace] control characters]
  [-y variable length type display width]
  [-Y fixed length type display width]
  [-p[1] print statistics[colon format]]
  [-R use client regional setting]
  [-b On error batch abort]
  [-v var = "value"...]   [-A dedicated admin connection]
  [-X[1] disable commands, startup script, enviroment variables [and exit]]
  [-x disable variable substitution]
  [-? show syntax summary]

C:\Users\jay>
```

Connect to SQL Azure from the DOS window

You must be running the computer from the same location for which you have set up
the firewall rules. In this case, it is assumed that the Service Principal is connecting
to the SQL Azure database Bluesky. The server name after the -S flag should be **tcp**:
servername.database.windows.net and the user name after the -U flag should be
<username>@<servername>. The command-line options are case sensitive.

Follow the indicated steps to run SQLCMD against the SQL Azure database. Make
sure you use SQL Azure-related items specific to your provisioning:

1. Bring up the DOS screen and enter the following at C:\ prompt:

   ```
   C:\Users\jay>sqlcmd -S tcp: XXXXXXXXX.database.windows.net -U
   <Username>@XXXXXXXXXX

     -P <Password> -d Bluesky
   ```

2. The command prompt changes form C:\Users\jay> to 1>****.

3. Try to query a table that does not exist using the select command.

4. The next command shows what happens when you query for a non-existent object.

```
1> Select * from MyTable
2>;
3> Go

Msg 208, Level 16, State 1, Server XXXXXXXX, Line 1
Invalid object name 'MyTable'.

Querying the table MyHobbies
Querying a table that is known to exist in the database.
1> Select * from MyHobbies
2> GO

ID          Name                                    Hobby     Date
Started
----------- --------------------------------------------------------------
--------------
------------------------------------------ ---------------------------------
--------------
--- ----------------

(0 rows affected)
```

Run queries using SQLCMD in SSMS

As previously mentioned, we can connect to a SQL Azure database and run queries in the query window.

1. Connect to SQL Azure in SSMS as discussed previously in *Chapter 2, SQL Azure Services*.

2. Click **New Query** in the main menu.

3. The Query menu item gets enabled.

4. Click **Query** and from the drop-down list choose the menu item **SQLCMD Mode** as shown in the next screenshot:

By default this is not turned on.

5. Click **Tools** | **Options** in the main menu. The **Options** window is displayed as shown:

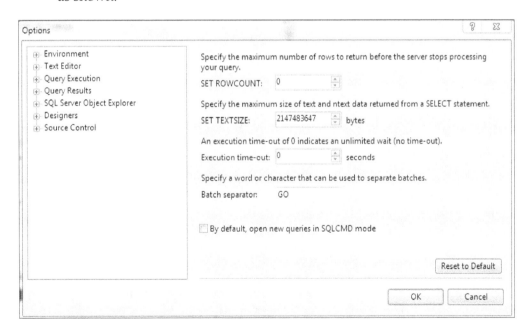

6. Choose **By default, open new queries in SQLCMD mode** and click **OK**.

7. Create new query in Bluesky as discussed in *Chapter 2, SQL Azure Services.*

8. Enter the following code in the query window:

```
:setvar tablename MyHobbies
go
select * from $(tablename)
go
```

9. Notice that the first line gets a grey background. Click **Execute** in the query window.

The result of the query output together with the query and the objects in the Bluesky database are shown in the following screenshot:

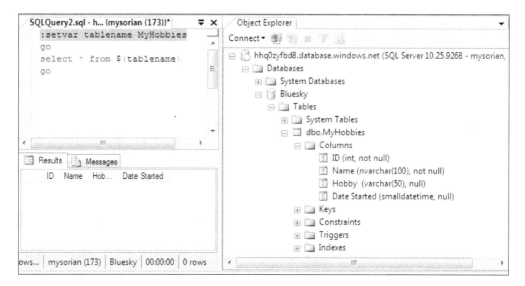

BCP Utility

BCP is a bulk copying utility copying data between SQL Server instances and a data file in a user-specified format. BCP utility can be used with SQL Azure. BCP is a veteran Export/Import utility known for its ease; capable of moving large amounts of data and speed. These features testify to its survival for so long.

It is used for copying a large set of rows out of tables to data files. It is not T-SQL dependent, except when used with the Query option. However, **Queryout** option, which would allow T-SQL, is not presently supported in SQL Azure. You need to understand file formats and table structures to work with BCP. For more details on BCP follow this link: http://msdn.microsoft.com/en-us/library/ms162802.aspx.

To create a backup of data you must first create a file to record the data format.

The syntax of BCP utility (from MSDN) is as follows:

```
bcp {[[database_name.][schema].]{table_name | view_name} | "query"}
    {in | out | queryout | format} data_file
    [-m max_errors] [-f format_file] [-x] [-e err_file]
    [-F first_row] [-L last_row] [-b batch_size]
    [-n] [-c] [-N] [-w] [-V (70 | 80 | 90 )]
    [-q] [-C { ACP | OEM | RAW | code_page } ] [-t field_term]
    [-r row_term] [-i input_file] [-o output_file] [-a packet_size]
    [-S server_name[\instance_name]] [-U login_id] [-P password]
h
```

For details of the various options please refer to the previous link to BCP on MSDN. The DOS help screen seems to have been created during SQL Server 2005 (90) and differs from the MSDN documentation.

BCP utility can be used with SQL Servers from version 7.0 (70) to 2008 (100) and if there is an older version of the database on the computer, you need to know which version is being used. You can find the BCP version using the following command in the DOS screen:

```
C:\Users\jay>bcp /v
BCP - Bulk Copy Program for Microsoft SQL Server.
Copyright (C) Microsoft Corporation. All Rights Reserved.
Version: 10.50.1352.12
```

Depending on the direction of data flow, you need permissions to work with the objects. For data going out of tables to files you need to select permission on the dataset going out. For inserting values into tables from files, you need to select and Insert permissions to the tables.

You can get oriented with calling this utility by following these steps:

1. Create the table MyTable in the Bluesky database and populate the table as described in *Chapter 2, SQL Azure Services* by executing the following statements in SSMS:

```
CREATE TABLE MyTable (
ID int PRIMARY KEY CLUSTERED,
FirstName varchar (20)
)
INSERT INTO MyTable VALUES('1','John')
```

```
GO
INSERT INTO MyTable VALUES('2','Mary')
GO
INSERT INTO MyTable VALUES('3','Kristine')
GO
```

2. Execute a SELECT Statement to verify the returned data.

3. You should see 3 rows returned, each having two columns.

4. Bring up the DOS screen by calling the command cmd from Run.

5. Now you will be running the BCP utility. This is an interactive utility where in, you need to have knowledge of the fields in your table; their data types, their field lengths, etc. as you will be asked to answer the questions in the interactive session.

6. Type-in the following at the command prompt:

```
C:\Users\jay>bcp Bluesky.dbo.MyTable out C:\Users\jay\testAzure.
dat -S tcp:<Your SQL_Azure_Server_Name.database.net> -U
<username>@< Your SQL_Azure_Server_Name > -P <Your Password>
```

7. Hit return.

8. The Interactive session starts as shown here, you will then need to type-in your answers (shown in red) after the prompt:

```
Enter the file storage type of field ID [int]: char
Enter prefix-length of field ID [1]: 1
Enter field terminator [none]: ,
Enter the file storage type of field FirstName [char]: char
Enter prefix-length of field FirstName [2]: 4
Enter field terminator [none]:
Do you want to save this format information in a file? [Y/n] Y
  Host filename [bcp.fmt]: bcpAzure.fmt
```

9. After entering bcpAzure.fmt hit return.

10. You get the following displayed in your DOS screen:

```
Starting copy...

3 rows copied.

Network packet size (bytes): 4096

Clock Time (ms.) Total    : 125    Average : (24.00 rows per
sec.)
```

11. You will find two files testAzure.dat and bcpAzure.fmt in the directory you specified in the bcp utility previously. Both are text files that you can open with **Notepad** or **WordPad**.

The next table shows the `bcpAzure.fmt` from the previous run. The table as well as the text in bold was added to the output (output is in a tab separated text format) to help in understanding the items:

10.0	BCP Version							
2	No of fields							
Data Field Position	Data Type	Prefix	Data file field length	Row or field terminator	Column position	Column Name	Column Collation
1	SQL Char	1	12	","	1	ID	""
2	SQL Char	4	20	""	2	First Name	SQL_Latin1-General_CP1_As

12. The `testAzure.dat` has the following content:

```
1,    John2,    Mary3,Kristine
```

The characters not in ASCII arise out of exporting data in Unicode representation: (`http://msdn.microsoft.com/en-us/library/ms188289.aspx`).

This can be improved by using the `-w` option as in:

```
C:\Users\jay>bcp Bluesky.dbo.MyTable out C:\Users\jay\testAzure.dat -S
tcp:<Your SQL_Azure_Server_Name.database.net> -U <username>@< Your SQL_
Azure_Server_Name > -P <Your Password> -w
```

In this case, there are no interactive sessions and you will get the output file right away.

The output of a BCP utility depends strongly on how the questions are answered in the interactive session. For additional information on the output format follow this link here:

`http://support.microsoft.com/kb/67409`

Only a very simple description of the usage of BCP is presented, for details please refer to the link here:

`http://msdn.microsoft.com/en-us/library/ms162802.aspx`

IIS7 Database Manager

Database Manager 1.0 for both x32 and x64 is an IIS 7.0 extension that supports managing SQL Servers from IIS 7 Manager. It may be downloaded from this location:

`http://www.iis.net/download/DatabaseManager`

IIS 7 Database Manager can automatically discover SQL Servers (it did not in the present installation) — both local and remote — and make them available in the IIS 7 Management Console. From the IIS 7 console you can manage all server objects such as tables, views, stored procedures, and so on.

In addition to SQL Server IIS, Database Manager also provides support for MySQL, the popular database product recently acquired by Oracle. This is a nice feature because IIS 7's Database Manager connects to SQL Azure as well as MySQL, and the SQL Azure server can get exported data from MySQL through the recent introduction of SSMA.

Herein, few of the details of practically using the Database Manager are provided as it lends itself to be a nice tool, especially to those operating systems where IIS 7.0 is available by default such as Windows 7.0.

Some of the advertised features are:

- Manage Microsoft SQL Server or MySQL databases
- Add, rename, drop, and edit tables
- View and manage primary keys, indexes, and foreign keys
- Edit data
- Establish connections to multiple databases
- Create and execute queries
- Create, alter, and delete stored procedures and views
- Manage both local and remote databases from your machine
- Backup and restore Microsoft SQL Server databases
- IIS 7 Manager provides remote management capabilities with a clean firewall-friendly option for managing a remote SQL Server
- Exposes a public extensibility platform that enables the development of providers to support other databases
- Compatible with SQL 2008/2005 and MySQL

To get some working experience with this tool, follow the indicated steps. These steps will help you in connecting to SQL Azure and run SQL queries on SQL Azure:

1. **Start | Search programs and files**. Enter **InetMgr**. Double-click **InetMgr** in the pop-up search list.

2. Internet Information Services (IIS) Manager is displayed as in the following screenshot:

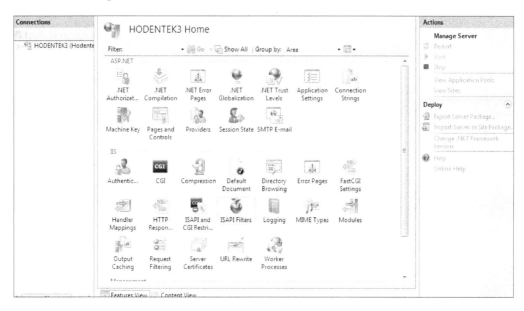

3. Click the **Connections**.

4. Under the **Management** Section you will find the **Database Manager,** as shown in the next screenshot.

 Database Manager will not be available if you did not install the extension from the website mentioned earlier. From the download site you must install the `iisdbmanager_x86_en-US.msi` `installer` package 595KB.

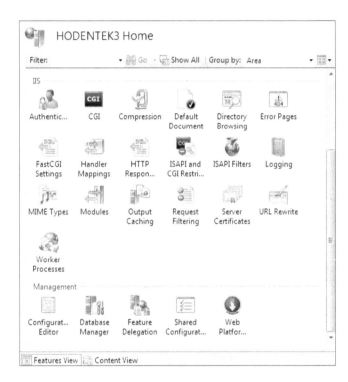

5. Double-click the **Database Manager** Icon to open the items as shown.

6. The **Database Manager** will open to reveal a single connection to an existing **LocalSqlServer**.

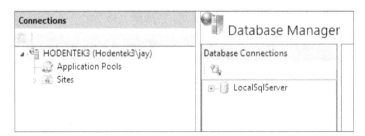

7. Double-click the **LocalSqlServer**. It may open to reveal the existing databases.

8. As it happened, it may display an error (although it is supposed to discover all servers, it did not).

9. Right-click on the icon above it (if you hover above it you can see it is an **Add Connection** link).

10. The **Add Connection** window will open as in the following screenshot:

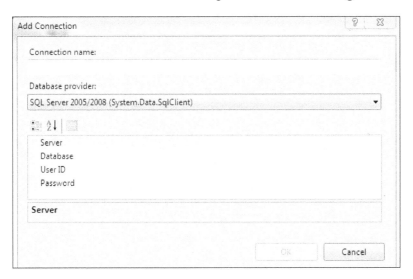

11. Enter the credentials for the SQL Azure Server database Bluesky with the appropriate values after providing a name of your choice (herein, SqlAzure01)@:

    Server: xxxxxxxx.database.windows.net

    Database: Bluesky

    User ID: <Username>

    Password: <Password>

12. Click **OK.**

13. The **SqlAzure01** connection gets added as shown (it is shown with the node fully expanded). You should observe that the columns are not displayed like they are in SSMS:

14. The five toolbar icons from left to right above **LocalSqlServer** are Add Connection, New Query, Open Table Definition, Show Table Data, and Delete.

15. In order to see the data in the MyTable, query the table as in the next step.

16. Click **MyTable** and click **Show Table Data** icon.

17. The **MyTable** data is displayed as shown in the next screenshot:

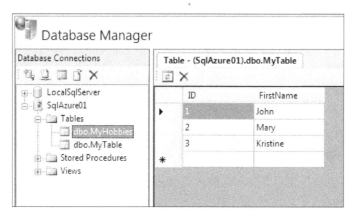

18. You can delete a row if you want to by highlighting a row and clicking the delete button in the pane. In addition, you can run a query using the **New Query** icon.

19. Click **New Query**.

20. The **SqlQuery_1** is displayed.

21. Enter the following query and click **Execute**:

```
Select * from MyTable for XML auto
```

22. The query result appears in the bottom pane as shown:

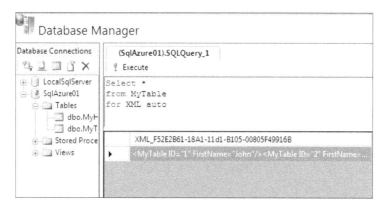

The Database Manager is another useful tool in working with SQL Azure. Presumably, it can deliver most, if not all, of the items when used with SQL Azure. The connection you created can be stored in IIS by going to **File | Save Connection**, so that it can be readily used the next time a connection is to be made.

OData and SQL Azure

OData uses well–known, existing technologies HTTP, Atom Publishing protocol, and JSON to provide access to information from a variety of services and stores of data including relational store in SQL Azure. The OData (`http://hodentek.blogspot.com/2010/03/microsoft-azure-and-open-data.html`) Portal and Service allows publishing SQL Azure databases as OData services using simple configuration. This way, the SQL Azure data can be URL-accessed using REST-based APIs. We will look at this in *Chapter 10, Recent Developments*.

Brand new tools

Microsoft has since added a few more tools as well as web-based tools, which appear to be very attractive to work with SQL Azure. The following are some of the tools and links to them:

- Microsoft Web Matrix, `http://www.microsoft.com/web/webmatrix/learn/`

- Microsoft LightSwitch, `http://www.microsoft.com/visualstudio/en-us/lightswitch`

Third-party tools

Even as the Windows Azure platform was evolving, third-party tools—either by individual developers or vendors—began to appear and there will be more appearing as this is being written. A few of the tools available today are highlighted in this section. Some of these have appeared on the CodePlex site, or have been discussed on forums.

SQL Azure Migration Wizard

SQL Azure Migration Wizard v3.2.1, is a migration tool that helps migrating on-site SQL 2005/2008 servers to SQL Azure. Under the hood, this tool will be using the BCP described earlier. The Migration tool can be downloaded from the following URL:

```
http://sqlazuremw.codeplex.com/
```

It is wizard-based and the wizard will walk you through the migration of the database allowing you to:

- Select SQL Objects you want to export
- Create SQL Scripts suitable for SQL Azure
- Migrate data

The SQL Azure Migration Wizard can migrate SQL Server<----->SQL Azure, as well as between SQL Azure instances. The source used for migration can be file-based, which may contain T-SQL and the wizard can check for incompatibilities and apply fixes where necessary. In doing this, the wizard analyzes the SQL Profiler trace files and T-SQL scripts.

For details, please visit the CodePlex site. To get a handle on practically using this for migrating data, an example is provided in the next chapter.

Installing the SQL Azure Migration Wizard

The SQL Azure Migration wizard needs to be installed by following these steps before it can be called:

1. Open the browser to the URL `http://sqlazuremw.codeplex.com` and click the **Download** button on the right.

2. This downloads the file `SQLAzureMW_v3.2.1_Release_Binary.zip` (88.6KB) file. You may open or save and later install the file.

3. The zip folder has the following files:
   ○ NotSupportedByazureFile
   ○ SQLAzureMW
   ○ SQLAzureMW.exe

4. In case you are running in an environment other than English, you should read the XML document SQLAzureMW.exe to make some configuration changes.

5. After unzipping, double-click SQLAzureMW. This immediately starts the wizard.

6. In the next chapter, you will step through the process of migration; a database from SQL Server 2008 R2 to SQL Azure.

SQL Azure Explorer

Created as an Add-in for Visual Studio 2010 Beta 2, SQL Azure explorer made it possible to view the objects on SQL Azure by configuring the Connections in the Server Explorer menu item. It may be recalled that this was not possible in Visual Studio 2008 SP1.

In order to use this tool, you need to download the add-in from the CodePlex site shown here: http://sqlazureexplorer.codeplex.com/

Installing the SQLAzure2010 Add-in

The file name of the add-in is, SQLAzure2010Addin.vsix (2.03 MB). Make sure you have VS2010. For the purposes of this book, the evaluation version of VS 2010 Ultimate was used.

Double-click the SQLAzure2010Addin.vsix to install the add-in:

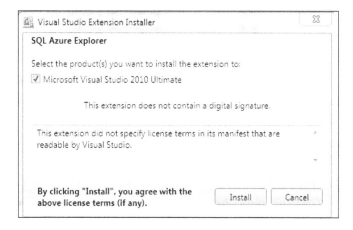

The recently introduced Visual Studio 2010 Express (a free program) does not need the add-in. It supports establishing a connection to SQL Azure from within its IDE. Follow this link for the free edition: `http://hodentek.blogspot.com/2010/06/get-these-web-development-tools-for.html`.

Exploring the SQL Azure in VS2010

Once the add-in is installed it is very easy to connect to the SQL Azure database. The following steps show you how to connect to SQL Azure from VS2010 IDE:

1. Open the VS2010 Ultimate IDE from its shortcut in **ALL Programs**.
2. The **VS2010 IDE** is displayed as shown:

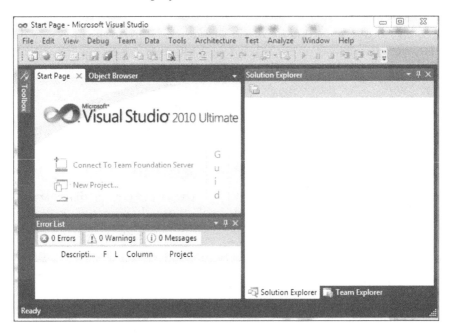

3. Click **View | Server Explorer**.

4. The **Server Explorer** window will display a data connection to an on-site SQLExpress server with the connection disabled.

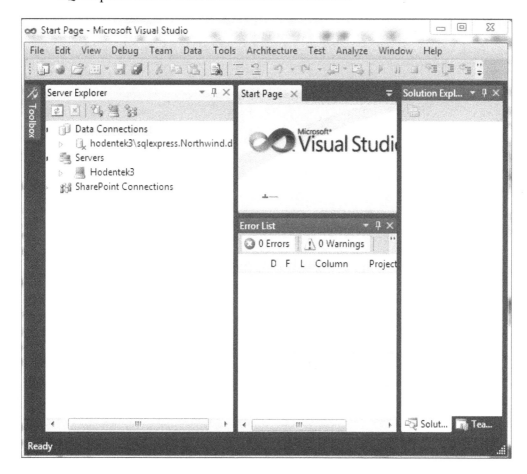

5. Right-click the **Data Connections** node in **Server Explorer,** and from the drop-down menu click on **Add Connection** menu item.

6. The **Add Connection** window is displayed as shown in the next screenshot:

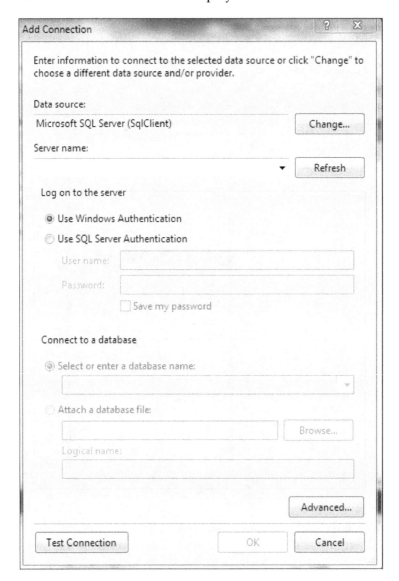

7. Enter or choose the following items:

   Server name: xxxxxxxxx.database.windows.net

   Choose **Use SQL Server Authentication**

   User Name: SQL Azure Database user name

   Password: SQL Azure Database password

   Save my password: Checked

8. If these are correct then you should be able to browse the databases on the SQL Azure server by clicking on the drop-down handle of **Select or enter a database name**.

9. Choose a database. Herein, the database **Bluesky** was chosen.

10. Click **Test Connection** button. You should see a **Test Connection succeeded** message.

11. Click **OK** on the message window and **OK** on the **Add Connection** window.

12. You will immediately see a new connection in the Data Connections node displaying the SQL Azure database name as in `Servername.databasename.dbo`.

13. Expand the new data connection node to display all the objects.

14. Presently, **Bluesky** has just one empty table as shown in the next screenshot:

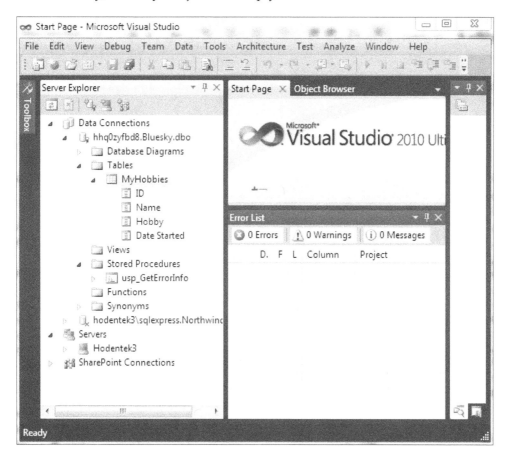

Running a query in VS2010

VS2010 IDE can be used to run queries against the SQL Azure database. Follow the steps to run the queries:

1. Right-click the **MyHobbies** table to reveal the following drop-down menu:

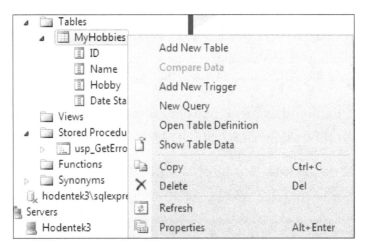

2. Click **New Query**. The **Add Table** window is displayed as shown:

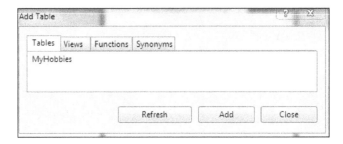

3. Click **Add** and click **Close**.

4. The query window, which has the same look and appearance of most of Microsoft's query windows, is displayed as shown displaying the table with columns; the SQL window, and the results window. Also the windows have contextual menus as shown for the SQL window (right-click empty area in SQL window):

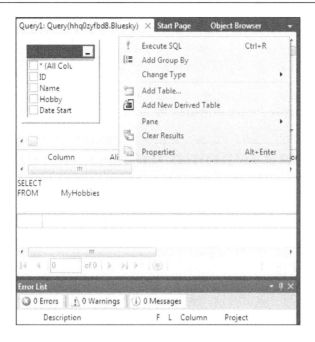

5. The **Change Type** menu item has submenu items, which are displayed by clicking on the drop-down handle as shown in the next screenshot. Using these, you can insert values to tables, update tables, and carry out delete operations.

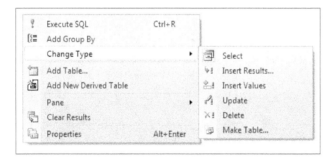

However, the interface does not support the dragging and dropping of objects from the server to the design interfaces.

SQL Azure Manager *à la community*

The starting point to work with SQL Azure Manager is the following URL: http://hanssens.org/tools/sqlazuremanager/

This tool, developed by community effort described in Hanssens.org, is a light weight tool that enables connecting to SQL Azure to perform some basic tasks.

Installing and running the SQL Azure Manager

When you browse to the previous address in IE (version 8 here) the UI for SQL Azure Manager is displayed as follows:

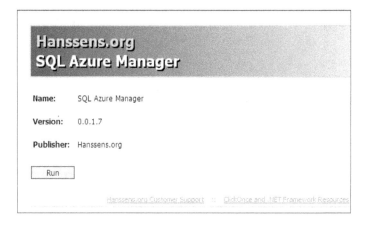

When you click the Run button the application launches displaying this window:

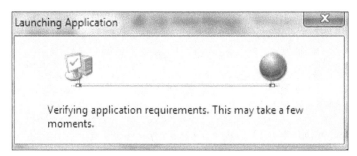

You may also get a security warning as shown here:

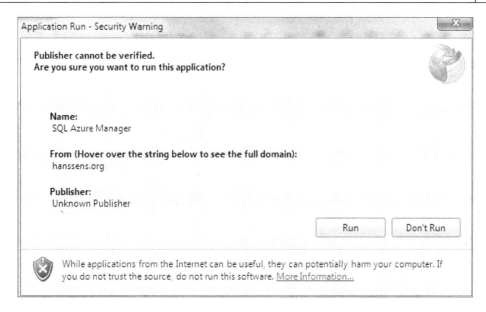

When you click Run, the program downloads to your computer as seen here:

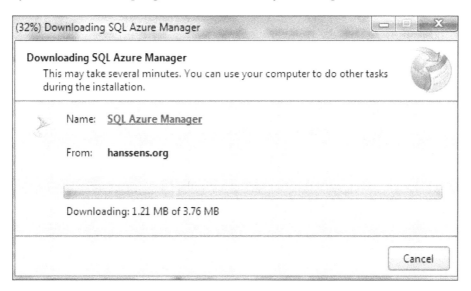

Now you can go back and browse the URL to launch the application as shown here:
`http://hanssens.org/tools/sqlazuremanager/`

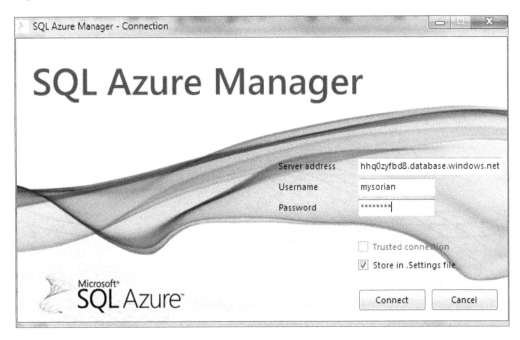

Now, insert the full server address in the format servername.database.windows.net; the username and the password of your server. Accept the default Store in settings file.

Click **Connect** and the SQL Azure server with the master database will be displayed. The drop-down list can reveal other databases too.

In this UI, you can create a New database, Delete a database, run queries as shown, and also open SQLCMD (appears to be inactive, probably work in progress). The MyHobbies table is empty as no data has been stored when queried in this interface, as shown in the following screenshot:

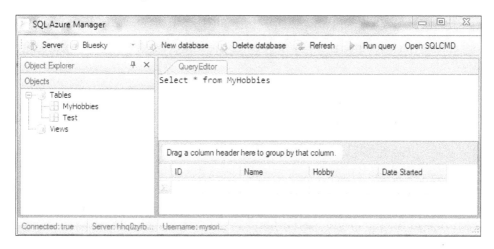

Cerebrata©

Cerebrata© is a browser-based application designed to interact with SQL Azure. The company also has other products for Windows Azure (its main product now) and in fact the SQL Azure application is not released. However, you may access this software from the following link: `http://www.cerebrata.com/Blog/post/Browser-based-SQL-Azure-Explorer.aspx`.

When you browse to the previous link, the following web page is displayed:

You first need to add the firewall settings (IP Address 74.63.196.42 to 74.63.196.46) on your portal as described in *Chapter 2, SQL Azure Services* so that you simulate running your application from the Cerebrata site.

You may leave this firewall setting ON only for the duration of your test drive and remove it as soon as you complete the test.

You start the Cerebrata program by accessing the following URL, after setting up the firewall:

```
https://onlinedemo.cerebrata.com/SQLAzureClient/default.aspx
```

The web interface is intuitive and easy to follow, and easy to work with the various database objects on SQL Azure.

DBArtisan©

For data existing on on-site data stores, a clear and easy migration path of data to SQL Azure is at the top of the wish list and DBArtisan is well-placed to address this scenario.

DBArtisan© for SQL Azure is an offering from Embarcadero Technologies, which you may access and download (an evaluation version) from the company's website at:

```
http://www.embarcadero.com/products/dbartisan/azure
```

After downloading the software you should get an activation code in your e-mail, which you need for activating the software.

This is one of the products that, according to Microsoft, can streamline data migration and management process for customers who wish to deploy Cloud-based solutions on SQL Azure. It provides both schema extraction and migration facilities.

The key features of DBArtisan as advertised on its site are:

- Full database administration capabilities for SQL Server 2000, 2005, and 2008
- Basic database administration for SQL Azure includes:
    - Object management
    - Object editing
    - SQL editing
    - Schema extraction and migration utilities

Explore SQL Azure with DBArtisan

You can explore your SQL Azure database using DBArtisan by following these steps:

1. Double-click the `dbart874_14325_ion.exe` file.

2. This opens up **the Embarcadero DBArtisan XE Pro** window, as shown in the next screenshot, displaying a **local (SQL Server)** in the **MS SQL Servers** group:

3. Click **Datasource** in the main menu and from the drop-down select **Register Datasource.**

4. The **Information** page of the Datasource Registration window is displayed.

5. Here, you can see the different database products to which DBArtisan can hook up in which SQL Azure is also included.

6. Choose **Microsoft SQL Azure** and click **Next**.

7. The **Connection information** page is displayed as shown:

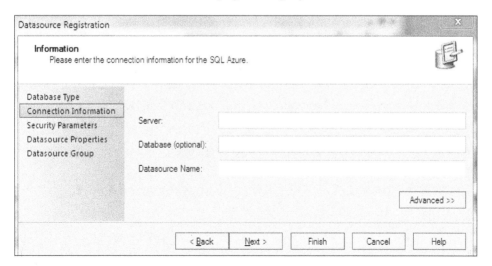

8. Enter the information which you have already used for connecting to SQL Azure several times in the first textbox alongside **Server**. The other two can be left blank. Then click **Next**.

9. This brings up the **Security Parameters** page as shown:

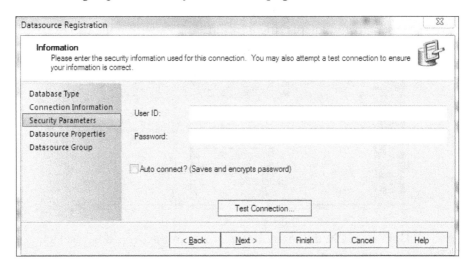

10. Enter the **User ID** and **Password** for connecting to a SQL Server (Herein, the Security Principal's information was entered).

> Enter the User ID by appending the servername as `<User ID>@<servername>`.

11. Click the **Test Connection** button.

12. You should get a **Connection succeeded** message in the message window.

13. Click **Next >** on the **Datasource Properties** page.

14. Click **Next >** on the **Datasource Group** page after reviewing its contents.

15. Click **Finish**.

16. You get a "new SQL Azure Datasource has been registered .....etc." message window.

17. Click **Yes** to connect to SQL Azure. A login window is displayed.

18. Enter the credentials (only Login ID and Password are sufficient) and once again choose auto connect and click **OK**.

19. You will see SQL Azure added to the DB Artisan's main window as shown (**Schema | Tables (2)** expanded):

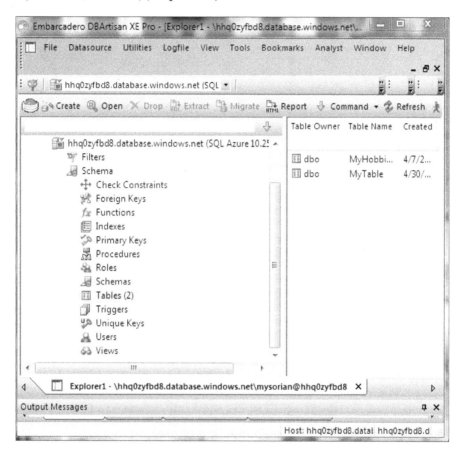

20. Click on each of the menu items to get acquainted with the user interface.

21. For example, **Utilities** helps you to extract schema and migrate schema and the Tools menu has lots of useful submenus as shown:

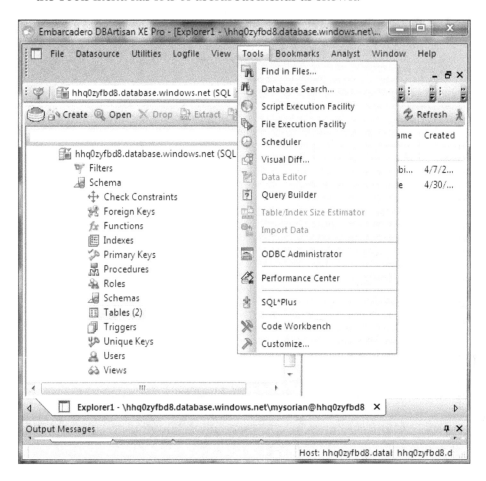

22. For example, here is an image of the Query Builder tool in DBArtisan displaying the results of running a simple query against the SQL Azure database:

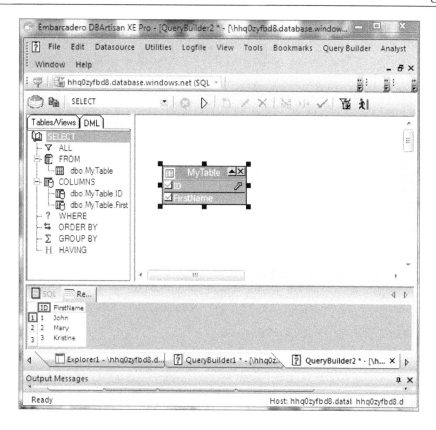

Indeed, DBArtisan has covered a lot of ground in managing and synchronizing SQL Azure.

Red Gate (SQL Compare©)

SQL Compare© is from Red-Gate's arsenal of SQLTOOLBELT that allows Synchronization of SQL Servers of different versions including SQL Azure. You can download SQL Compare 8.1.3.14 (a password protected zip file) from this location after registering at the Red-Gate's website: `http://www.red-gate.com/index.htm`.

You can unzip and run SQL Compare. SQL Compare allows you to compare two Microsoft SQL Server databases 2000, 2005, 2008, and SQL Azure 2008.

Here is an image of a **New Project** you will be creating in Red-Gate's SQL Compare. The user interface is very intuitive as it depicts the source and target clearly. The Source is the on-site SQL Server 2008 and it is compared to the SQL Azure:

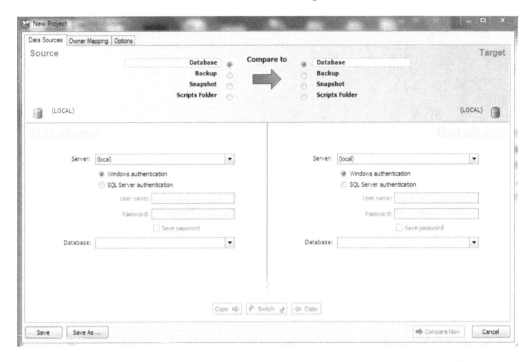

On the left, you enter the details of the on-site server and on the right, the details for the SQL Azure. When you hit the **Compare Now**, the request will be processed and a results window will be presented, as shown, for two databases not having any common objects:

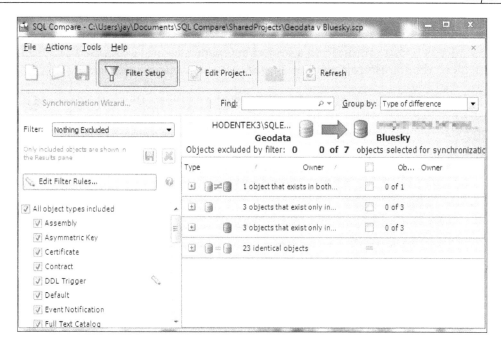

You can save this to a file (`Geodata v Bluesky.scp`) from the main menu. This is another option to the Microsoft Sync described earlier.

ToadSoft©

Toadsoft's© Toad for SQL Server Beta Version 5.0.0.370, has a new functionality that supports SQL Azure. Details may be obtained from the following URL:

```
http://www.toadsoft.com/toadsqlserver/ReleaseNotes/Beta/
ToadSqlServBetaRN.htm#Welcome
```

Toadsoft Version 5 allows you to connect to SQL Azure the same way you do in SSMS and supports the following features:

- Group Execution
- Export/Import
- Query Builder
- Master Detail Browser
- Schema Reports
- Data Reports
- Execution Plans (both actual and estimated)
- Stored Proc/Function Execution

SQL Azure and OpenOffice

OpenOffice is both a product and a project at OpenOffice.org supported by Oracle. Learn more about this project at this site: `http://about.openoffice.org/index.html`.

OpenOffice has the major functionality of the Office Suite that includes all the components shown in the splash page of this product:

We will work with the SQL Azure database using the programs in OpenOffice.org in *Chapter 10, Recent Developments*. We will see how you may access SQL Azure using OpenOffice and create useful reports. It may be noted that accessing SQL Azure using MS Access became available much later, after a long debate in the forums.

Summary

In this chapter, we looked at tools that can be used with SQL Azure, which includes tools from Microsoft, third party, and open source. Microsoft's tight integration of SQL Server 2008 R2 with two versions of Visual Basic as well as its Management Studio-related tools such as SSMS, Import/Export, and Data; SyncFramework; SSMS; scripting support for SQL Azure; SQLCMD; BCP Utility; IIS7 Database Manager and ODATA service are described, some of them with examples. Several third-party tools such as those from SQL Azure Migration wizard, SQL Azure Explorer, SQL Azure Manager, Cerebrata, DBArtisan, Red Gate, and ToadSoft are also described.

In the next chapter, we will be using some of the tools mentioned in this chapter to migrate data from an on-site server to SQL Azure.

5
Populating SQL Azure Databases

In order to work with databases you need a database(s), which can be created from scratch or by migrating data from another source. Migration of data is a reality of enterprise businesses. The reasons may vary; migrating from an older version to a more recent version to harvest the benefits of software improvements, from one vendor product to another vendor product due to cost benefits or a changed business environment such as a merger, or from a departmental server to a central data store.

Most of the vendors support migration of data from other vendors to their own servers. Oracle, Sybase, MySQL, and many others have their own Migration Wizards, Migration Assistants, and so on. Microsoft also has a variety of tools to address migration not only between its servers, but also between its various version using integration components such as SQL Server Integration Services and Export/ Import wizard.

This chapter will cover transferring data in and out of SQL Azure, to in and out of on-site SQL Servers and will consider the following methods of migrating or moving data from/to SQL Azure databases. Besides these methods, there are other ways to move data such as using SQL Server Integration Services, BCP, SQL Azure DataSync, Data-Tier Components, and many other third party tools. However, we will be focusing on the following topics:

- Using SQL Server Management Studio with scripts
- Using the SQL Server Import and Export Wizard
- Using SQL Azure Migration Wizard
- Migration from MySQL to SQL Azure using SQL Server Migration Assistant 2008 for MySQL
- Using SqlBulkCopy

Sample databases used in this chapter

In order to get a handle on the practical aspects discussed in this chapter, you need sample databases. The default installation of SQL Server 2008 R2 does not come with the samples.

There are a number of database source samples available on the internet. Microsoft samples used in this book (SQL Server 2000 Sample DBS, as well as Microsoft Sample Databases) can be downloaded from the CodePlex site here: `http://sqlserversamples.codeplex.com/#databases`. The SQL 2005 (top right of the URL) and SQL Server 2008 R2 databases can be downloaded from the following URL: `http://msftdbprodsamples.codeplex.com/releases/view/37109`.

After downloading them you will have to attach them to your server. For this you can use SSMS, and use the attach menu item (right-click databases node and choose the attach drop-down menu), or use the system stored procedures: `sp_attach_db` and `sp_detach_db` (if you want to remove the database). A sample of the procedure to attach a database is available here: `http://hodentekmsss.blogspot.com/2010/05/using-sample-databases-with-sql-server.html`. A similar procedure is also detailed here: `http://www.aspfree.com/c/a/MS-SQL-Server/Moving-Data-from-SQL-Server-2000-to-SQL-Server-2005/3/`.

Using SQL Server Management Studio with scripts

SQL Server Management Studio can be used to create scripts for all database objects including databases. This can be used to move a database from your on-site SQL Server 2008 R2 to SQL Azure. This is a general procedure that can be used with databases on other server versions as well. For running scripts on SQL Azure in SQL Server 2008 R2 using SSMS, please read the *Scripting support for SQL Azure* section in *Chapter 4*, *SQL Azure Tools*.

Creating a script for the Northwind database

We will now migrate the **Northwind** database from the on-site server (HODENTEK3\KUMO) to SQL Azure. Make sure you have configured **Script for server version** to SQL Server 2008 R2 from **Tools | Options** in SSMS, as described in *Chapter 4*, *SQL Azure Tools*. Also make sure that you have configured the scripting in **Tools**, such that the script option is **Script for database engine type** to **SQL Azure Database** and that the **Tools** window appears, as shown in the following screenshot:

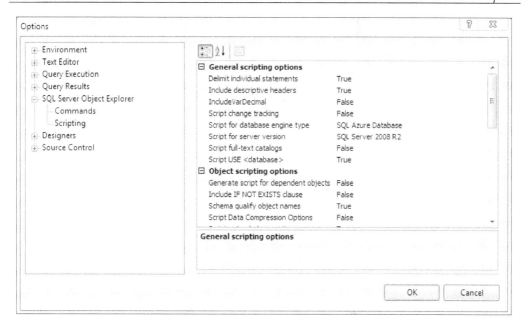

1. In SSMS, click on the **Northwind** database under the **Databases** node, and from the drop-down menu click on **Tasks**.

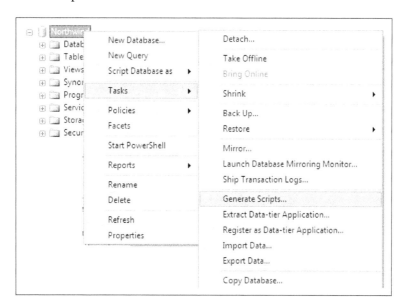

2. Click on the sub-menu item **Generate Scripts....**

3. The **Generate and Publish Scripts** window gets displayed. Make sure you read the information in this window and click on **Next >**.

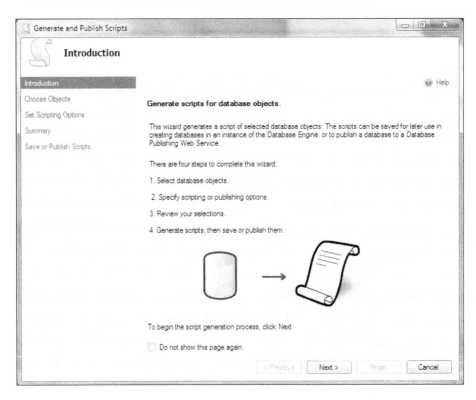

4. The **Choose Objects** page gets displayed, where-in you need to choose the objects to be scripted and click on **Next >**. Here, all objects were chosen to be scripted, which happens to be the default.

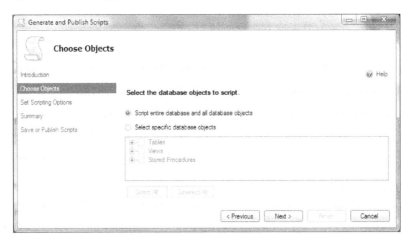

5. This brings up the **Set Scripting Options** page, as shown in the following screenshot:

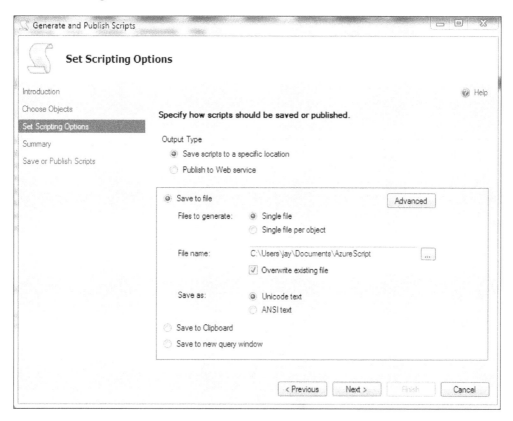

6. Change the default file name in the **Save to file** option by choosing to generate a **Single file**. Choose a location to save the file using the ellipsis (**...**) button. Accept other defaults. The new location of the SQL file is `C:\Users\jay\Documents\AzureScript` but this will obviously be different in your case.

7. Click on **Next >**.

8. You get a summary of what has been accomplished so far in the **Summary** page. Both the source and target are shown clearly, including whatever you have scripted (the nodes shown are expanded). Click on **Next >**.

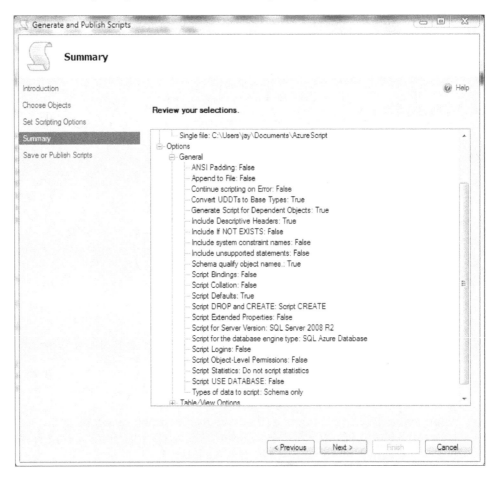

9. The wizard generates the script and the **Saving or publishing scripts** (progress) page shows the result of scripting.

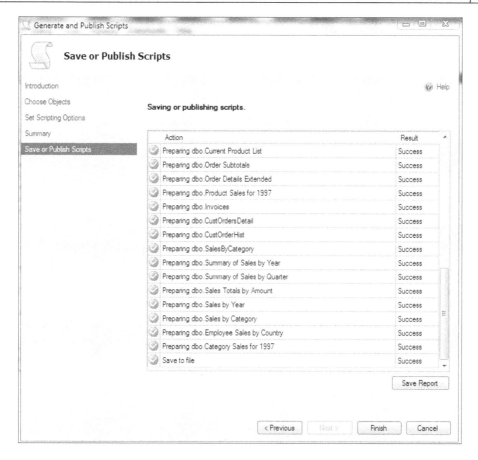

10. Click on **Finish**.

11. The script generated, `AzureScript.sql` is saved to the location
    you indicated.

You will see that in `AzureScript.sql` everything that is not supported by SQL
Azure is stripped out, including the `Create database` statement, as it involves files
and so on.

Running the scripted query in SQL Azure

In order to get all the tables into a database on SQL Azure use the `Create database`
statement to create a database in SQL Azure and run the scripted query in the new
database, as described in the following steps:

1. Create a database `AzureNorthwind` in SQL Azure when logged into the
   `master` database as detailed in *Chapter 2, SQL Azure Services*.

2. Create a new query in AzureNorthwind and run the generated script, as shown. The script runs without errors, as seen in the following screenshot:

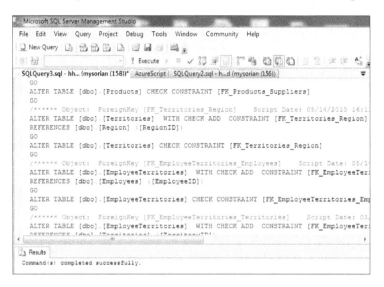

3. Verify that the database is migrated to SQL Azure, to the **AzureNorthwind** database, as shown in the following screenshot:

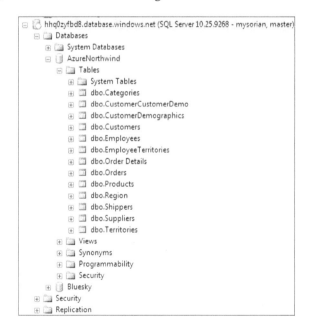

Using the SQL Server Import and Export Wizard

Using this tool, we will copy a table from SQL Server 2008 R2 to the **AzureNorthwind** database on SQL Azure. This tool was described in *Chapter 4, SQL Azure Tools*.

Populating a table

We will use the **Customers** table shown here from the **Northwind** database on SQL Server 2008 R2. The table has 91 rows of data.

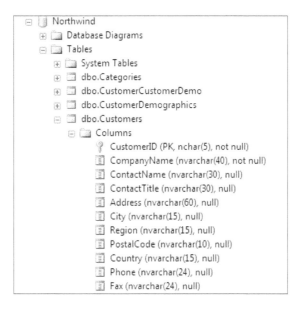

Using the Import and Export Wizard

Three provider options were discussed in *Chapter 4, SQL Azure Tools* to use the Import and Export Wizard. In the present example, we need to move the database table **dbo.Customers** from SQL Server to SQL Azure database **AzureNorthwind**, as shown in the following screenshot:

1. Click on **Start | All Programs | Microsoft SQL Server 2008 R2 November-CTP** and click on **Import and Export Data (32-bit)**.

2. This brings up the **Welcome to SQL Server Import and Export Wizard** page. Make sure you read the information on this page and click **Next >**.

3. The **Choose a Data Source** page is displayed, which changes to the display shown after a short interval. The page comes with default entries for **Server name**, **Data source**, and **Authentication**. All of these are appropriate for the local server on the machine.

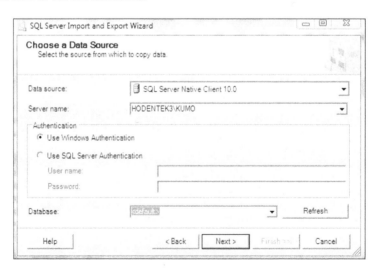

4. Click the drop-down handle for the **Database** field and choose **Northwind** from the list of databases and click **Next >**.

5. This brings up the **Choose a Destination** page of the wizard, as shown in the following screenshot:

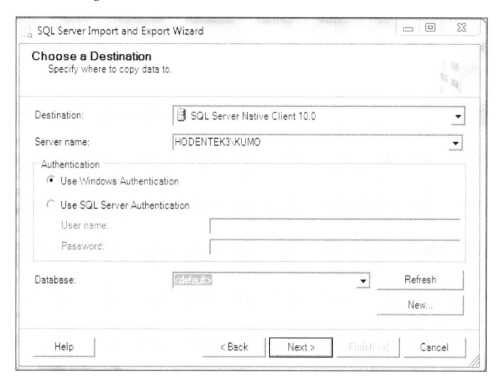

6. Use the drop-down handle for **Destination** and choose **.Net Framework Data Provider for SqlServer**. The window changes to the following:

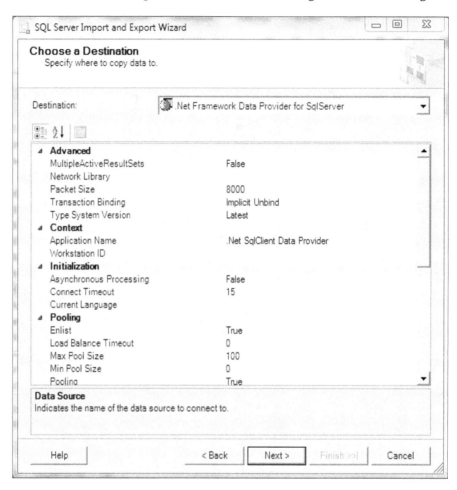

7. Make changes to the following by typing them to the right of the items:
    ° **Password**: Your password for SQL Azure
    ° **User ID**: Your User ID for SQL Azure
    ° **Data Source**: Your full server name
    ° **Initial Catalog**: The database you want to specify

This is displayed in the following screenshot:

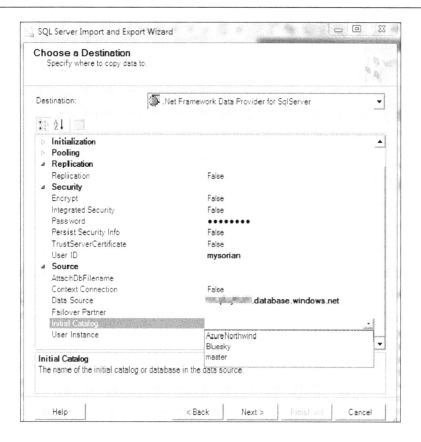

8. Choose **AzureNorthwind** from the drop-down for the **Initial Catalog** and click **Next >**.

9. The **Specify Table Copy or Query** page of the wizard with a default choice for **Copy data from one or more tables or views** is as follows:

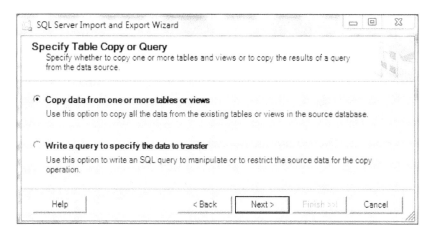

10. Click on **Next >**.

11. The **Select Source Tables and Views** page is displayed, as shown in the following screenshot:

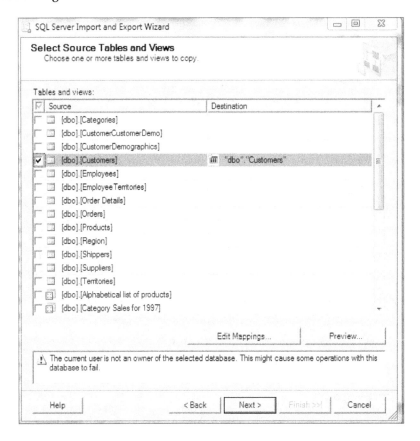

12. Place a check mark for **[dbo].[Customers]** on the left in the list.

13. A corresponding **"dbo"."Customers"** appears on the right, which happens to be the correct name of the table on **AzureNorthwind**. There could be a problem due to the user not having permission (bottom of the previous screenshot). If needed, we will come back and fix this later. Click on **Next >**.

14. The **Save and Run Package** page is then displayed. Accept the entries and click on **Next >**.

15. The **Complete the Wizard** page is displayed, summarizing the choices made for the package. Click on **Finish**.

16. The **Performing Operation** page is displayed momentarily. It goes through establishing the connection, validating, and so on, but the operation gets stopped.

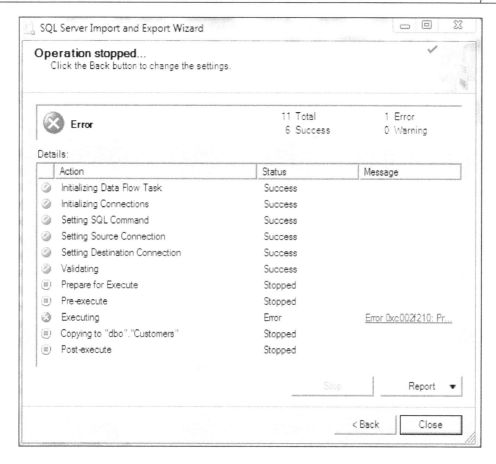

17. Click on the error link in blue, along the line **Executing** in the previous screenshot.

18. The error message page from the wizard is displayed, as shown in the following screenshot:

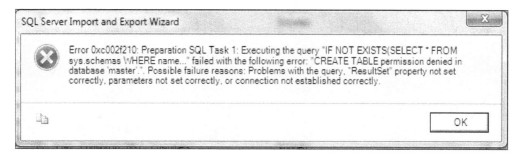

Error messages do not always provide the proper guidance, although most of the times they do, but we did see earlier that there could be a permissions problem.

 For a database that is attached to the server, as in this case, the permissions on the database itself are the default permissions.

19. Place the user of the computer in the db_creator role using the SSMS and refresh the database node (if you do not know how, consult the SQL Server Books Online: http://technet.microsoft.com/en-us/library/ms130214.aspx).

20. Now you can either start from the beginning or go back to the previous screens by repeatedly clicking the **< Back** button until you come to the **Specify Copy Table or View** page of the wizard. You can then continue from there by clicking **Next >**.

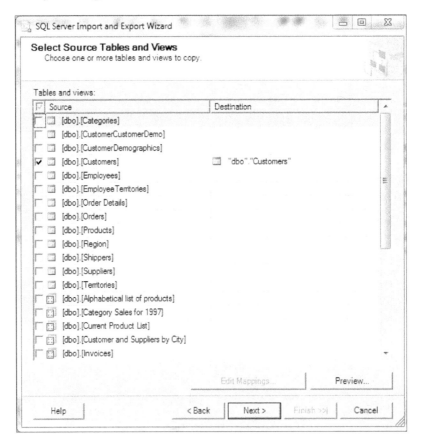

21. Observe that there is no message at the bottom of the previous screenshot.

22. Click **Next >** twice and click on **Finish**. This will bring you to the **Performing Operations** page after processing is rendered.

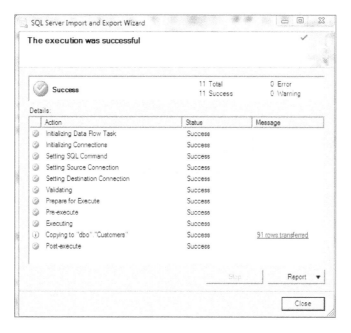

23. The message clearly shows that 91 rows of data, from **Northwind** database on the on-site SQL Server 2008 R2 November-CTP, were transferred to the **Customers** table of the **AzureNorthwind** database of the SQL Azure server.

24. Verify by running the query, as shown in the following screenshot:

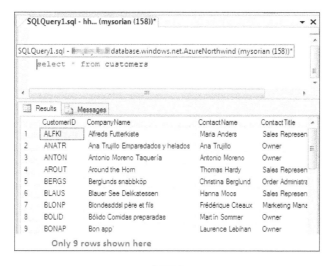

Using the SQL Server Migration wizard

In the previous chapter, the SQL Azure Migration wizard was introduced, herein the practical implementation of using it to migrate from on-site SQL Server 2008 R2 November-CTP (SQL Server 2008 R2 can also be used) to SQL Azure server will be described. In order to do this, you will need to perform the following steps:

1. Click `SQLAzureMW` application file from its location on your computer.

2. The following **Select Process** of the **ScriptWizard** is displayed. You have several options in using this tool, as shown in the following screenshot:

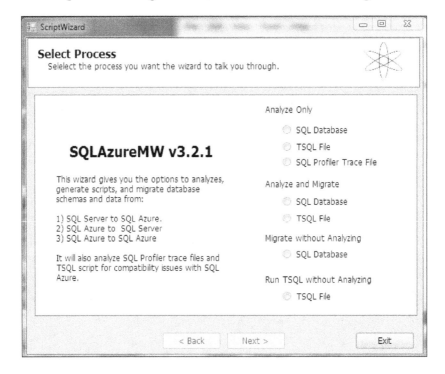

3. Choose the **SQL Database** option under **Analyze and Migrate** category and click **Next >**.

4. The **Connect to Server...** window is displayed, as shown in the following screenshot, with **localhost** as a default for **Server name**. The drop-down handle reveals all the servers.

5. Choose the server (herein **HODENTEK3\KUMO**). Accept the default **Authentication,** as it is appropriate for the installation, and click the **Connect** button.

6. The **Select Source** page of the wizard is displayed as shown, with all the databases listed:

7. Highlight the **[pubs]** database, as shown in the previous screenshot and click **Next >**.

8. The **Choose Objects** page of the wizard is displayed with the default **Script all database objects** selected. All objects in the **pubs** database are listed, as shown in the following screenshot:

While it is possible to choose object(s) to migrate, the whole database can be migrated. This option is chosen here. The **Advanced** button gives more options when it is clicked. We will not use this button except to show what is possible, as shown in the following screenshot:

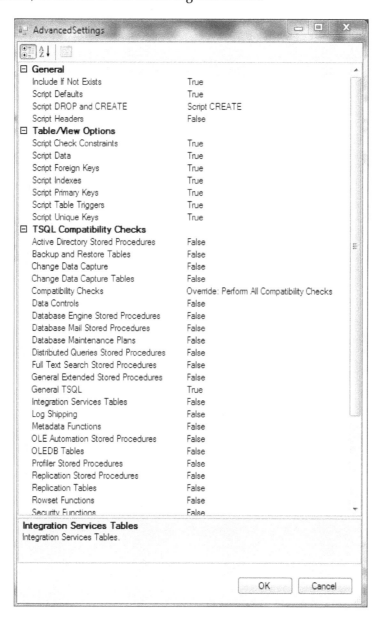

9. Click **Next >** on the **Choose Objects** page after choosing all objects.

10. The **Script Wizard Summary** page is displayed, as shown in the following screenshot. All elements are shown expanded. Click on **Next >**.

11. The **Ready to Generate Script?** message is displayed in a message box. Click on **Yes**.

12. The scripting starts as in the following screenshot, shown at an intermediate state of the process:

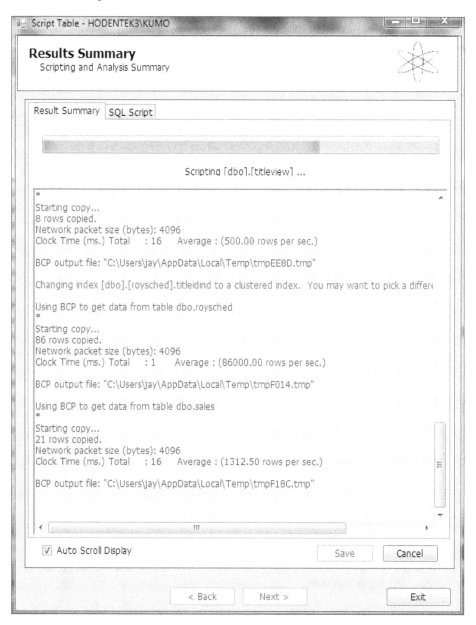

13. The window also shows the SQLScript generated if the **SQL Script** tab is chosen.

14. It is instructive to study the generated script as it shows all the differences that need to be accounted for, while going from SQL Server 2008 to SQL Azure, then click **Save**.

15. The save to folder options of the computer opens, with rich text format (*.rtf) as an option. Change it to SQLAMW.sql and save it to a location of your choice and click **Next >**.

16. The **Connect to Server...** window is displayed, this time seeking information about the target server, as shown in the following screenshot:

17. Enter the **Server name**, **User name**, and **Password** of your provisioned SQL Azure and click on **Connect**.

18. The **Setup Target Server Connection** page is displayed, as shown in the following screenshot:

19. Click the **Create Database** button.

20. The **Create Database** window is displayed where you can specify the name and size of the database. Herein, **AzurePubs** is chosen for a **1 GB Database**. The database sizes have undergone changes with the business edition, ranging from 10 GB to 50 GB, and the web edition 1 GB or 5 GB. Please refer to this URL for database sizes and pricing information: `http://www.microsoft.com/windowsazure/pricing/#sql`.

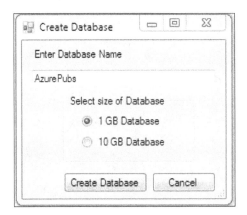

21. Click the **Create Database** button. **AzurePubs** is created and is displayed in the previously shown **Setup Target Server Connection** page. Highlight **AzurePubs** and click **Next >**.

22. The **Execute script against the destination server?** message is displayed in a message box. Click **Yes**.

23. The process starts and the results are written to the window, as shown in the following screenshot:

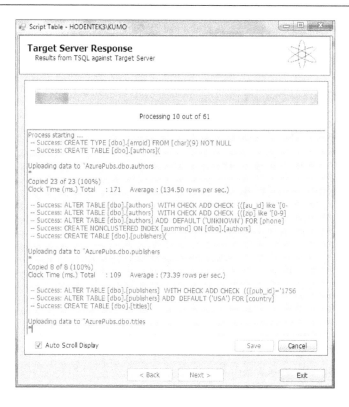

24. Click on **Exit** when the process is completed.

25. Verify the database migration in SSMS, as shown in the following screenshot. Also, use queries to verify that data is also migrated to the tables. The other tables, views, and stored procedures are also tested:

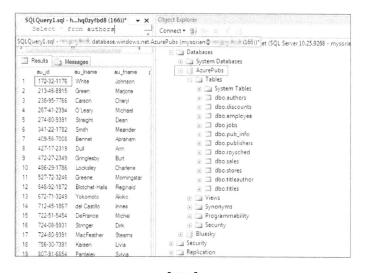

Migration from MySQL to SQL Azure using SQL Server Migration Assistant 2008 for MySQL

With **SQL Server Migration Assistant 2008 for MySQL (SSMA)**, introduced in the previous chapter, you can accomplish the following:

- Connect to both MySQL and SQL Azure
- Convert MySQL schemas to SQL Azure
- Upload MySQL database schemas to SQL Azure
- Migrate MySQL data to SQL Azure

Another option available for the target server is SQL Server 2008.

You need to have both servers available and you should make sure you can connect to the servers using SSMA. The details of MySQL programs installed for use in this section are as follows:

- MySQL 5.1.36, this version can be downloaded from here: `http://dev.mysql.com/downloads/mirror.php?id=387719#mirrors`
- mysql-connector-odbc 5.1.6, available here: `http://dev.mysql.com/downloads/connector/`
- `Create and populate sample databases on MySQL`
- Install SSMA after downloading it from the following location: `http://www.microsoft.com/downloads/en/confirmation.aspx?familyId=0e6168b0-2d0c-4076-96c2-60bd25294a8e&displayLang=en`

After these installations, you can proceed to migrate the data on a table (`from2k8`) from MySQL to SQL Azure. A `SELECT` query is used to display data in the `from2k8` table in the DOS screen. It is assumed the reader has familiarity working with MySQL.

```
C:\Program Files\MySQL\MySQL Server 5.1\bin>mysql -u root -p
Enter password: ********
Welcome to the MySQL monitor.  Commands end with ; or \g.
Your MySQL connection id is 4
Server version: 5.1.46-community MySQL Community Server (GPL)
Copyright (c) 2000, 2010, Oracle and/or its affiliates. All rights
reserved.
This software comes with ABSOLUTELY NO WARRANTY. This is free software,
```

and you are welcome to modify and redistribute it under the GPL v2 license

Type 'help;' or '\h' for help. Type '\c' to clear the current input statement.

```
mysql> show databases
    -> ;
+--------------------+
| Database           |
+--------------------+
| information_schema |
| mysql              |
| test               |
| testmove           |
+--------------------+
4 rows in set (0.00 sec)

mysql> use testmove
Database changed
mysql> show tables;
+--------------------+
| Tables_in_testmove |
+--------------------+
| employees          |
| from2k8            |
| mypet              |
| otherconnector     |
| testconnector      |
| testing            |
| testonly           |
+--------------------+
7 rows in set (0.01 sec)

mysql> Select * from from2k8
    -> ;
    •  +------+-----------+-------------+------------+
    •  | Id   | Month     | Temperature | RecordHigh |
    •  +------+-----------+-------------+------------+
```

```
|    1 | Jan          |          40 |          60 |
|    2 | Feb          |          32 |          50 |
|    3 | Mar          |          43 |          65 |
|    4 | Apr          |          50 |          70 |
|    5 | May          |          53 |          74 |
|    6 | Jun          |          60 |          78 |
|    7 | Jul          |          68 |          70 |
|    8 | Aug          |          71 |          70 |
|    9 | Sep          |          60 |          82 |
|   10 | Oct          |          55 |          67 |
|   11 | Nov          |          45 |          55 |
|   12 | Dec          |          40 |          62 |
+------+--------------+-------------+-------------+
12 rows in set (0.01 sec)
mysql>
```

The steps in migrating this table are easy to follow as shown here:

1. Double-click the SSMA from its shortcut in **Start | All Programs** and if it is not in the shortcuts find the file SSMAforMySql.exe on your computer.

2. The SSMA user interface is displayed, as shown in the following screenshot. It has an intuitive menu, toolbar menu items to connect to MySQL, and SQL Server as well as other migration-related items:

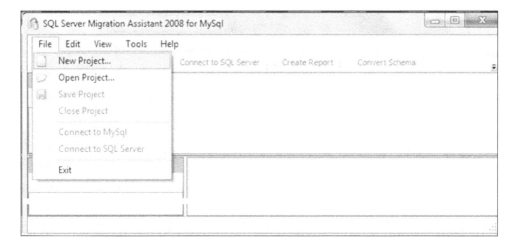

3. Click on **File | New Project...**, as shown in the previous screenshot.

4. The **New Project** window is displayed. Change the default name to one of your choice; choose a location to save files by browsing, and choose whether you want to migrate to SQL Server or SQL Azure. Herein, a project name `Take6` (**SqlMigration 1** renamed) was chosen to migrate a MySQL database table to **SQL Azure**.

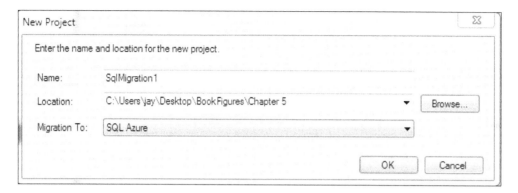

5. Click on **OK**. The connection toolbar items will be enabled.

6. Click on **Connect to MySQL**.

7. The **Connect to MySQL** window is displayed, as shown in the following screenshot. All fields are filled except for the MySQL Server database password (use the one created during installation):

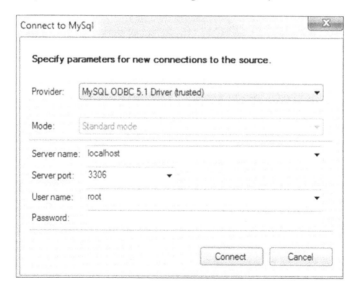

8. Enter the password created during installation in the **Password** field and click on **Connect**.

9. You will be connected to the MySQL database on the computer, as shown in the following screenshot. The **testmove** database is shown expanded to show all the tables in the **MySql Metadata Explorer**. Review all menu and toolbar items, as well as tabbed pages for each of the explorer items, to get a clear understanding of this interface. The **Help** menu item describes all there is to know about this user interface.

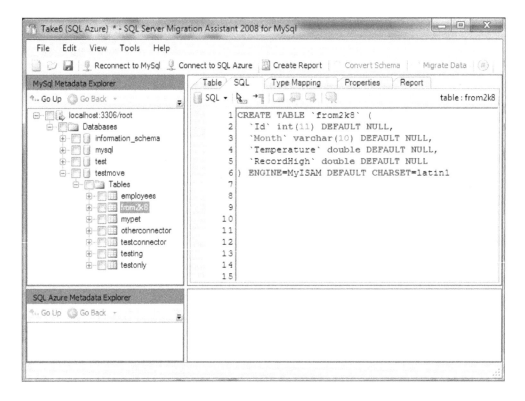

10. Click on the **Connect to SQL Azure** toolbar item.

11. The **Connect to SQL Azure** window is displayed, as shown in the following screenshot:

12. Enter the required information and click **Connect** when the button gets enabled (after all fields are filled). Herein, the `Bluesky` database on SQL Azure was chosen.

13. The SSMA UI will display an explorer-type menu for SQL Azure database-related objects, as shown in the following screenshot:

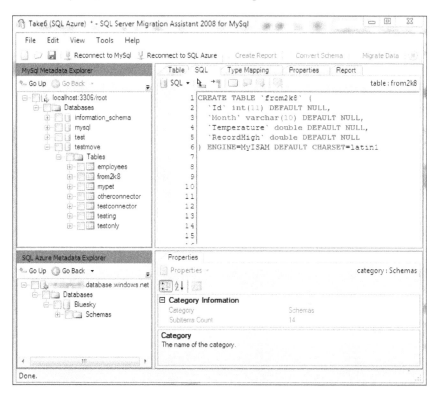

14. Click on **from2k8** in **MySQL Metadata Explorer**.

15. The toolbar items **Create Report**, **Convert Schema**, and **Migrate Data** are enabled.

16. Click on **Create Report**.

17. The schema conversion starts and the results of the conversion are in the report, as shown in the following screenshot. Note the location of this file at the bottom of this screenshot. Since the original table did not have a primary key, a **RowId PRIMARY KEY** has been added to the target. The left pane shows the MySQL table **from2k8**. The right pane shows the **testmove. from2k8** in SQL Azure.

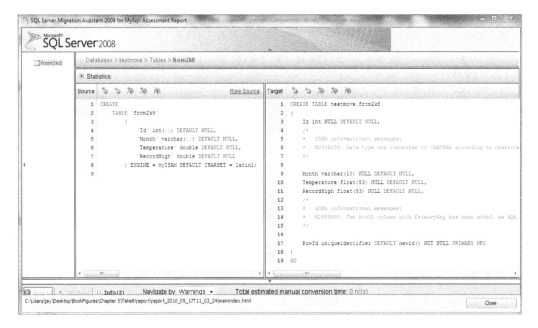

18. Click on + **Statistics**.

19. The conversion statistics are displayed. There were no errors, as shown in the following screenshot:

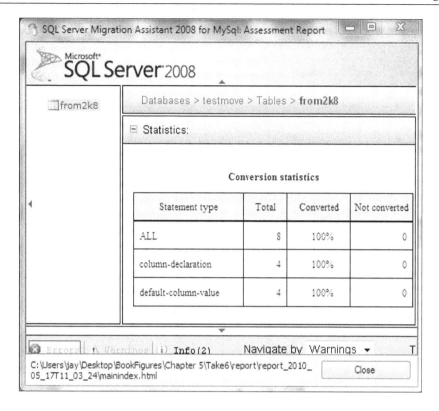

20. Click on **Close** to close the **Assessment Report**.

21. Highlight **from2k8** in **MySQL Metadata Explorer** and click the menu toolbar item **Convert Schema**.

22. The following message is copied to output:

    Starting conversion...

    Analyzing metadata...

    Converting table testmove.from2k8 ...

    Information: M2SS0055: Data type was converted to VARCHAR according to character set mapping for latin1 character set

    Information: M2SS0058: The RowID column with PrimaryKey has been added, as SQL AZURE does not allow the table without Primarykey or Clustered Index.

    Conversion finished with 0 errors, 0 warnings, and 2 informational messages.

The schema of from2k8 appears in the **SQL Azure Metadata Explorer**, as shown in the following screenshot:

After the conversion of schema, you need to load the database objects to SQL Azure. There are two ways of doing this. You can copy the SQL (right of **SQL Azure Metadata Explorer**) and run the script in SQL Azure, or you can synchronize the databases in SSMA. Here, the second option is described.

1. Right-click **from2k8** in **SQL Azure Metadata Explorer** and from the drop-down choose **Synchronize with Database**.

2. You may need to provide authentication for the SQL Azure server. Although you may get a message that does not indicate synchronization has taken place, if you open SSMS and connect to SQL Azure database (Bluesky) you will notice that a table **testmove.from2k8** is displayed in the Bluesky database, as shown in the following screenshot (here, schema is transferred but not data):

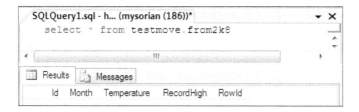

3. Click the **Migrate Data** toolbar item in the main menu.

4. You have to login to MySQL and SQL Azure again, after which the data is moved. It may take time to migrate, depending on the size and number of tables, after which a report is displayed, as shown in the following screenshot:

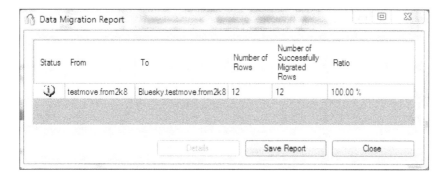

5. Run the previous query again in SSMS. The query returns the migrated rows, as shown in the following screenshot. It has added **RowId** to conform to SQL Azure. Note that the sort order is not maintained.

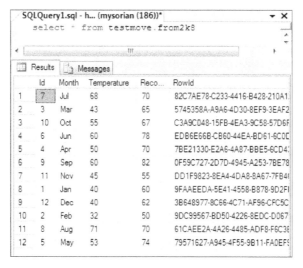

While a very simple table was migrated, the interface has all the required elements for migrating from MySQL to SQL Azure. The **Help** menu that is part of the user interface has more details and you are encouraged to review it.

Using SqlBulkCopy

We will be using SqlBulkCopy; a class supported from .NET Framework 2.0, to copy data from a table in SQL Express to a table with the same schema in SQL Azure.

The details of SqlBulkCopy class displayed in Visual Studio 2010 RCs Object Browser is shown in the following screenshot:

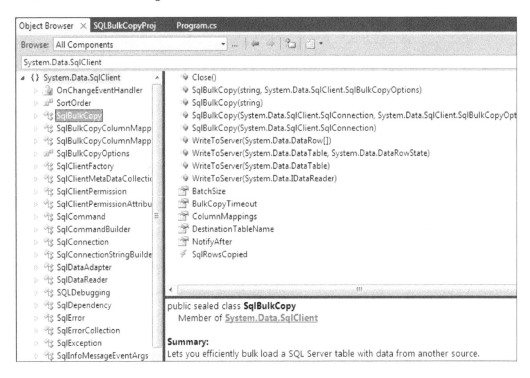

The data transfer takes place from one database object on one server, to a database object with a similar schema on another server. We will transfer the data from the Shippers table in Northwind on SQL Server 2008 Express, to a table in the Bluesky database on SQL Azure.

Create a table in the destination server

In the next step, we will create a table in the SQL Azure's `Bluesky` database.

1. Login into SQL Azure's `Bluesky` database and create a table called `AzureShippers` using the following statement:

```
CREATE TABLE [dbo].[AzureShippers](
[ShipperID] [int] IDENTITY(1,1) NOT NULL,
[CompanyName] [nvarchar](40) NOT NULL,
[Phone] [nvarchar](24) NULL,
 CONSTRAINT [PK_Shippers] PRIMARY KEY CLUSTERED
(
[ShipperID] ASC
)
)
```

This creates the **AzureShippers** table in the **Bluesky** database, as shown in the following screenshot:

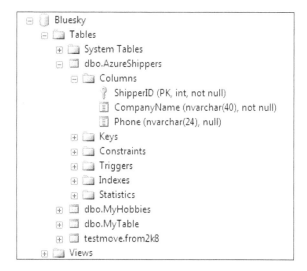

Create a console application in VS2010

We will be using VS2010 RC for creating the application. It can also be created using VS2008. We first create a C# console application as follows:

1. Open VS2010 RC using **Run as administrator** and create a new console project in C#.

2. Remove the default using statements and insert the following code in the Program.cs code page:

```
using System;
using System.Data.SqlClient;
using System.Data.Common;

namespace SqlBulkCopyProj
{
    class Program
    {
        static void Main(string[] args)
        {

            // Indicate connection string and set up
connections.
            //Connection strings to SQL Express and SQL Azure
are:
            String strsource = "Data Source=HODENTEK3\\
SQLEXPRESS;" +
                "Initial Catalog=Northwind;Integrated
Security=True";
            String strDest = "Server=tcp:<Servername>.database.
windows.net;" +
                "Database=Bluesky;User ID=<username>@<Servernam
e>;Passwordpassword;" +
                "Trusted_Connection=False;Encrypt=True;";
            //Open the connections to source and destination
            SqlConnection source = new
SqlConnection(strsource);
            SqlConnection dest = new SqlConnection(strDest);
            source.Open();
            Console.WriteLine("Source Open");
            dest.Open();
            Console.WriteLine("Destination Open");
            // fill up a data table with 3 rows from Shippers
table in SQL Express:
            System.Data.DataTable tmp = new System.Data.
DataTable();
            SqlCommand cm = new SqlCommand(@"select * from
Shippers", source);
            Console.Write("Loading sql data from
Shippers...");
```

```
            SqlDataAdapter da = new System.Data.SqlClient.
SqlDataAdapter(cm);
                da.Fill(tmp);
                Console.WriteLine("done.");
                // Make sure that our destination table is empty
by deleting data:
                new SqlCommand("delete from AzureShippers",
dest).ExecuteNonQuery();
                DateTime start = DateTime.Now;
                Console.WriteLine("Beginning Copy ....");

                // copy the data:
                SqlBulkCopy scopy=new SqlBulkCopy(dest);
                scopy.DestinationTableName = "AzureShippers";
                scopy.WriteToServer(tmp);

                Console.WriteLine("Copy complete in {0}  seconds.
Good Bye", DateTime.Now.Subtract(start).Seconds);
                Console.ReadLine();


            }


        }
}
```

The lines of code are explained within the code.

3. Build and run the application. The result appears, as shown in the following screenshot:

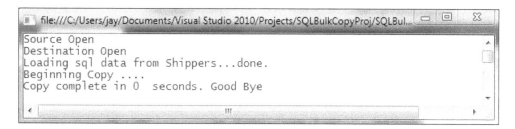

4. In SQL Azure, verify that the data has been transferred to the `AzureShippers` table, as shown in the following screenshot:

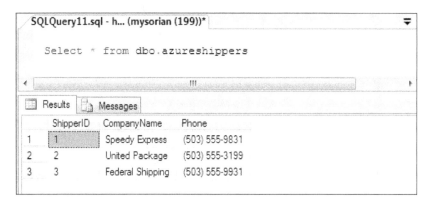

Summary

In this chapter, a number of methods to move schema, data, and schema and data were described, such as generating scripts to move schemas in SSMS, using the Export/Import Wizard to move schema and data, using SSMA to move schema and data, and using SqlBulkCopy. While the examples by themselves are quite simple, they describe the proof of principle and usage.

In the next chapter, we will be working with **SQL Server Integrated Services (SSIS)** and **SQL Server Reporting Services (SSRS)**, which are components of the **Business Intelligence Development Studio (BIDS)**. While SSIS is used to move data between SQL Azure and an on-site database, SSRS will be used to author a report using data on SQL Azure.

6
SSIS and SSRS Applications Using SQL Azure

Microsoft **SQL Server Integration Services 2008 (SSIS)** is a full service Extract, Transform, and Load (ETL) program tightly integrated with SQL Server 2008 with a **Rapid Application Development (RAD)** user interface. Microsoft **SQL Server Reporting Services 2008(SSRS)** is a third generation reporting program that is also tightly integrated with SQL Server 2008, which hosts the Report Server providing full support with a web service frontend for a variety of reporting needs—from web-based reporting to embedded reporting.

SSIS and SSRS are not presently supported on SQL Azure. However, this is one of the future enhancements that will be implemented. While they are not supported on Windows Azure platform, they can be used to carry out both data integration and data reporting activities.

In this chapter, we will be leveraging SSIS, SSRS, and the tools used in earlier chapters to address ETL processes, and Report authoring with SQL Azure as the source of data. We will be looking at the following data-related items in some detail:

- Merging sharded data
- Moving a MySQL database to SQL Azure database
- Creating a report using SQL Azure as data source
- Accessing SQL Azure from Report Builder 3.0

While working with these, we will also use some of the other tools described in earlier chapters.

Merging sharded data

One of the major concerns in using SQL Azure is the security of data such as credit card numbers, Social Security Numbers, salaries, bonuses, and so on. The degree to which data needs to be protected is to be determined by each business entity but generally, on-site data is more secure than data stored in the cloud (perhaps in the opinion of enterprises).

We start off with this scenario: The fictitious company SecureAce wants to place one of their employee tables on SQL Azure, but they do not want to keep any sensitive information such as employee salaries. However, from time to time they need to generate reports of their employees and salaries to the management.

The solution to this scenario is divided in two parts. In the first part, the on-site data in the employee table is partitioned in such a way that the sensitive information stays on-site and the larger, non-sensitive data is stored on SQL Azure. In the second part, SSIS is used to bring the two pieces of data together and loaded on an Access database (on-site), which is used as a frontend for reporting information to the management, an entirely realistic process of data management. Although a Microsoft Access database is used, any other destination handled by SSIS can also be used, such as another SQL Server database. Herein, we used MS Access as it is a very common product used in many small businesses.

It may be noted however, that Microsoft now supports connecting SQL Azure to MS Access directly, review this link for details: http://social.msdn.microsoft. com/Forums/en-US/ssdsgetstarted/thread/05dd7620-f209-43d2-8c41- 63b251c62970. With the availability of Microsoft Office Professional Plus 2010, it is possible to directly connect to SQL Azure using an ODBC connection.

Splitting the data and uploading to SQL Azure

This is also a preparation for the SSIS task that follows. We will be using the Northwind database's Employees table and splitting it in two parts each containing different columns, using a vertical partition. One part will remain on-site, which contains the salary information of the employees and the other, which is loaded to SQL Azure will contain most of other information. In the Northwind database, the employee table does not have a salary column and hence, an extra column will be added for this simulation. The procedure is described in the following steps:

1. Create a database VerticalPart in SSMS.

2. Create a table Employees in VerticalPart using the following statement:

```
CREATE TABLE [dbo].[Employees](
[EmployeeID] [int] PRIMARY KEY CLUSTERED NOT NULL,
[LastName] [nvarchar](20) NOT NULL,
[FirstName] [nvarchar](10) NOT NULL,
```

```
[HomePhone] [nvarchar](24) NULL,
[Extension] [nvarchar](4) NULL,
[Salary] [money] NULL
)
```

3. Use the Import/Export Wizard to populate the columns (except `Salary`) of the previous table using the `Employees` table from the `Northwind` database.

4. Modify the table by adding the salary for each employee.

   There are only a few employees and this should not be a problem. When you want to save the table, you may not be able to do so unless you have turned on this option (**Tools** | **Options** | **Designers** | **Table** | **Database Designers** and uncheck **Prevent saving changes that require table-recreation**), in the **Tools** menu of SSMS. You will get a reply after you save the `Employees` table, as shown in the following screenshot:

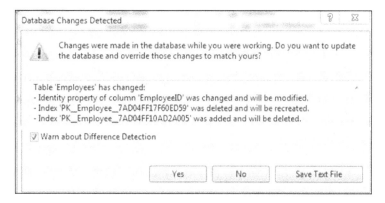

5. Now run a `SELECT` query to verify that the **Salary** column has been populated, as shown in the following screenshot:

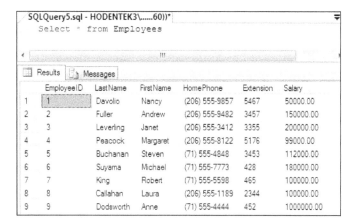

6. Copy the script for the Employees table of the Northwind database and modify it by changing the table name and removing some columns resulting in the following statement:

```
CREATE TABLE [dbo].[AzureEmployees](
[EmployeeID] [int] PRIMARY KEY CLUSTERED NOT NULL,
[LastName] [nvarchar](20) NOT NULL,
[FirstName] [nvarchar](10) NOT NULL,
[Title] [nvarchar](30) NULL,
[TitleOfCourtesy] [nvarchar](25) NULL,
[HireDate] [datetime] NULL,
[Address] [nvarchar](60) NULL,
[City] [nvarchar](15) NULL,
[Region] [nvarchar](15) NULL,
[PostalCode] [nvarchar](10) NULL,
[Country] [nvarchar](15)
)
```

 Note that the table name has been changed to AzureEmployees. This is the table that will be stored in the Bluesky database on SQL Azure.

7. Login to SQL Azure and create the table in the Bluesky database by running the previous create table statement. The table will be created with the previously mentioned schema, which you may verify in the Object Browser.

8. Use Import and Export Wizard to populate the columns of AzureEmployees with data from Northwind. Use the query option to move data from the source to destination using the following query:

```
SELECT EmployeeID, LastName, FirstName,
Title, TitleOfCourtesy, HireDate,
Address, City, Region, PostalCode,
Country
FROM
Employees
```

9. Save the query results to the AzureEmployees table you created earlier, as shown in the following screenshot:

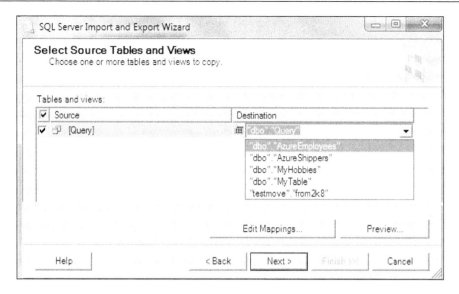

10. Follow the wizard's steps to review data mapping, as shown in the following screenshot:

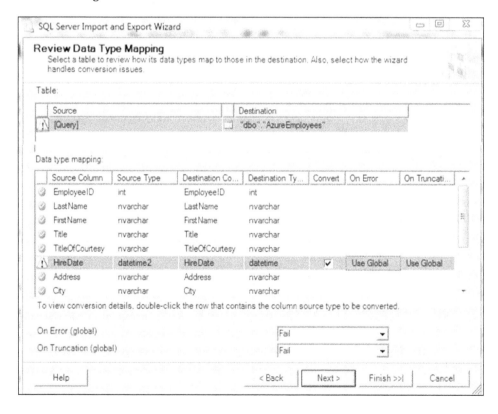

11. Complete the wizard's steps, as shown in the following screenshot:

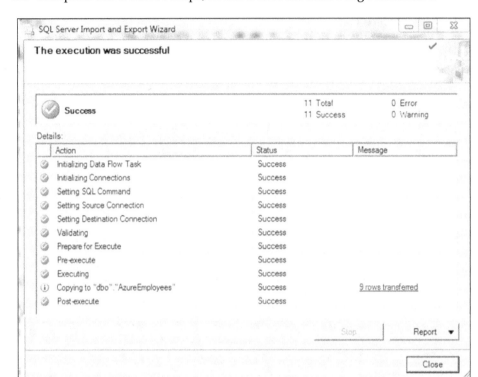

12. Verify the data in `AzureEmployees` in the `Bluesky` database on SQL Azure by running a `SELECT` statement.

By following the previously mentioned steps we have created two tables, one on-site and the other on SQL Azure.

Although, data transformation of string data types did not present any error, due to string length it could present some problems if the string length is over 8000, if the strings are of type varchar (max), and text. In these cases, just change them to nvarchar (max) to overcome the problem. For details review the following link: http://blogs.msdn.com/b/sqlazure/archive/2010/06/01/10018602.aspx.

Merging data and loading an Access database

In this section, we will reconstruct the `Employees` table on-site by retrieving data from SQL Azure as well as SQL Server's `VerticalPart` database and merge them. After merging them, we will place them in an MS Access database so that simple reports can be authored.

In order to do this, we perform the following steps:

1. Click open **BI Development Studio (BIDS)** from its shortcut.

2. Create an Integration Services project after providing a name for the project. Change the default name of the package file. The project folder should appear as shown in the following screenshot. Project name and package name were provided.

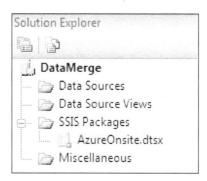

3. Drag-and-drop a **Data Flow** task to the **Control Flow** tabbed page of the package designer surface.

4. At the bottom pane in **Connection Managers**, configure the connection managers one each for SQL Azure database, VerticalPart database on SQL Server 2008, and an MS Access database, as shown in the following screenshot:

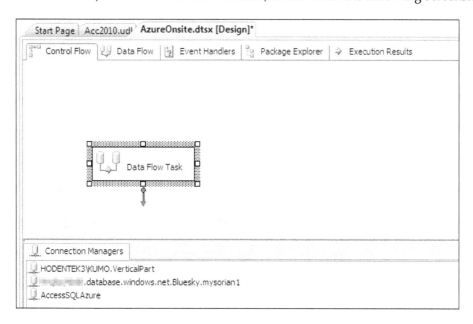

5. The following screenshot shows the details of the connection manager
   HODENTEK3\KUMO.VerticalPart. Note that **SqlClient Data Provider**
   is used. The SQL Server **HODENTEK3\KUMO** is configured for
   Windows Authentication.

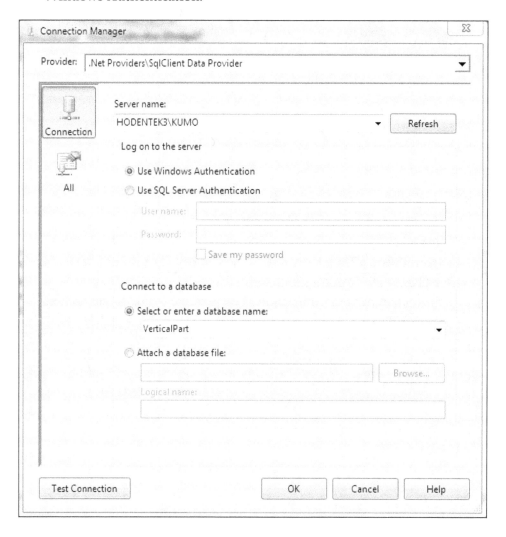

6. The following screenshot shows the connection xxxxxxxxxx.database.
   windows.net.Bluesky.mysorian1 for the Bluesky database on SQL Azure.
   The authentication information is the same one you have used so far, and if it
   is correct you should be able to see the available databases.

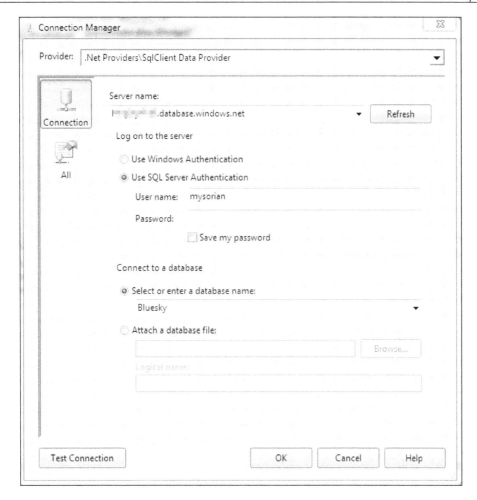

7. Create an MS Access database (Access 2003 format) and use it for this connection.

Later, we also create a table in this database to receive the merged fields from SQL Azure and the on-site server.

For this connection manager we use the following settings and verify by clicking the **Test Connection** button:

- ° **Provider**: Native OLE DB\Microsoft Jet 4.0 OLE DB Provider
- ° **Database file** is at: C:\Users\Jay\AccessSQLAzure.mdb
- ° **User name**: Admin
- ° **Password**: <empty>

> It is assumed that the reader is familiar with using SSIS. The author recommends his own book on SSIS for beginners, which may be found here: https://www.packtpub.com/sql-server-integration-services-visual-studio-2005/book.

Each of the connections mentioned here can be tested using the **Test Connection** button on them.

Merging columns from SQL Azure and SQL Server

You will use two ADO.NET data flow sources, one each for SQL Azure and SQL Server. The outputs will be merged.

1. Add two ADO.NET data flow sources to the tabbed designer pane **Data Flow**.

2. Rename the default names of the source components to read **From SQL Azure Database** and **From SQL Server 2008 database**.

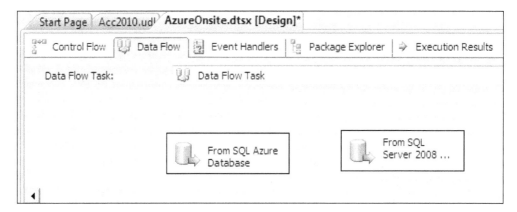

3. Configure the **ADO.NET Source Editor** connected to SQL Azure to display the following, as shown in the following screenshot.

   ADO.NET connection manager: XXXXXXX.database.windows.net.Bluesky. mysorian1

   Data access mode: Table or view

   Name of the table or view: "dbo"."AzureEmployees"

   You must use the server name appropriate for your SQL Azure instance.

4. Configure as shown and you should be able to view the data in this table with the **Preview…** button.

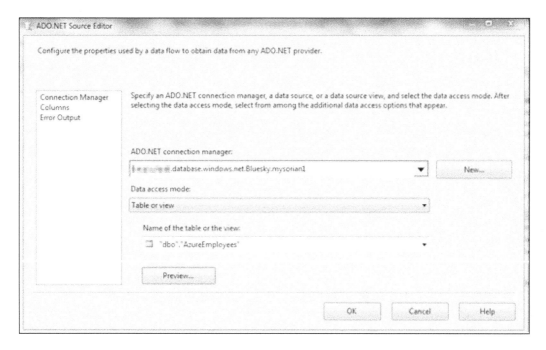

5. Configure the **ADO.NET Source Editor** connected to SQL Server to display the following, as shown in the next screenshot. Use the following details to configure the **From SQL Server 2008 database** source used in the **ADO.NET Source Editor**:

ADO.NET connection manager: HODENTEK3\KUMO.VerticalPart

Data access mode: Table or view

Name of the table or view: "dbo"."Employees"

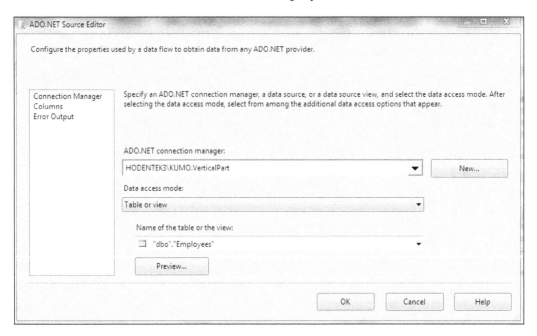

6. Again, you should be able to view the data in this table with the **Preview...**button.

Sorting the outputs of the sources

Since the data coming at the exit point of the sources is not sorted, it is important to get the sorting correct and the same in both sources before they can be merged.

1. Drag-and-drop two **Sort** dataflow controls from the **Toolbox** to the design surface just below the ADO.NET data sources.

2. Start with the one that is going to be receiving its input from the **From SQL Azure Database** source control.

3. Click **From SQL Azure Database** and drag-and-drop the green dangling line on to the **Sort** control below it, as shown in the following screenshot:

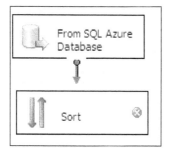

4. Double-click the **Sort** control to display the **Sort Transformation Editor** and place a check mark for **EmployeeID**, as shown in the following screenshot:

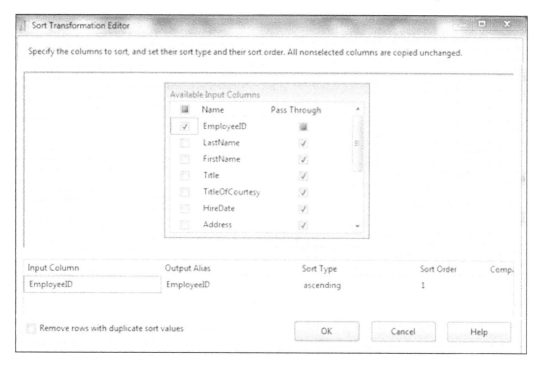

5. Repeat the same procedure for the **From SQL Server 2008 database** source. Now we have two sort controls receiving their inputs from two source controls with outputs sorted.

6. Drag-and-drop a **Merge Join** data flow transformation from the **Toolbox** on to the design surface.

7. Click the **Sort** data flow transformation on the left (connected to **From SQL Azure Database**) and drag-and-drop its green dangling line on to the **Merge Join** data flow transformation.

   The **Input Output Selection** window will be displayed, as shown in the following screenshot:

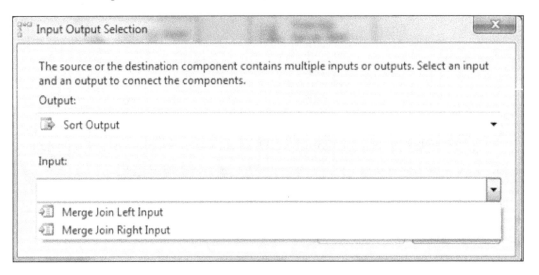

8. Select **Merge Join Left Input** and click on **OK**.

9. Repeat the same for the other Sort on the right (this time select **Merge Join Right Input**).

10. This merge control now merges the output from the two sort controls (merges left input and right input) and provides a merged output.

You still need to configure the **Merge Join**.

1. Double-click **Merge Join** to open the **Merge Join Transformation Editor** page as shown.

2. Read the instructions on this window.

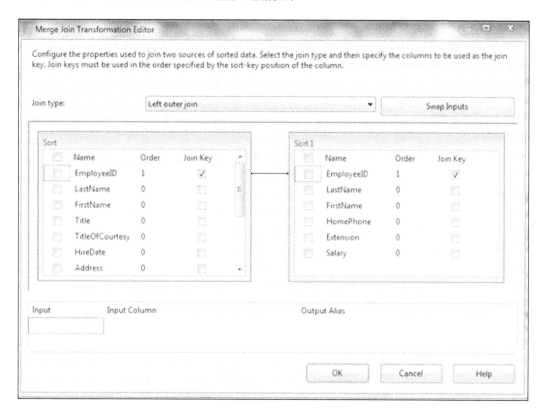

3. Place a check mark for **EmployeeID** in both the **Sort** lists shown in the top pane. The bottom pane gets populated with Input columns and Output aliases. Make sure the join type is **Left outer join** as in the previous screenshot (use the drop-down handle if needed).

 We can add a Data Viewer for each flow path so that we can monitor the flow of data at runtime by momentarily stopping the flow downstream. We are skipping this diagnostic step.

Porting output data from Merge Join to an MS Access database

We will be using the merged data from the two sources to fill up a table in an MS Access 2003 database.

1. In the MS Access database you created while setting up the Connection Managers, create a table, SalaryReport with the design parameters shown in the following screenshot:

Field Name	Data Type
EmployeeID	Number
LastName	Memo
FirstName	Memo
Title	Memo
TitleOfCourtesy	Memo
BirthDate	Date/Time
HireDate	Date/Time
Address	Memo
City	Memo
Region	Memo
PostalCode	Memo
Country	Memo
HomePhone	Memo
Extension	Memo
Photo	OLE Object
Notes	Memo

General Lookup

Field Size	Long Integer
Format	
Decimal Places	Auto
Input Mask	
Caption	
Default Value	
Validation Rule	
Validation Text	
Required	Yes
Indexed	No
Smart Tags	
Text Align	General

2. Drag-and-drop an **OLE DB Destination** component from the **Toolbox** on to the package designer pane just underneath the **Merge Join** component.

3. Drag-and-drop the green dangling line from **Merge Join** to the **OLE DB Destination** component.

4. Double-click the **OLE DB Destination** component to open its editor and fill in the details as follows:

   OLEDB connection manager: AccessSQLAzure

   Data access mode: Table or view

   Name of the table or view: SalaryReport

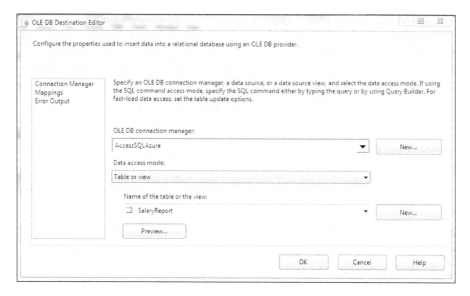

5. Click on **Mappings** to verify all the columns are present.

6. Build the project and execute the package.

7. The package elements turn yellow and later green, indicating a successful run.

8. You can verify the table in the access database for the transferred values. This should have all the merged columns from the two databases. Note that, in the screenshot, columns have been rearranged to move the **Salary** column into view.

Moving a MySQL database to SQL Azure database

Realizing the growing importance of MySQL and PHP from the LAMP stack, Microsoft has started providing programs to interact with and leverage these programs. For example, the SSMA described previously and third-party language hook ups to Windows Azure are just the beginning. For small businesses who are now using MySQL and who might be contemplating to move to SQL Azure, migration of data becomes important. In the following section, we develop a SQL Server Integration Services package, which when executed transfers a table from MySQL to SQL Azure. This may be compared with what we achieved using the SQL Server Migration Assistant for MySQL in the previous chapter.

Creating the package

The package consists of a dataflow task that extracts table data from MySQL (source) and transfers it to SQL Azure (destination). The dataflow task consists of an ADO.NET Source connecting to MySQL and an ADO.NET Destination connecting to SQL Azure. In the next section, the method for creating the two connections is explained.

Creating a package and adding source and destination data flow components is exactly the same as in the previous example.

Creating the source and destination connections

In order to create the package we need a connection to MySQL and a connection to SQL Azure. We use the ADO.NET Source and ADO.NET Destination for the flow of the data.

In order to create an ADO.NET Source connection to MySQL we need to create an ODBC DSN as we will be using the .NET ODBC Data Provider. Details of creating an ODBC DSN for the version of MySQL are described here: `http://www.packtpub.com/article/mysql-linked-server-on-sql-server-2008?utm_source=rk_jay1_0909&utm_medium=content&utm_campaign=ramsai`. Configuring a Connection Manager for MySQL is described here: `http://www.packtpub.com/article/mysql-data-transfer-using-sql-server-integration-services-ssis?utm_source=rk_jay2_1109&utm_medium=content&utm_campaign=ramsai`.

The Connection Manager for SQL Azure Destination uses a .NET SQLClient Data Provider and this is described here (when SQL Azure was in CTP but no change is required for the RTM): `http://www.packtpub.com/article/ground-to-sql-azure-cloud-migration-using-ms-ssis?utm_source=rk_jay2_1109&utm_medium=content&utm_campaign=ramsai`. The authentication information needs to be substituted for the current SQL Azure database.

Note that these procedures are not repeated step-by-step as they are described in great detail in the referenced links. However some key features of the configuration details are presented here:

- The ODBC DSN created is shown here with the details:

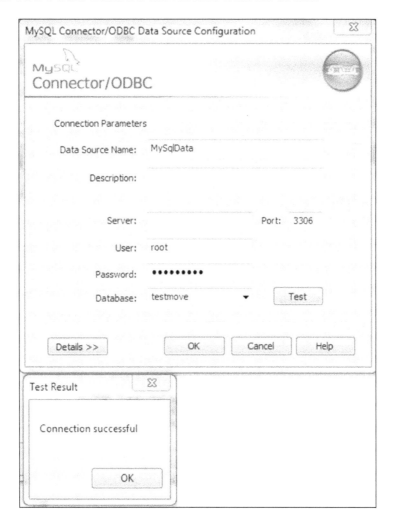

- The settings used for the MySQL **Connection Manager** are the following:

  Provider: .NET Providers\Odbc Data Provider

  Data Source Specification

  Use user or system data source name: MySqlData

  Login Information: root

  Password: <root password>

- The settings for the SQL Azure are the following:

  Provider: .Net Providers\SQLClient Data Provider

  Server name: xxxxxxx.database.windows.net

  Log on to the server

  Use SQL Server authentication

  User name: mysorian

  Password: ********

  Connect to a database

  Select or enter database name: Bluesky (if authentication is correct, it should appear in the drop-down)

Creating the package

We begin with the source connection and after configuring the **Connection Manager**, by editing the source as shown in the following screenshot. You may notice that the **SQL command** is used rather than the name of the table. It was found however, that choosing the name of the table results in an error. Probably a bug, and as a workaround we use the **SQL command**. With this you can preview the data and verify it.

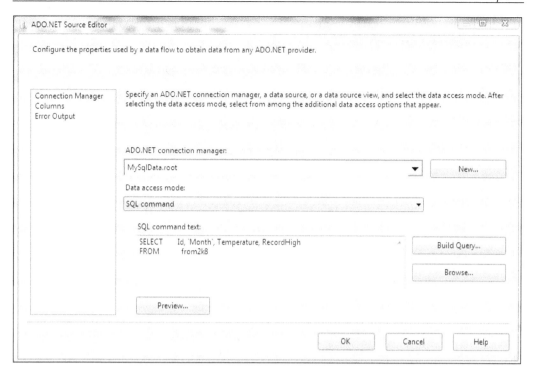

After verifying the data from the source, drag-and-drop the green dangling line from the source to the ADO.NET Destination component connected to SQL Azure. Double-clicking the destination component brings up the **ADO.NET Destination Editor** with the following details:

> **Connection manager: XXXXXXXX.database.windows.net.Bluesky. mysorian2**
>
> **Use a table or view: "dbo"."AzureEmployees"**
>
> **Use Bulk Insert when possible**: checked

There will be a warning message at the bottom of screen: **Map the columns on the Mappings page.**

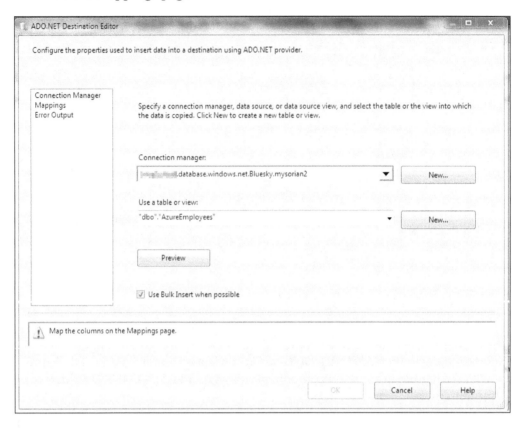

The **ADO.NET Destination Editor** window comes up with a list of tables or views displaying one of the tables. We will be creating a new table. Clicking **New…** button for the field **Use a table or view** brings up the **Create Table** window with a default create table statement with all the columns from the source table and a default table name, ADO.NET Destination. Modify the create table statement as follows:

```
CREATE TABLE fromMySql(
    "Id" int Primary Key Clustered,
    "Month" nvarchar(11),
    "Temperature" float,
    "RecordHigh" float
```

When you click on **OK** in this screen you will have completed the configuration of the destination. There are several things you can add to make troubleshooting easier by adding Data Viewers, error handling, and so on. These are omitted here but best practices require that these should be in place when you design packages.

The completed destination component should display the following details:

Connection manager: XXXXXX.database.windows.net.Bluesky.mysorian2

Use a table or view: fromMySql

Use Bulk Insert when possible: Checked

The columns from the source are all mapped to the columns of the destination, which can be verified in the **Mappings** page, as shown in the following screenshot:

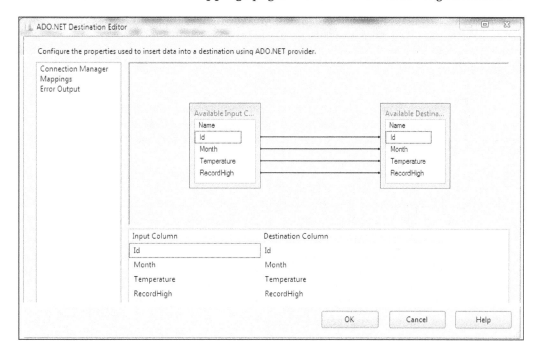

When the source and destination are completely configured as described here you can build the project from the main menu.

When you execute the project, the program starts running and after a while both the components turn yellow and then go green indicating that the package has executed successfully. The rows (number) that are written to the destination also appear in the designer.

You may now log on to SQL Azure in SSMS and verify that the table `fromMySql2` has been created and that 12 rows of data from MySQL's data have been written into it.

Creating a report using SQL Azure as data source

Although Reporting Services is not installed in the Cloud as of this writing, Microsoft is considering placing it in the near future. Moving SQL Server Reporting Services has the main advantage of reduced latency as the data is directly accessed in the datacenter. This may entail providing access to the database to a larger group of report authoring personnel. Given the fact that Reporting Services is not in the cloud, does not prevent the generation of reports based on the data on SQL Azure. In fact, SQL Azure is included as one of the data sources that can be configured using SSRS. In the following section, a procedure is described to connect to SQL Azure from BIDS to generate the report.

 The author recommends his book *Learning SQL Server Reporting Services 2008* published by Packt Publishing, which explains report authoring in greater detail.

In order to generate a report using BIDS, perform the following steps:

1. Start the SQL Server Business Intelligence Development Studio (BIDS) and create a **Report Server Project** in the **Business Intelligence Projects** type. Provide a custom name for the project.

2. Herein it is named **CloudReport**.

3. Click on **OK**.

4. This creates the **CloudReport** project with three folders, **Shared Data Sources**, **Shared Datasets**, and **Reports**.

5. Highlight the **Report** folder, right-click and choose **Add New Report** from the drop-down menu.

   This wakes up the **Report Wizard** and displays the **Welcome to the Report Wizard** page. Make sure you read the information on this page.

6. Click on **Next**.

7. The **Select the Data Source** page of the **Report Wizard** is displayed as shown in the following screenshot. Observe that you can connect to a variety of data sources including those from third parties.

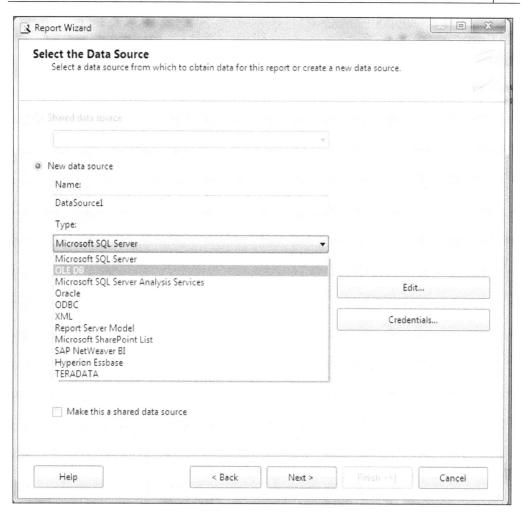

We have the option to make this a shared source or not. We do not check this box. We use the default data type source, which is Microsoft SQL Server. We choose a name for the data source. Herein it is named SQLAzureDS.

Copying the connection string for ADO.NET from the portal, saving it to clipboard, and pasting it in the text area reserved for the connection string in the previous screenshot will not work as this is a connection string that will be constructed by the wizard.

8. Click on **Edit...**.

9. The **Connection Properties** window is displayed, as shown in the following screenshot:

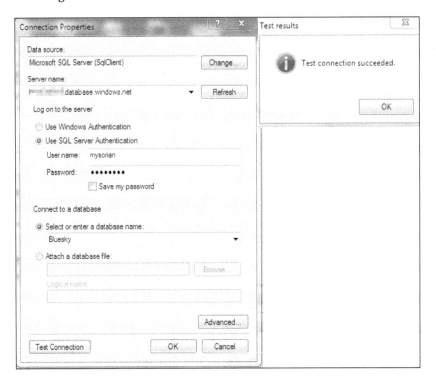

10. Enter the details for **Server name**, **User name**, and **Password** after choosing **Use SQL Server Authentication** and the **Select or enter a database name**. You may test the connection. Click on **OK**.

    The **Connection string** field of the **Select Data Source** page gets updated with the server name and the database name.

11. Click on **Next**. The **Enter Data Source Credential** window pops up.

12. Enter the credentials once again and click **OK** on this window.

13. The **Design the Query** page of **Report Wizard** is displayed.

14. Click the **Query Builder** button. The **Query Designer** is displayed. This is a common interface in most of Microsoft's database products (for example, Microsoft Access and Query Designer in SSMS).

15. Dismiss the **Query Designer** by closing it.

    We will not use the **Query Designer** but directly enter the following statement in the **Design the Query** window.

    ```
    Select * from fromMySql2
    ```

Here, the table `fromMySql2` on the SQL Azure database, `Bluesky`, is used. You could use any other table you might have on your SQL Azure database as long as the connection string correctly points to the data source.

16. Click on **Next**. The **Select the Report Type** page of the **Report Wizard** is displayed with two options **Tabular** or **Matrix** with **Tabular** being the default.

17. Click on **Next**. The **Design the Table** page of the wizard is displayed. `fromMySql2` is a simple table with four columns and 12 rows.

    Pick each of the items in the **Available fields**, drag-and-drop it on the **Displayed fields** area of the page (alternatively, you could also use the **Details>** button to achieve the same after highlighting all items in the area of the **Available fields**).

18. Click on **Next**. The **Choose the Table Style** page of the wizard is displayed.

19. Choose a style and click on **Finish**.

    The `Report1.rdl` file generated by the Report Wizard is displayed in the Visual Studio 2008 IDE. The **Report Data** window with **Built-in Fields**, **Data Sources**, and **Datasets** folders are also displayed, as shown in the following screenshot:

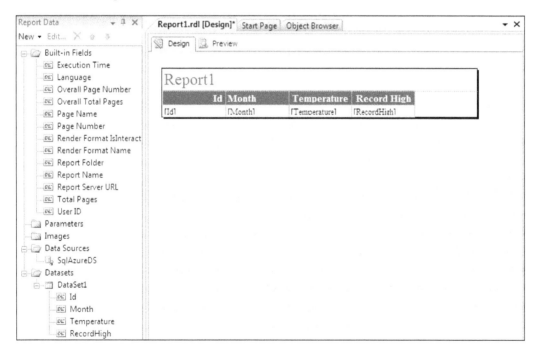

At this point the report is essentially complete.

20. Right click the **Report1.rdl** in the project folder and click the **Run** menu item from the drop-down. The **Report1.rdl - Report Preview** page is displayed.

21. Enter authentication information at the top of this page and click **View Report**.

The report will be processed and will be displayed, as shown in the following screenshot:

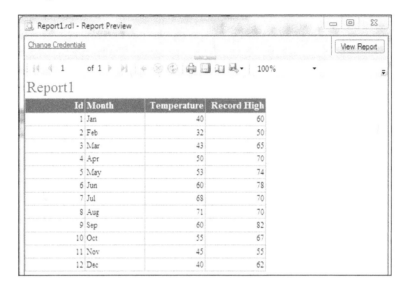

This can now be deployed to the Report server.

22. Right click the report file in the project folder and choose **Deploy**.

23. You need to provide the correct target URL for deployment. The URL for the present installation is: http://hodentek3/ReportServer_KUMO.

Accessing SQL Azure from Report Builder 3.0

Report Builder 3.0 is a standalone report authoring and deploying tool that is totally integrated with SQL Server 2008 R2. It can be downloaded from the link given here although it can also be installed when you install SQL Server 2008 R2: http://www.microsoft.com/downloads/details.aspx?FamilyID=D3173A87-7C0D-40CC-A408-3D1A43AE4E33&displaylang=en.

For the purpose of the following example, it is assumed that Report Builder 3.0 is installed on the computer. It is also assumed that the Report Server has been configured. By following these steps we can develop a report using data on the SQL Azure server.

We start with Report Builder 3.0 and use it to connect to SQL Azure data source and obtain a dataset from one of its tables. After obtaining the data, we will create a report based on the data and then deploy to the Report Server.

1. Start Report Builder 3.0 from its shortcut.

    The first time it takes some time to connect to the Report Server. Make sure you run it as administrator. When you get connected to the Report Server you should see the server you are connected to, at the bottom of the window.

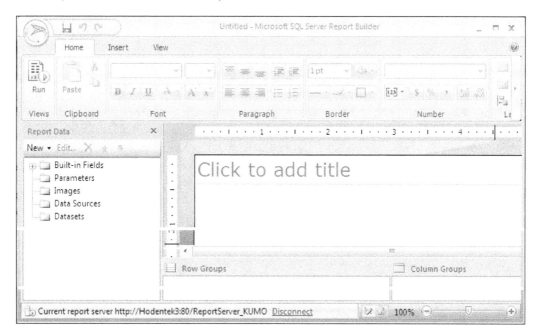

2. Right-click on the **Data Sources** folder and choose **Add New Data Source....**

3. This opens the **Data Source Properties** page where you can choose the connection type (of the data source) that includes SQL Azure.

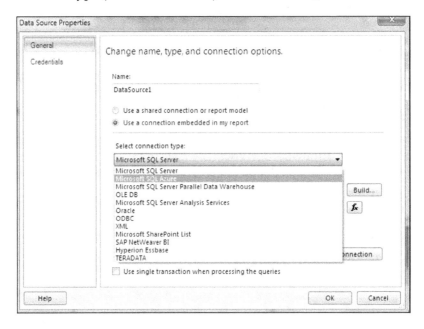

4. Choose **Microsoft SQL Azure.**

5. The **Data Source Properties** window is displayed.

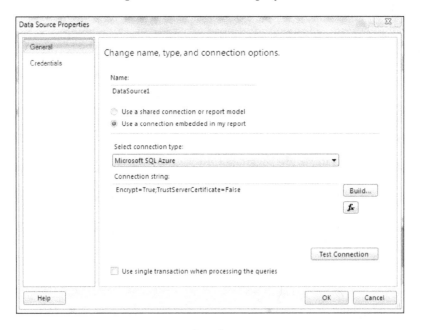

6. Click on the **Build...** button.

7. The **Connection Properties** page is displayed, as shown in the next screenshot.

8. Fill in the details as shown here. Click on **Test Connection** and verify if the connection is ok.

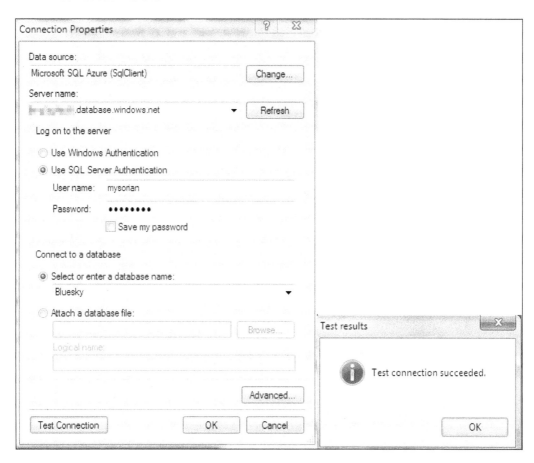

9. Click on **OK** in the two screens.

The **Connection string** information gets updated as shown. Note that the default **Datasource1** is changed to **BuilderSRC**.

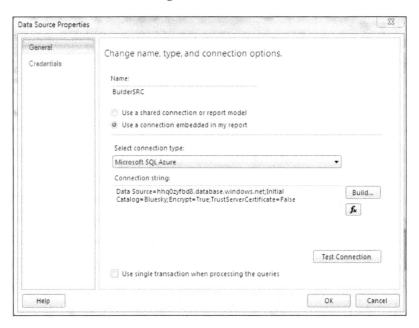

10. Click on **Credentials**.

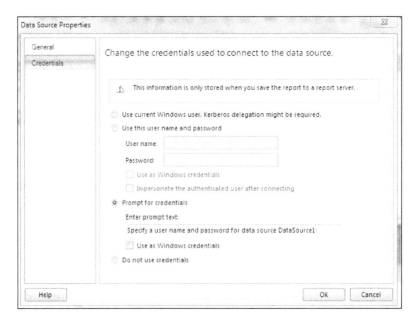

With this choice of the credential, the user will be asked to provide login information every time he/she accesses the report.

11. Click on **OK**.

Now you can drag-and-drop a table (or you can start with a Table Wizard) and drag-and-drop fields from the dataset onto the report to author a report. The user can refer to the SSRS online references to learn about authoring reports. The following URLs provide detailed examples of creating a report using Report Builder 2.0, which is not very different from using Report Builder 3.0.

- `http://www.packtpub.com/article/report-builder-in-microsoft-sql-server-2008-part1`

- `http://www.packtpub.com/article/report-builder-in-microsoft-sql-server-2008-part2`

Reporting Services is treated in more detail in another book by the author published by Packt Publishing. The details are available here: `https://www.packtpub.com/learning-sql-server-2008-reporting-services/book`.

A complete view is shown in the following screenshot where three items from the dataset were dragged-and-dropped on the table designer interface:

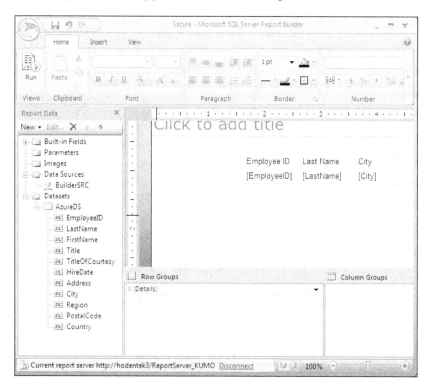

The designed report can be saved on the Report Server. It may be noted however, that this report will not render due to the fact that the data extension SQLAZURE – which is needed for validation and rendering – is not supported in the CTP edition. You will typically get the error shown in the following screenshot when you try to display the report in Report Builder.

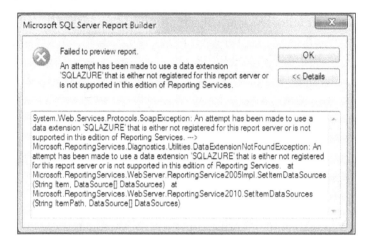

Note that a report created in Visual Studio will not have this problem. In the RTM version of SQL Server 2008 R2, this is known to work.

 In Windows 7, even if you are the owner of the computer, you need to open the browser explicitly as owner of the computer to view the folders and files on the Report Manager and the Report Server.

Summary

This chapter described in detail how SSIS and SSRS are used in creating BI projects using SQL Azure data. Using some of the tools described in the previous chapter, a table on the on-site server was partitioned to keep sensitive data on the site and non-sensitive data on SQL Azure. A SSIS package was created to merge data from an on-site location and SQL Azure for internal reporting. A second SSIS project showed how easy it is to migrate data from a MySQL database to SQL Azure. Two reporting services projects were described in this chapter: one using BIDS and the other using Report Builder 3.0, to author a report using data on SQL Azure.

Chapter 7, Working with Windows Azure Hosting lays the basis for the following chapter where details of how web facing projects deployed to Windows Azure Cloud access relational data.

7
Working with Windows Azure Hosting

Businesses typically create web facing applications on their site or hosts on third-party Internet service provider sites that usually display their business-related information, allow users to manipulate objects, or do some buy/sell transactions. The businesses may want to move sites to the Windows Azure cloud platform for the various advantages mentioned in *Chapter 1, Cloud Computing and Microsoft Azure Services Platform.*

In this chapter, we will look at hosting web facing applications as Windows Azure Hosted Service introduced in *Chapter 1, Cloud Computing and Microsoft Azure Services Platform.* To recapitulate, we created a hosted service in Windows Azure by setting up an account for the hosted services.

We will start off from this point and create web facing applications. These applications are created using Visual Studio 2008 SP1 or Visual Studio 2010. After the applications are created and tested in Visual Studio they will then be deployed to Windows Azure platform. Visual Studio has all the nuts and bolts to simulate the cloud platform on the ground (a simulated environment, which has almost 90 percent of the cloud functionality) and then deploy the application to Windows Azure cloud platform.

We will also look at the details of hosting an application, that can register users by storing their credentials on SQL Azure and authenticate them by forms authentication when they access the website during their subsequent visits.

In this chapter, we will be describing the following:

- Tools needed to develop and host Cloud Service applications
- Create and deploy an ASP.NET web application
- Windows Azure ASP.NET application with forms authentication

Tools needed to develop and host Cloud Service applications

We need to install Windows Azure Tools for Microsoft Visual Studio 1.1 (February 2010) to develop scalable web facing applications that can be:

- created
- configured
- built
- debugged
- run
- packaged
- deployed

You can download the Windows Azure Tools for Microsoft Visual Studio 1.1 from here:

`http://wareseeker.com/download/microsoft-windows-azure-tools-for-microsoft-visual-studio-1.1.30131.1501-february-2010.rar/3714010fb.`

The previous installation also includes the required Windows Azure SDK.

However, as this book is being written, a new version of Windows Azure SDK has been released in June 2010. Details of this version, as well as the express editions of Visual Studio 2010 Express and SQL Server 2008 R2 Express (both are free) may be found here: `http://hodentek.blogspot.com/2010/06/windows-azure-working-set-of-programs.html.`

Due to this latest software iteration, the software set we will be using for this chapter is the following:

- Microsoft Visual Studio 2008 SP1
- Microsoft SQL Server 2008 R2 Express
- Windows Azure Tools for Microsoft Visual Studio 1.2 (June 2010)

In lieu of Visual Studio 2008 SP1, the Visual Studio 2010 Express can also be used for developing cloud applications.

The Microsoft Azure Tools for Microsoft Visual Studio also includes the Windows Azure SDK (if the development platform is not Microsoft Visual Studio then Windows SDK can be downloaded separately).

Create and deploy an ASP.NET application

In Visual Studio IDE you can create the following two types of applications for the Web:

- An ASP.NET website, which creates a website on your local IIS web server
- An ASP.NET web application that can be tested within the IDEs internal web server — the ASP.NET Development Server with a port other than 80

With the Microsoft Azure Tools for Microsoft Visual Studio installed, you can create web facing applications in Visual Studio and test them in the IDE, *debug* them in the development fabric (the environment, which simulates the cloud), and after verifying its performance you can *publish* the application to the cloud. When the cloud application is published, the project files are bundled and kept ready in a specific folder on the computer.

After creating and developing the application you will then deploy the application to your hosted site on Windows Azure, by initiating the deployment process. This process consists of pointing to the aforementioned bundled programs on your machine and providing a name for the application. The deployment will be first made to the 'staging site' (it is possible to host the project directly on the production site), which is private to the user deploying the application. When the application is promoted using a control on the Windows Azure Portal, the application moves over to the production site, which is, in general, public facing (if there is already an existing application hosted on the production site, they get interchanged).

In the following section, we will be creating a cloud application consisting of a single web page. This will then be tested in the IDE, debugged in the development fabric, and later deployed to the cloud. The main steps envisaged are the following:

- Create a cloud project in Visual Studio 2008 SP1
- Test and debug in the development fabric
- Deploy the application to the cloud from the portal

Create a cloud project in Visual Studio 2008 SP1

Following are the few steps you needed to create a cloud project in Visual Studio 2008 SP1 (similar procedure in Visual Studio 2010):

1. Open Visual Studio 2008 from its shortcut with the option to run it as an administrator.

    You should see Windows Azure Tools listed in the program on the splash screen.

2. Click on **File | New | Project...**.

3. In the **New Project** window that opens, choose to create a project of the type **Cloud**, as shown in the following screenshot:

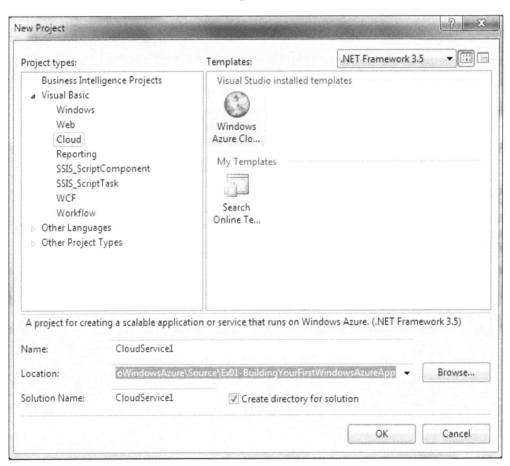

The **Cloud** project type uses the **Windows Azure Cloud Services** template and would create a project with a default name **CloudService1**. You have to provide a distinct name of your choice and when you click on **OK** you will be saving the files to a location of your choice.

4. Change the name of the project to one of your choice (herein **PlainsboroClub**), accept the default location for the files and click on **OK**.

The program starts creating the template files and after some processing the **New Cloud Service Project** window is displayed, as shown in the following screenshot:

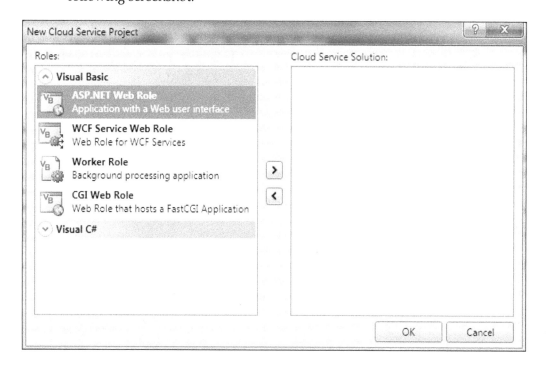

As explained in *Chapter 1, Cloud Computing and Microsoft Azure Services Platform* the cloud service is a hosting service that works in a multi-tenant architecture by design and each tenant works inside its own boundary. The hosted service is served by web roles and worker roles whose functionality was also described in *Chapter 1, Cloud Computing and Microsoft Azure Services Platform*. There are three different types of web roles for processing web requests and a worker role that does the background processing. These web roles (**ASP.NET Web Role**, **WCF Service Web Role**, and **CGI Web Role**) and the **Worker Role** are shown in the previous screenshot.

In Visual Studio 2010 there is an additional ASP.NET MVC2 Web Role and F # Worker Role.

Of the three web roles, the **CGI Web Role** is used to host a **FastCGI Application**, such as a PHP application. The web role bestows functionality analogous to the functionality of a web page and the worker's role functions analogous to a Windows Service. These programs are available for both C# and VB.NET developers.

1. Highlight **ASP.NET Web Role** and add it to the **Cloud Service Solution** by hitting the **>** button in the middle.

   An **ASP.NET Web Role, WebRole1** gets added into the **Cloud Service Solution**. It can be renamed by clicking the rename button shown as an icon in the following screenshot:

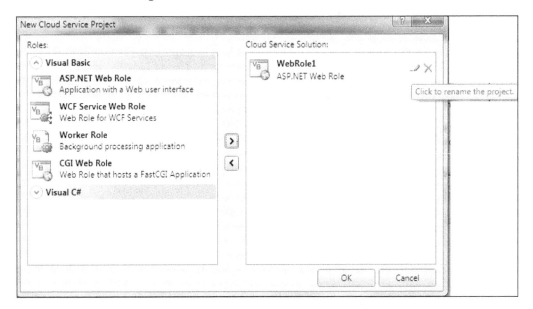

2. After renaming the **WebRole1** (herein **demoRole**) click on **OK**.

   The **PlainsboroClub** solution will be created with all the folders and files as shown in the next screenshot. It consists of two related projects, the **PlainsboroClub** cloud service project consisting of the various roles and the **demoRole** web application project. Notice the familiar **Default.aspx** page in the **demoRole** project.

The **PlainsboroClub** cloud service project's principal element is the **ASP.NET Web Role** – the **demoRole**.

The configuration and settings information for the web role are contained in the `ServiceDefinition.csdef` and `ServiceConfiguration.cscfg` files, which are both XML files. Changes can be made directly in these files or by invoking the properties of the web role by right-clicking the web role and making modifications in the UI that gets displayed.

> There are four kinds of web roles and two kinds of worker roles that determine how your Windows Azure Services application functions when deployed to the cloud using Visual Studio 2010. Visual Studio 2008 supports three web roles and a worker role.
>
> More detailed information about the roles and their default properties is briefly described here: `http://hodentekhelp.blogspot.com/2010/06/what-are-default-properties-of-aspnet.html`.

For the purposes of this section, we will assume just a single instance of the web role and all the default web role properties (configuration, settings, endpoints, local store, and certificates) and their attributes. As no data will be used, there will be no local storage of the data.

The **demoRole** project is similar to an ASP.NET Web Application except that it has an extra file `WebRole.vb`, which supports changing the configuration information without stopping the service (if desired).

> "You can update your service's configuration while the service is running in Windows Azure, without taking the service offline. The service's configuration is described in the service configuration (`.cscfg`) file.
>
> To change configuration information, you can either upload a new configuration file, or edit the configuration file in place and apply it to your running service".
>
> Details of this are taken from Microsoft documentation and described in the link: `http://msdn.microsoft.com/en-us/library/ee848064.aspx`.

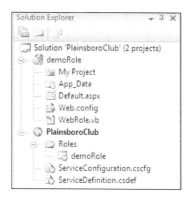

3. Add some text to the design view of Default.aspx. Click **Build** and after it succeeds, browse by making a right-click and choosing **View in Browser**.

The **Default.aspx** page is displayed as shown in the following screenshot. Notice that the development web server with a program assigned port number is displaying the page as shown in the following screenshot. The text that was added to the **Default.aspx** page is just the text that is displayed.

Test and debug in the development fabric

As mentioned earlier, Windows Azure hosted service uses the IIS server and to set up an equivalent simulation environment, the local web server is used. This comes into play when you debug the Cloud Service application in Visual Studio (2008 as well as 2010 versions) and at the same time a development fabric console is displayed, which stays in the task bar of the computer. The development fabric, which is a simulation of the Windows Azure fabric (simulating more than 80 percent of the Windows Azure fabric) should start when you start the debug process. The messages generated during the debug process are written to this console and as debugging an application on the hosted site is not supported, the development fabric is the only means available for debugging without going through hoops to log messages to the Windows Azure Storage containers and retrieving them for evaluation.

In the latest (June 2010) Windows Azure Tools SDK (there are two versions, one for 2008 and the other for 2010), there is a new feature called the IntelliTrace, which requires .NET 4.0 and Visual Studio 2010 Ultimate that allows you to debug problems you may face in the cloud. For details look here:

http://www.cloudtweaks.com/2010/06/using-intellitrace-to-debug-windows-azure-cloud-services/.

1. Click on **Solution 'PlainsboroClub' (2 projects)** in the **Solution Explorer** and click **Debug | Start Debugging...** in the main menu.

   A number of events get started and the messages are written to the status line at the bottom of the screen and the development fabric would have started indicating by spawning an icon, which when clicked, appears as shown in the following screenshot. The Windows Azure icon will be on the taskbar. The simulation environment displays that both the development fabric and the development storage, have started. For this section, we are not using the development storage.

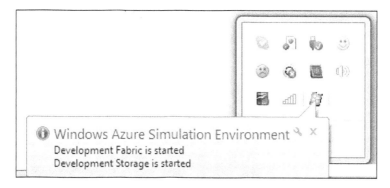

2. Right-click on the **Windows Azure Simulation Environment** icon.

   The contents of the development environment as well as controls to shutdown these services are displayed, as shown in the following screenshot:

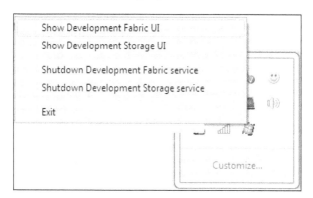

3. Click on **Show Development Fabric UI**.

4. The **Development Fabric** UI is displayed, as shown (all nodes shown expanded) in the following screenshot:

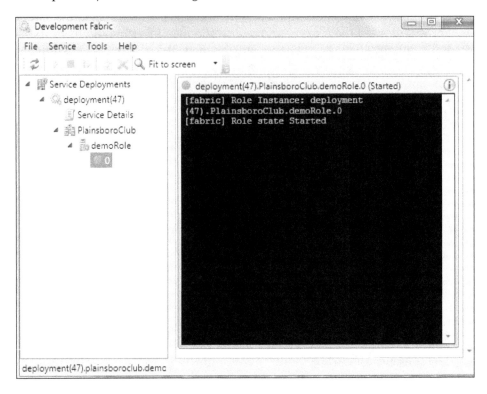

The previous screenshot shows that the role instance was deployed with the role deployment ID shown in the parenthesis and there is just one role. In addition to the one role 0, additional roles will be displayed if more than one role was configured.

The development fabric is a service and the contract details are shown in the node **Service Details**. When this is clicked, the service details are displayed, as shown in the following screenshot:

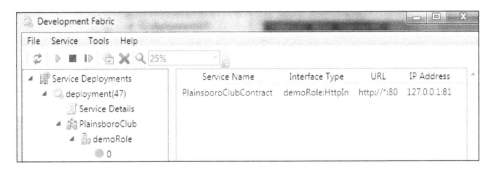

5. Together with the starting of the role state, the web application is processed, and displayed on the browser, as shown in the following screenshot:

The page is displayed in the local web server (127.0.0.1) on a port different from that of the localhost.

The messages that were displayed on the status line such as Build Started, Build Succeeded, Initializing the Service Deployment, and so on, progress one after another. During this process, *Packaging the Deployment* also takes place. This is because the deployment needs a specific type of formatting. It is these packages that will be deployed to the Windows Azure cloud platform.

The package files (`PlainsboroClub.csx` and the `ServiceConfiguration.cscfg`) are located in the **PlainsboroClub** folder in its `bin/debug` subfolders. It is these files, which after they are modified by the *Publish* process, get deployed to the Windows Azure hosted site.

Deploy the application to the cloud from the portal

Once the Cloud Service Project is debugged in the development fabric as described previously, it is ready for deployment to the Windows Azure hosted site. The publishing process converts the `PlainsboroClub.csx` and `ServiceConfgiuration.cscfg` files into deployable files for the Windows Azure Cloud fabric and places them in the `debug/Publish` folder of **PlainsboroClub** project folder.

With the release of Windows Azure Tools for Microsoft Visual Studio 1.2 (June 2010), the Publish process has slightly changed. The following describes the process of publishing while using the June 2010 version for Visual Studio 2008.

The procedure to publish starts with the following steps:

1. Right-click on the **PlainsboroClub** project and click **Set as StartUp Project**. Again right-click **PlainsboroClub** project and click on **Publish...**.

2. The **Publish Cloud Service** window is displayed, as shown in the following screenshot:

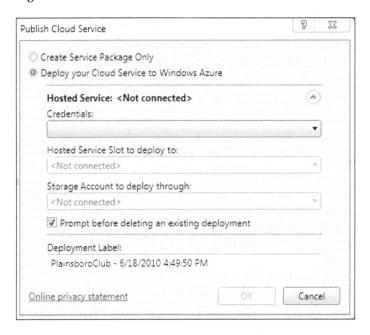

There are two options but we will just use the **Create Service Package Only** option. The other option lets you upload a certificate and authenticate the portal (this has been left out of the present discussion to keep the explanation simple).

3. Choose the suggested option and click on **OK**.

You get a *Publish* related message in the **Output** window of Visual Studio, and the folder to which the deployment files were published, opens up, displaying two files, **PlainsboroClub** (notice the icon), a **Service Package file**, and the **Cloud Service Configuration file**, as shown in the following screenshot. These will be placed in the project's bin/Publish folder. The service package file is the **PlainsboroClub** folder we encountered in the development fabric.

Name	Date modified	Type	Size
PlainsboroClub	6/18/2010 5:00 PM	Service Package file	1,542 KB
ServiceConfiguration	6/17/2010 6:22 PM	Cloud Service Configuration file	1 KB

In the following steps, these will be deployed to the Windows Azure's hosted site:

1. Right-click on **PlainsboroClub** and click on **Browse to Portal…**.

    The **Welcome to Windows Live** page is displayed. Enter the credentials to your account. The Windows Azure Portal opens with the following URL, as shown in the following screenshot: `https://windows.azure.com/Cloud/Provisioning/Default.aspx`.

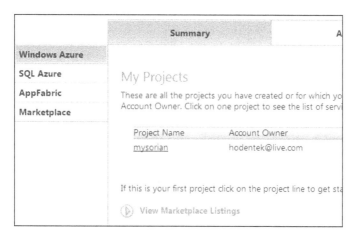

2. Click the name of your project (**mysorian** in this case) in **Windows Azure** under the **Project Name.**

    This brings up the project page displaying the Windows Azure hosting icon. (**Moda** in this case. This name was given during provisioning.)

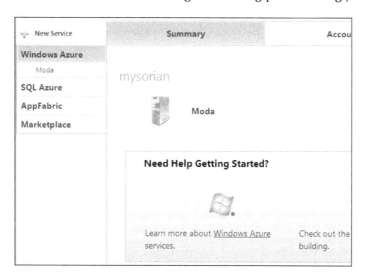

3. Click on the **Moda** icon. The **Hosted Service** page is displayed.

   We shall deploy the application to the staging area first and after confirming we will promote it to **Production**.

4. Click the black arrowhead pointing left to bring the **Staging** to the view, as shown in the following screenshot:

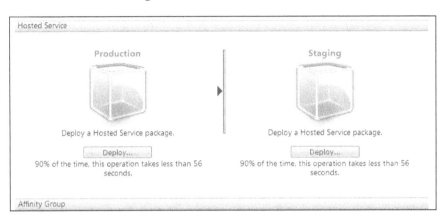

5. Click on **Deploy....** The **Staging Deployment** page is displayed, as shown in the following screenshot:

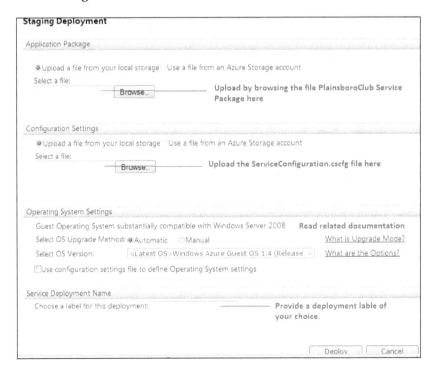

6. As suggested in the previous screenshot, browse and bring in the indicated files to the portal. Also, provide a name for the label and click on **Deploy**.

The page reverts to the previous page showing a progress bar, which after processing is displayed, as shown in the following screenshot and the label (**PlainsboroClubTest**) provided is shown for this deployment.

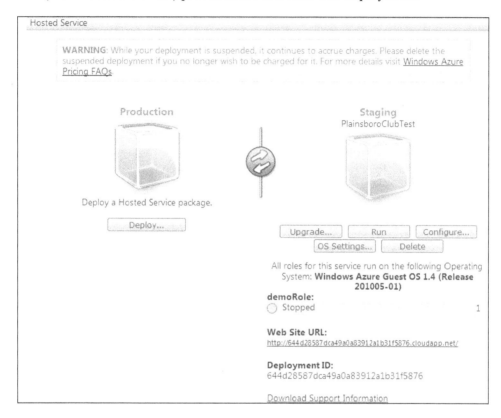

Note that the deployment has stopped. You may access the deployed application after you click on **Run** and after the command has been processed (indicated by the **demoRole** changing from **Stopped** to **Ready**). Before changing to **Ready** it may go through other intermediate states, *Initializing, Busy,* and so on.

 Also make sure you read the warning as it may result in charges that you may want to avoid.

7. Click on **Run**. The **Stopped** icon should change to **Ready**.

8. When the icon reads **Ready** click on the **Web Site URL:** shown in the previous screenshot:

Now the web application (which has just the `Default.aspx` page) is deployed to the staging site and the ID of the staging site is shown in the URL shown in the previous screenshot.

9. Now go back to the portal and click on the control between **Staging** and **Production**.

You may get a message asking you whether or not you want to promote the deployment to production. If you promote it, it becomes a public URL and any one can look at the page by browsing to your production site.

Assume that you want to promote it.

10. Click on **OK**. The hosted service starts working again and may go through the same states as **Staging** and when the role states get ready you get the following display:

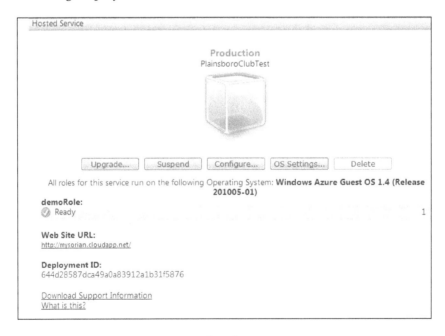

Your application is now live on your Windows Azure provisioned site.

11. Click on the **Web Site URL** link.

    Your website's Default.aspx is now displayed on your cloud site, as shown in the following screenshot. Notice the web page URL.

This completes the deployment of the application to the production site. You could make changes to the configuration using the **Configure...** button. We will not make changes to this deployment.

12. Click on **Suspend**, after a while your request is processed (the hosted site processes the request).

13. The **Production** site's **demoRole** enters a stopping, stopped state. The **Delete** button gets enabled.

14. Click on the **Delete** button. Your site is removed from the cloud.

Why should you take all this trouble to create and then delete? This is just a demo, but it is sitting on a site, which is accruing charges by the minute. Hence after it is verified that it is functioning, there is no need to leave it there.

Windows Azure ASP.NET site with forms authentication

ASP.NET sites can come in all sizes, from the biggest ones in large enterprises to smaller ones in small businesses. With small businesses moving into the cloud, forms authentication appears attractive and universal as it is less restrictive than Windows authentication, not restricted to Windows environment, and less expensive than passport authentication.

With the authentication credentials stored in SQL Azure, the standard ASP.NET Membership/Role Provider can be used for authenticating users accessing the ASP.NET websites. Please review the following link if you are not conversant with the SQL Server membership provider concepts. Please review this link for ASP.NET membership provider: http://msdn.microsoft.com/en-us/library/yh26yfzy.aspx. It may be mentioned that for on-site ASP.NET website authentication with ASP.NET Membership/Role Provider, the Membership information is stored in SQL Server Express (or SQL Server). A discussion of other possible methods of authentication or, more generally, methods of access control available are described here: http://cm-bloggers.blogspot.com/2009/02/what-are-options-azure-and-access.html.

In the following section, the procedure for setting up the ASP.NET Membership/Role Provider database for use with forms authentication and configuring the ASP.NET application will be described. The Visual Studio IDE is equipped with appropriate interfaces and controls for interacting with the membership database. The main steps involved in creating such an authentication scheme consist of the following:

- Create an ASP.NET website for authentication with a form
- Create an ASP.NET Membership Provider on SQL Azure
- Configure the site to support forms authentication
- Test and verify

We start creating an ASP.NET Cloud Service Project with an ASP.NET Web Role, as we did earlier along the following lines.

Create Windows Azure Cloud Service Project in Visual Studio 2008

Since we already have a Windows Azure Cloud Service Project that we created earlier, we can use the same site for our authentication. We will add an extra web page to the **demoRole** project in the **PlainsboroClub** solution.

1. Right-click on **demoRole** in the Solution Explorer and click on **Add | New Item...**.
2. In the **Add New Item – demoRole** window pick the **Web Form** template and change its default name to **login.aspx**. Then click on **Add**.
3. A new web page **login.aspx** will be added to the **demoRole** project in the Solution Explorer.

Add a Login control to the login.aspx page

Out of the box, ASP.NET provides fully functional forms authentication in the form of prebuilt login web pages or login controls that you can use in your applications. Please review the following link to learn about the ASP.NET Login controls: `http://msdn.microsoft.com/en-us/library/ms178329.aspx`.

In the following steps we will be using the **Login** control from the **Toolbox** in Visual Studio 2008:

1. Drag-and-drop a Login control from the **Toolbox** under **Login** on to the **login.aspx** page you added earlier.

2. The **Login** control adds a set of UI controls to the page for providing user information.

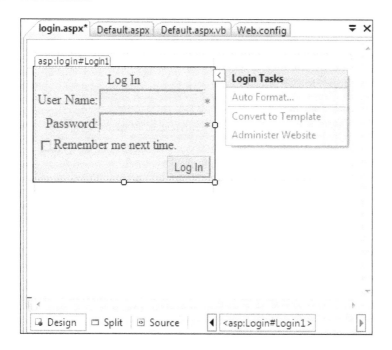

The textboxes and the button are the common features of most form-based authentication schemes. The **Remember me next time** checkbox, if checked, will store the inserted information in the ASP.NET Membership Provider and will authenticate the user when he/she logs in. Adding the following tag to the `login.aspx` would have the same effect:

```
<asp:Login ID="Login1" runat="server"></asp:Login>
```

Add a control to login.aspx for new users to register

Users new to the site must have a way to register so that their name can be registered in the Membership database. Visual Studio provides the control **CreateUserWizard** for this purpose.

In the following step, add a **CreateUserWizard** control to the **login.aspx** page:

1. Drag-and-drop the **CreateUserWizard** control on to the design view of the **login.aspx** page just below the **Login** control, as shown in the following screenshot:

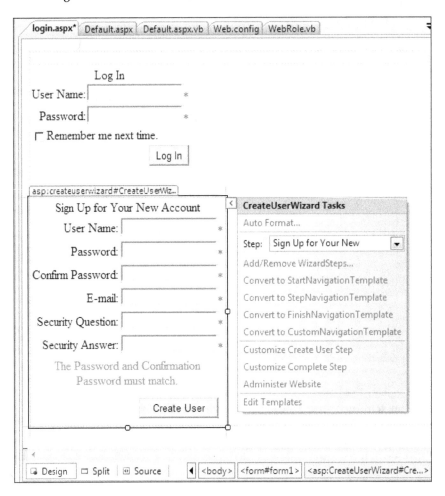

With this a new user can sign up and the next time the user logs in, he/she gets admitted to the website. The various items on this page such as **E-mail**, **Security Question**, and so on will all get into the database when the user clicks the **Create User** button at runtime. There is also coded validation for password checking (in red) in this control.

So far, only two login-related controls were added.

Configure authentication mode

The authentication is configured in the web.config file. Presently, the part of the web.config file related to authentication is shown here:

```
<authentication mode="Windows" />
```

This needs to be changed. The authentication mode has to be set to Forms. The configuration should explicitly deny users who are unauthenticated (denoted by a **?**) and allow all others (denoted by a *****) who are authenticated. Furthermore, unauthenticated users are directed to the login.aspx page and those who pass authentication are directed to the page they wish to go to. The loginURL attribute of the <forms> tag directs unauthenticated users to the login.aspx page. The default setting of loginURL is login.aspx.

The changes to the web.config page are as shown here:

```
<authentication mode="Forms">
  <forms loginUrl="login.aspx">
  </forms>
</authentication>
<authorization>
  <allow users="*"/>
  <deny users="?"/>
</authorization>
```

Create Membership database in SQL Azure

As the hosted application will be looking up membership information in the SQL Server database (since we choose to do so), the `Membership` database needs to be created in SQL Azure. In the case of a membership database for on-site usage, the membership information is stored in the SQL Express database `aspnetdb`. This database is created running the following executable code from the command line: `aspnet_regsql.exe`. The details of this utility can be reviewed by accessing help from the command line as shown here:

`C:\Windows\Microsoft.NET\Framework\v2.0.50727>aspnet_regsql /?`

You will find the details of this help file here: `http://hodentekhelp.blogspot.com/2010/06/what-does-utility-aspnetregsqlexe-do.html`.

However, due to the differences between SQL Azure and SQL Express, `aspnet_regsql.exe` would result in an error. Moreover, another downside of using SQL Azure database is that the user's session will not expire as *SQL Server Agent* is not supported in SQL Azure. This agent runs the stored procedures for session state management. Session state management is outside the scope of this section, sufficient to say that there are third party programs addressing this issue with some restrictions. These issues and workarounds are described in this article here: `http://code.msdn.microsoft.com/KB2006191`, where you can also download modified scripts to create the `aspnetdb` database on SQL Azure.

[This `aspnetdb` may also be created in SQL Azure by migrating the tables from an on-site SQL Server (SQL Server Express) to SQL Azure.]

We will use the `aspnet_regsqlzure.exe` from the KB article download to create the required tables in SQL Azure by running the command in the console as follows:

1. Execute `aspnet_regsqlazure.exe` with the options as shown:

   `C:\Users\jay\Desktop\ASPNET_Membership>aspnet_regsqlazure`

   `-S <Servername>.database.windows.net -U <loginname> -P <your password> -A mp`

   If the command runs without errors, you will have created the database with the required tables and your display after running the command is as shown in the following screenshot:

```
----------------------------------------
Starting execution of InstallCommon.SQL
----------------------------------------
Creating the aspnet_Applications table...
Creating the aspnet_Users table...
Creating the aspnet_SchemaVersions table...
Cannot grant, deny, or revoke permissions to sa, dbo, entity owner, information_
schema, sys, or yourself.
Cannot grant, deny, or revoke permissions to sa, dbo, entity owner, information_
schema, sys, or yourself.
Creating the vw_aspnet_Applications view...
Creating the vw_aspnet_Users view...
Cannot grant, deny, or revoke permissions to sa, dbo, entity owner, information_
schema, sys, or yourself.
----------------------------------------
Completed execution of InstallCommon.SQL
----------------------------------------

----------------------------------------
Starting execution of InstallMembership.SQL
----------------------------------------
Creating the aspnet_Membership table...
Creating the vw_aspnet_MembershipUsers view...
Cannot grant, deny, or revoke permissions to sa, dbo, entity owner, information_
schema, sys, or yourself.
Cannot grant, deny, or revoke permissions to sa, dbo, entity owner, information_
schema, sys, or yourself.
----------------------------------------
Completed execution of InstallMembership.SQL
----------------------------------------

----------------------------------------
Starting execution of InstallProfile.SQL
----------------------------------------
Creating the aspnet_Profile table...
Creating the vw_aspnet_Profiles view...
Cannot grant, deny, or revoke permissions to sa, dbo, entity owner, information_
schema, sys, or yourself.
Cannot grant, deny, or revoke permissions to sa, dbo, entity owner, information_
schema, sys, or yourself.
----------------------------------------
Completed execution of InstallProfile.SQL
----------------------------------------
```

2. Login to SQL Azure in SSMS. **Refresh** the **Databases** node.

   You should be able to see the **aspnetdb** database created with a number of tables, as shown in the following screenshot:

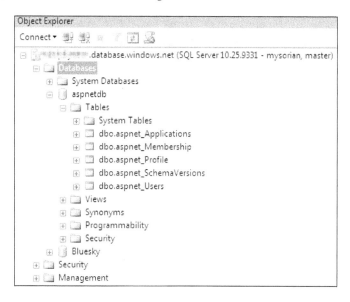

All tables will be empty except the **aspnet_SchemaVersions** table. As members register the other tables would be populated.

Configure the connection string

Now that the **aspnetdb** is created in SQL Azure, the **PlainsboroClub** application should have the appropriate connection string information in its `web.config` file.

Make changes to the `web.config`, which is presently empty, as shown. In the locations between '<>' shown in italics insert items appropriate to your SQL Azure installation.

1. Open the `web.config` file and modify `<connectionStrings>` tag as shown here:

```
<connectionStrings>
    <add name="some_name" connectionString="Data Source=<server_
name>.database.windows.net;Initial Catalog=aspnetdb;User ID=<your
user ID>;Password=<your password>"
        providerName="System.Data.SqlClient" />
</connectionStrings>
```

Modify system.web to access the Membership Provider

With the `aspnetdb` in SQL Azure and the connection string modified as described previously, the web application has to be modified so that it can access the `Membership Provider` database.

Now modify this section of `web.config` as follows:

1. Add the following XML inside the `<system.web/>` tag:

```
<membership defaultProvider="SqlAzureMembershipProvider">
    <providers>
      <clear/>
      <add name="SqlAzureMembershipProvider"
          connectionStringName="some_name"
          applicationName="demRole"
          type="System.Web.Security.SqlMembershipProvider,
System.Web, Version=2.0.0.0, Culture=neutral, PublicKeyToken=b03f5
f7f11d50a3a"/>
    </providers>
</membership>
```

Modify the Default.aspx page

We are almost finished except for some changes to the **Default.aspx** page, which is displayed first when the website is accessed. The page will display *Hi, User* if the name is not empty (if he/she is already registered) otherwise it sends the user over to the login page where he/she can register.

We will insert the snippet shown in `Default.aspx.vb` page as detailed here:

1. Open the `Default.aspx.vb` page and insert the following code in the page's load event:

```
Protected Sub Page_Load(ByVal sender As Object, _
              ByVal e As System.EventArgs) Handles Me.Load
       If Not User.Identity.Name = "" Then
           Response.Write("Hi, " + Server.HtmlEncode(User.
Identity.Name) + "<br />")
       Else
           Server.Transfer("login.aspx")
       End If
End Sub
```

Test and verify application authentication

Once the previous step is completed, build the project and verify that it allows the users who are already registered, to log in. It is also important to verify that SQL Azure is correctly registering the users. To start with, there are no users as yet.

Register users

The `aspnetdb` is all empty as no users are present initially. As users try to access the site they will register. In general, users will access the *Production* site in Windows Azure and they will be registering there.

In the following section, we shall create users and verify that their information gets entered in the `aspnetdb` database. Since we are testing the program we will register new users at several stages of the development.

1. Browse the **Default.aspx** page in the **PlainsboroClub** project in Visual Studio IDE. The login page is displayed, as shown in the following screenshot:

2. Enter the details for the new account and click on **Create User**.

   You should get a reply as shown in the following screenshot. Note that the **Continue** button is created by the program for which we will not be writing any code. Ignore this button.

3. Repeat the same in the development fabric as described earlier.

   You will again get a message like the previous one, but the URL will be that of the development fabric.

4. Publish the project to the cloud's Staging slot as described earlier and create a new user from there.

   You will again get a message similar to the previous one, but the URL will be that of the Staging site.

5. Promote from Staging to Production and create yet another user.

   You will again get a similar message but the URL will be that of the Production site.

   Now that a number of users have been created, let us take a look at the `aspnetdb` in SSMS as shown here:

6. Open SSMS. Log on to SQL Azure's `aspnetdb` in the **Connect to Server** dialog.

7. Run the following query in `aspnetdb` and review the returned rows.

   The query and results are as shown in the following screenshot:

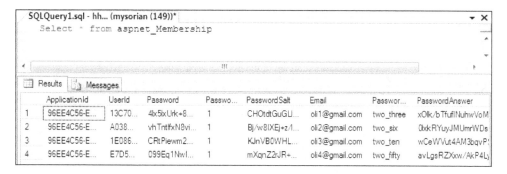

   The four users created are all present in the `aspnetdb` database against which the users will be authenticated.

8. Verify the users using the following query and review the results:

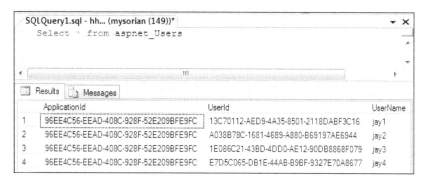

   These are the same users as in the **aspnet_Membership** table.

Test authentication of registered users

Typically, a user would be accessing the website (web application) in the cloud by way of its URL. In the present case however, we will test at each stage of the development and make sure authentication works. The next four screenshots in the table are the response to one of the logins from the previous screenshot to the site in the development server, the development fabric, the staging site, and the production site, respectively.

URL	Displayed page

Development Server
 	
`http://`
`localhost:53269/`
`default.aspx`
	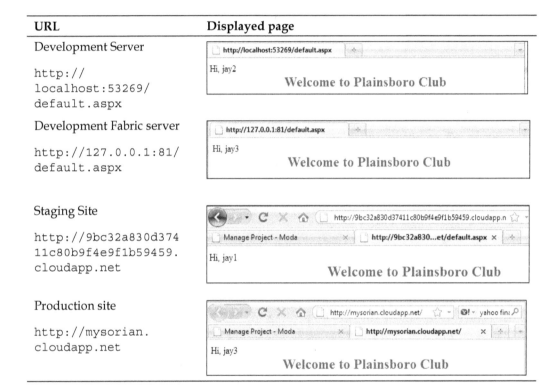

Development Fabric server
 	
`http://127.0.0.1:81/`
`default.aspx`	

Staging Site
 	
`http://9bc32a830d374`
`11c80b9f4e9f1b59459.`
`cloudapp.net`	

Production site
 	
`http://mysorian.`
`cloudapp.net`	

Summary

In this chapter, the process of creating a cloud service application in Visual Studio 2008 SP1 was described with details about the development fabric, the simulated Windows Azure hosting service. Details of deploying the application to the cloud were also described. Web applications deployed to the cloud or otherwise often require some form of authentication and one widely used method of authenticating users is the forms authentication. In forms authentication, user information can be stored in an SQL Server database. For authenticating an ASP.NET application hosted on the cloud platform this information can be stored in SQL Azure. This chapter described the details of authenticating ASP.NET web applications using the `Membership` database in SQL Azure.

In the next chapter, we will be looking at various approaches to interacting with data on SQL Azure using Microsoft web technologies, such as ASP.NET, WCF, and so on.

8
Database Applications on Windows Azure Platform Accessing SQL Server Databases

In this chapter, we look at the different kinds of projects that can be hosted on Windows Azure. Only data-centric applications with their data originating from either local (in-house) or on SQL Azure databases are considered. Working with Windows Azure Storage-related applications is not discussed.

In the case of applications that use relational data store there are a couple of possibilities. Both data and applications can stay either on the cloud or in-house. Businesses may want to store only data or part of their data on the cloud and keep their business applications in-house. On the other hand, they may want to keep both applications and data on the cloud.

In this chapter, we will be specifically looking at three different scenarios as detailed in the following table:

Scenario	Application by location	Database	Database authentication	Notes
Ground-to-Cloud	On-site Application	SQL Azure	SQL Server	Using a LinqDataSource Control
Cloud-to-Cloud	Windows Azure Hosted Application	SQL Azure	SQL Server	Using a GridView Control
Cloud-to-Ground	Windows Azure Hosted Application	On-site SQL Server 2008 R2	Windows Authentication	Using Service Bus, a component of Windows Azure AppFabric

Ground-to-Cloud access

In this case, a client on site will be retrieving data from SQL Azure. The application for this scenario will be using Visual Studio 2008 SP1. However, Visual Studio 2008 does not allow creating a connection to SQL Azure in its IDE. What is described here is a workaround, which is not necessary if you are using Visual Studio 2010 Express. The workaround consists of creating an ASP.NET web application, which retrieves data (or manipulates data) from an on-site SQL Server 2008 R2 and after making sure it works, the connection string is now set to point to the SQL Azure. It is necessary to have the table schema on SQL Azure the same as that of the table in the on-site server.

Using Linq to retrieve data from SQL Azure

Linq to SQL, a component of Visual Studio was designed to provide a run-time infrastructure for managing relational data as objects without losing the ability to query efficiently. Linq to SQL is an object-relational model that you can leverage in Visual Studio 2008. Your connection to SQL Server 2008 database is through a new control in Visual Studio 2008, the `LinqDataSource` control. This control needs a data context. The data context is provided by the Linq to SQL classes, a class generator that maps SQL server objects to the model. The class files generated support Create, Read, Update, and Delete (CRUD) operations.

The easiest way to understand retrieving data from SQL Azure using LINQ is to use the Linq Data Control that is available in Visual Studio 2008 SP1's Toolbox. In the following, a Linq Data Control will be used as described.

Create an ASP.NET web application project

You will create an ASP.NET web application project and add a `LinqDataSource` control.

1. Open Visual Studio 2008 SP1 as an administrator and create an ASP.NET web application (.NET Framework 3.5) after providing a name for the application. Herein it is named `LinkAzure`.

In order to use this control to retrieve data from the SQL Server Database, we should establish a data context. In the following, we will create a data context.

Creating a data context

A data context is very similar to a connection in ADO.NET. In fact, to establish a data context you need to create a data connection. You can easily set up a data context using `LinqDataSource` control as described here.

1. Right-click the project and choose to add a new item.

   The **Add New Item** window is displayed as shown in the next screenshot.

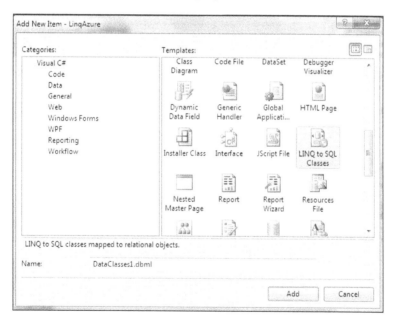

   In this window, we will choose **LINQ to SQL Classes** template and change the default name. This allows us to do the required mapping between SQL and LINQ.

2. Choose **LINQ to SQL Classes**; change the default name (herein `Azure.dbml`). Click **Add**.

   Azure.dbml is added to the project as shown in the **Solution Explorer**.

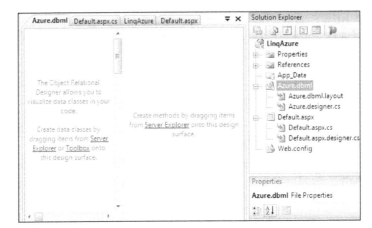

The **Object Relational Designer** (ORD) permits two kinds of procedures; you can create data classes by dragging and dropping objects from Server Explorer (or Toolbox) or, create methods by dragging-and-dropping items (typically stored procedures) from the Server Explorer.

In the following subsection, we establish a data connection to the SQL Server 2008 R2 in the Server Explorer of Visual Studio 2008 SP1.

Create a new data connection

1. Click the icon for Data Connections to connect to a database shown in the following screenshot:

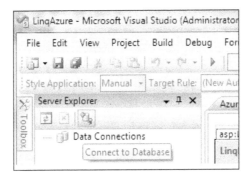

2. This brings up the **Add Connection** window as shown in the following screenshot (initially most fields are empty).

3. Connect to a SQL Server 2008 R2 (or SQL Express), which has a Northwind database.

In the previous screenshot, the Northwind database is in a SQL Server 2008 R2, which has been configured for Windows Authentication. Your choices will depend on your server and its configuration. If the SQL Server name is correct and the authentication is valid, you should be able to see the databases as shown in the next screenshot.

4. Choose **Northwind** and test the connection clicking the **Test Connection** button. After verifying that the connection is good, click **OK**.

The connection now appears in **Server Explorer** as shown in the next screenshot. The name of the computer is **hodentek3** and the server name is **kumo**. You can also review the connection string (it is also stored in the web. config file) by looking at the properties of this connection.

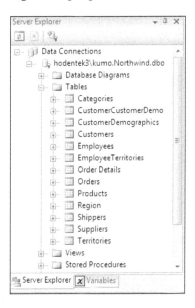

 Note that this procedure of establishing a connection is not supported while connecting to SQL Azure—one of the present limitations of Visual Studio 2008 SP1. However, this is now possible in Visual Studio 2010 Express.

Linq to SQL mapping

We will map the Employees table to the classes using the OR designer we saw earlier.

1. Drag-and-drop the **Employees** table from the connection in the **Server Explorer** and drop it into the left-hand side of the OR Designer as shown in the following screenshot.

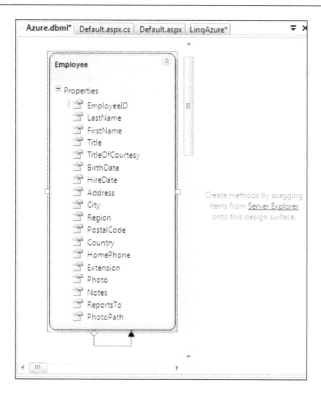

With this accomplished you have created a data context and created the **Employee Data Class** for Linq as shown in the following screenshot, looking at the properties of **Employee** in the OR Designer.

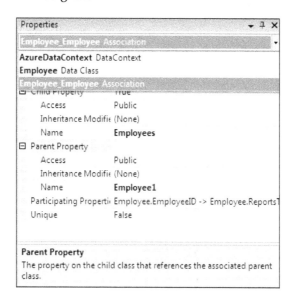

Please review the file, `Azure.Designer.cs` as it clearly describes the data context.

Add a LinqDataSource control

To display the data we will use a `LinqDataSource` control. This is available in Visual Studio's Toolbox.

1. Drag-and-drop a **LinqDataSource** control from **Toolbox | Data** onto the design pane of **Default.aspx** as shown in the following screenshot:

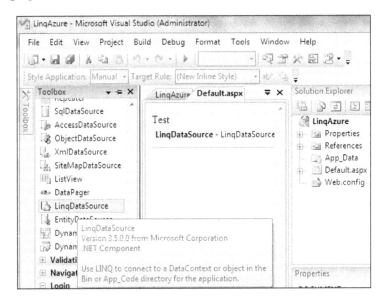

2. Click the smart tasks handle to bring up the task list as shown in the following screenshot:

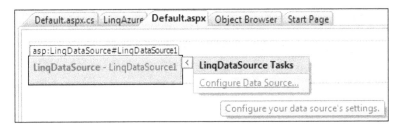

3. Build the project. Click **Configure Data Source....**

    The **Configure Data Source –LinqDataSource1** window is displayed as shown in the following screenshot.

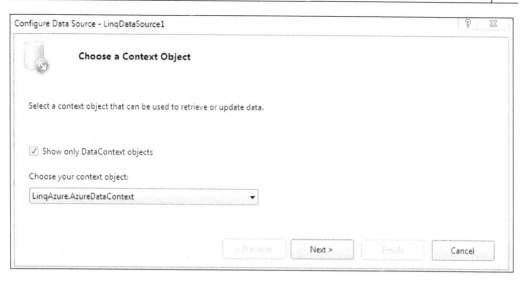

The `AzureDataContext` configured earlier comes up correctly as shown in the previous screenshot.

1. Click **Next >**.

    The **Configure Data Selection** page of the wizard is displayed as shown in the following screenshot:

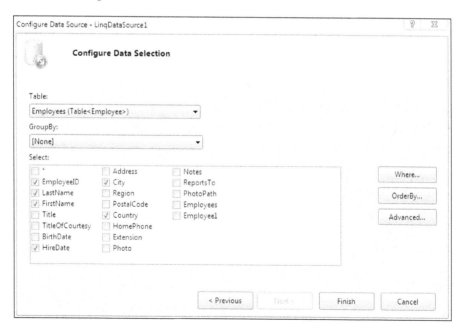

Here you can make a selection of the columns; filter; sort and order them. Using the **Advanced...** option you can carry out DML operations as shown in the next screenshot. Herein, only a few columns are chosen to keep it simple.

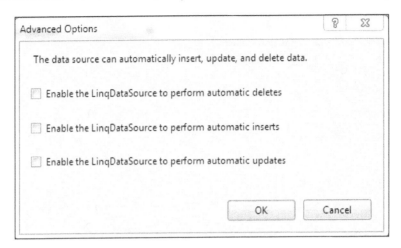

2. Click **Finish** on the **Configure Data Selection** page.

   The **LinqDataSource1** control you added will now have the source, as shown in the next listing.

```
<asp:LinqDataSource ID="LinqDataSource1" runat="server"
  ContextTypeName="LinqAzure.AzureDataContext"
  Select="new (EmployeeID, FirstName, City, Country, HireDate,
    LastName)"
    TableName="Employees">
```

Display data with a GridView control

Now that the data source is ready, all that we need is to have a control (or code) to display the selected columns.

1. Drag-and-drop a **GridView** control from the **Toolbox** below the **LinqDataSource** control.

2. From the drop-down of the **GridView Tasks** choose the **LinqDataSource1** as shown in the next screenshot.

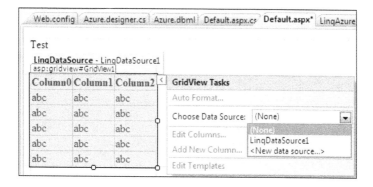

The `GridView` changes to the image shown in the following screenshot:

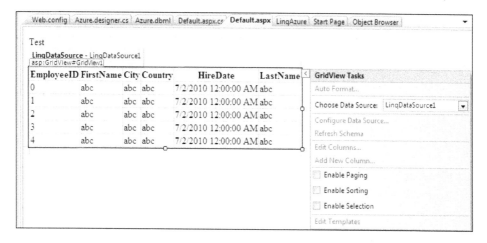

3. Build the project and bring up the `Default.aspx` page in the browser. The selected data is displayed as shown in the following screenshot:

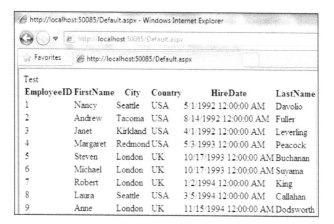

Swap connection to SQL Azure

This workaround is only necessary if you are using Visual Studio 2008. This will not be necessary if you use Visual Studio 2010 Express as it supports browsing the databases on your SQL Azure.

1. Swap the following connection string shown in `web.config`.

   ```
   connectionString="Data Source=HODENTEK3\KUMO;Initial
   Catalog=Northwind;Integrated Security=True"
   ```

   with the following:

   ```
   connectionString="Data Source=<your server name>.windows.
   net;Initial Catalog=Bluesky;User ID=<your user id>;Password=<your
   password> "
   ```

 The 'Bluesky' database on SQLAzure has an Employees table. This table was actually migrated to 'Bluesky' from SQL Server 2008 R2's Northwind database. However, the `FirstName` and `LastName` columns were altered to have different values.

The first connection string refers to the on-site SQL Server 2008 R2 and the second is that of the SQL Azure.

2. Build the project and browse the `Default.aspx` page.

   You will see the following displayed:

Cloud-to-Cloud access

In this scenario, we consider the simplest case of an ASP.NET application hosted in the Cloud retrieving data from SQL Azure. This scenario is likely in cases where the Internet client may want to access the SQL Azure database through a hosted application on Windows Azure.

We saw in the previous case that using Visual Studio 2008 SP1 we need to swap the connection string to connect to SQL Azure, as the platform does not allow direct connection to SQL Azure. However, if we use Visual Studio 2010 Express (which is a free version) we avoid this workaround of swapping the connection string. In working through this scenario, we will use Visual Web Developer Express 2010. You may download a copy of this from the following URL: `http://www.microsoft.com/express/Downloads/#2010-Visual-Web-Developer`.

Using the Microsoft Web Platform Installer available from the same link, it is very easy to install other related programs as well.

In order to create a Cloud Service we also need to install the Windows Azure Tools for 2010 1.2, which (`VSCloudService.exe 1.2.30517.1601`) can be downloaded from this site: `http://www.microsoft.com/downloads/details.aspx?FamilyID=2274a0a8-5d37-4eac-b50a-e197dc340f6f&displaylang=en`. After installing the software, we will be running Visual Studio as the administrator. Well, if you don't see a Cloud Service project template in Visual Studio, it means you have not installed the tools.

Default template Cloud Service Project

In the following procedure we will be creating a `Cloud Service` project in Visual Studio 2010 Express from its `File` menu item by choosing to create a **New Project** as shown in the following screenshot:

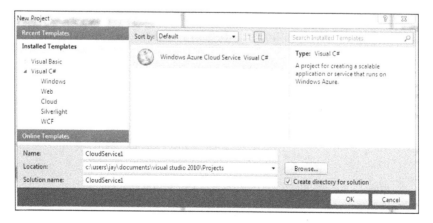

In the following screenshot it can be seen that the `CloudService1` project name has been changed to `CloudToCloud`. The default name of the ASP.NET Web Role has been renamed to `CloudWebRole`. The project is ready to go with a *Site Master* already designed as shown in the next screenshot. Also the `CloudWebRole` project is complete with the service configuration and service definition files, the same files needed for hosting the web application on Windows Azure Hosting sites.

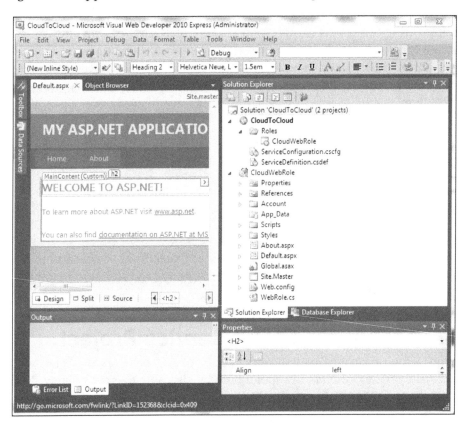

We can build the solution (right-click **Solution Explorer** and choose **Build Solution**), which builds both the projects. This is a cloud-ready project. You can see the **Development Fabric** console being displayed after pressing *F5* as shown in the following screenshot:

Simultaneously, the Default.aspx page would pop up in the browser as shown in the following screenshot:

As this is cloud-ready, it can be hosted on the *Staging* and *Production* slots on Windows Hosting Services.

Displaying data from SQL Azure

We will use an ASP.NET `GridView` control to display the data from a provisioned SQL Azure Database. In particular, we will display a couple of columns from the `Employees` table in the `Northwind` database on the provisioned SQL Azure, shown in the following screenshot:

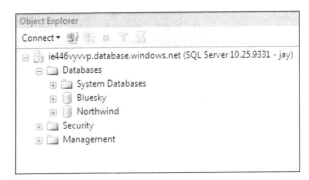

Data from SQL Azure can be easily displayed by dragging-and-dropping a **GridView** from the **Toolbox** on to the `Default.aspx` page as shown. The **GridView** can be easily designed using the **Grid View Tasks** handle, shown in the following screenshot:

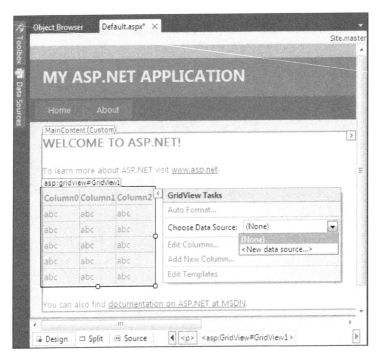

The very first thing to take care of is to connect to SQL Azure. Clicking on the **<New data source...>** item, as shown in the previous screenshot, wakes up the Data Source Configuration wizard's **Choose a Data Source Type** page as shown in the following screenshot. The ID of the SQL Database has been renamed as `SqlAz`.

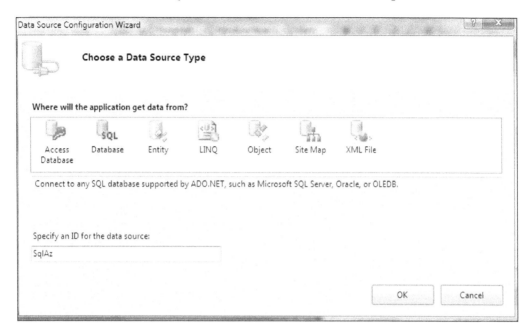

Clicking the **OK** button brings up the **Choose Your Data Connection** page of the wizard as shown in the following screenshot:

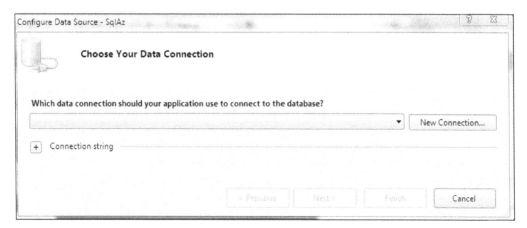

You establish a connection to the SQL Azure database by clicking the **New Connection...**button, which brings up the window where you can insert the SQL Azure database-specific information as shown in the next screenshot. The provisioned server is a temporary server and as such the full connection is shown for clarity. Once the correct authentication information is entered into this window, the databases show up promptly. Of course the connection can be tested as well with the **Test Connection** button.

Clicking **OK** after choosing **Northwind** will register the connection string (Data Source=ie446vyvvp.database.windows.net; Initial Catalog=Northwind;User ID=jay; Password=XXXXXXXX) in the previous screen. Clicking the **Next >** button takes you to **Save the Connection String to Application Configuration File** page of the wizard. It is a recommended practice to save the Connection string to the application configuration.

Clicking **Next >** on the page takes you to the **Configure the Select Statement** page of the wizard as shown in the next screenshot. We will be using a custom SQL Statement.

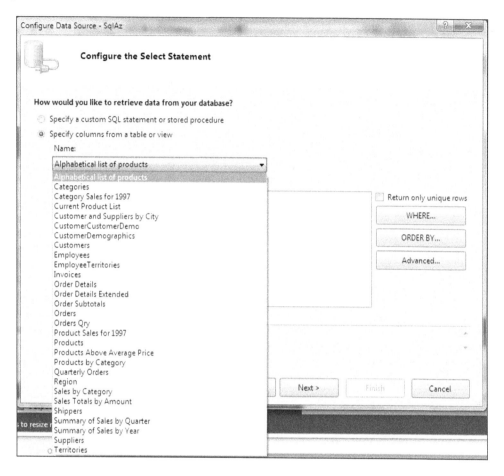

Clicking **Next >** on the previous page after making the selection takes you to the **Define Custom statements or Stored Procedures** page as shown in the following screenshot. Here, there are two options. You could type in a **Custom Statement** or evoke the **Query Builder** by hitting the button at the bottom of this page. To keep it simple, a custom SQL statement will be used here as shown. It should be remembered that you can carry out insert, update, or delete operations as well.

Clicking **Next >** takes you to the **Test Query** page where hitting the **Test Query** button would display the selected data from the query. Clicking the **Finish** button on the **Test Query** page brings in all the selected columns into the **GridView,** as shown in the next screenshot:

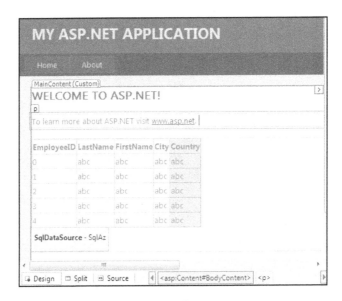

After building the application, this would display the `Default.aspx` page as shown in the developmental server.

Choosing **CloudToCloud** as the startup project (right-click **CloudToCloud** and choose from the menu) and start debugging (or hitting the *F5* button) will host the application in the `Development Fabric`, as was previously shown. The **CloudToCloud** project's **Default.aspx** page then gets displayed, as shown in the browser after the role has started.

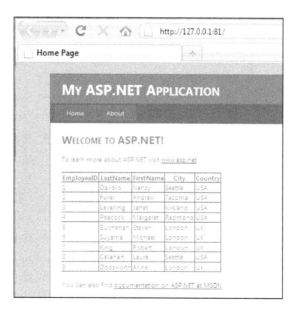

Deploying the application to the hosting site

In *Chapter 7, Working with Windows Azure Hosting,* deploying a web application to Windows Azure hosting site was described in detail. Here, a brief summary of deployment is described. Before deploying the project, comment out (use <!-- -->) the default connection string of the template related to SQL Server Express shown, as this is not required here. If your IDE does not show this, you may skip this task.

```
<add name="ApplicationServices" connectionString="data
  source=.\SQLEXPRESS;Integrated
  Security=SSPI;AttachDBFilename=|DataDirectory|\aspnetdb.mdf;User
  Instance=true"
  providerName="System.Data.SqlClient" />
```

Right-clicking the **CloudToCloud** project and choosing **Publish** will begin the publishing process by displaying the **Publish Cloud Service** window, shown in the following screenshot. Choose the **Create Service Package Only** option.

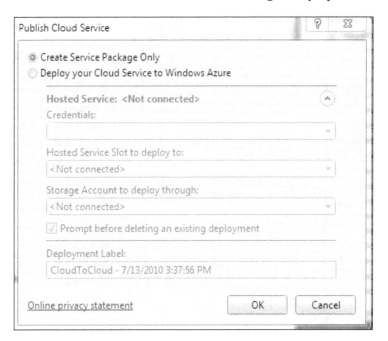

Clicking the **OK** button starts the process. Publishing starts, as described in detail in *Chapter 7, Working with Windows Azure Hosting* and the `Service Package` file and the `Cloud Service Configuration` files get created in the default directory of the project (`C:\Users\jay\Documents\visual studio 2010\Projects\CloudToCloud\CloudToCloud\bin\Debug\Publish`).

Now, bring up your Windows Azure hosted site (`http://windows.azure.com`) after logging into your windows Live ID site as described in *Chapter 7, Working with Windows Azure Hosting*. Follow this up by getting to the hosted service as shown in the following screenshot:

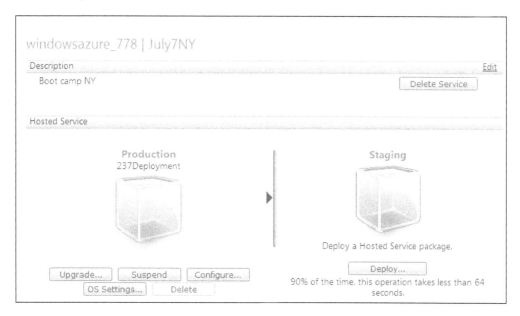

Click the **Deploy...** button in the **Staging** slot and deploy the **CloudToCloud** service as described in *Chapter 7, Working with Windows Azure Hosting*.

After some cycles of *Initializing, Busy,* and so on, the status turns to ready. At this point, the application can be accessed by the staging URL, which for the present deployment was as shown in the following screenshot:

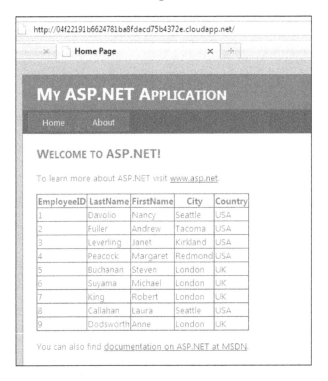

This can be promoted to the **Production** site by clicking the switch between Production and Staging slots.

Cloud-to-Ground access

 This section requires knowing the following concepts and it is recommended that the readers review the following related information.

WCF Data Services

Service Bus

In this case, an ASP.NET application hosted on the Windows Azure site would provide access to data on an on-site SQL Server database. It is further assumed that the database is set for Windows authentication. As there are firewalls protecting Windows Azure as well as the computer accessing the ASP.NET hosted site, there are natural impediments to data communication. This is overcome by using a relay service provided by the Windows Azure AppFabric component, the Service Bus. We are not using the other component of AppFabric, namely the Access Control Service. Also, in this section we will only expose local SQL Server Data to the intranet as a WCF Data Service that is Internet accessible. The client part of the data access is not described here, but the user can find a client project to access this service in the code bundle.

In this following schematic scenario, we consider the simplest case of an ASP.NET application hosted in the cloud, retrieving data from a database in the on-site SQL Server 2008 R2. This scenario is likely in cases where the internet client may feel comfortable in keeping his/her data on the on-site server. Firewalls prevent data access as indicated in the following figure:

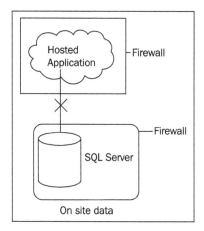

In order to expose local, on-site data, we will build a WCF Data Service. If you are new to this subject you may want to review my previous article, that had an earlier data access technology similar to the present one at the following URL: http://www. packtpub.com/article/data-access-with-ado-dot-net-data-services.

WCF Data Services serves up data as a web service over HTTP using the objects in the Entity Model of the data and conforms to the principles of REST (Representational State Transfer). In it, everything is a kind of resource with a name, and they can be manipulated using the well-known HTTP Verbs; Get, Put, Post, and Delete. The data can be returned in a number of formats including RSS and ATOM. An architectural schematic of a WCF service accessing data from an SQL Server is shown in the following figure. The client can URL-access this service from the Internet or from another hosted application.

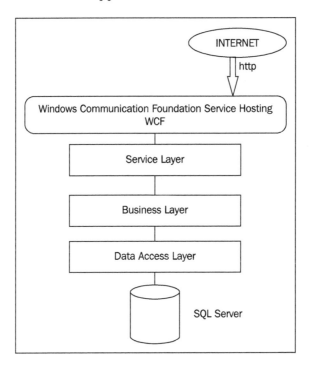

For services built using WCF technology the Service Bus can be used as shown in this section. However, if the service is built with a different technology, then using Service Bus is not easy. For such cases, one may use the idea of a Port Bridge, which you may review at this URL: http://blogs.msdn.com/b/clemensv/archive/2009/11/18/port-bridge.aspx.

In order to use the Windows Azure AppFabric, you need to download and install the Windows Azure AppFabric SDK V1.0 - July Update from the following link (download all of them as they include the SDK, documentation, and samples in C# and VB):

http://www.microsoft.com/downloads/details.aspx?FamilyID=39856a03-1490-4283-908f-c8bf0bfad8a5&displaylang=en.

Create a console project in Visual Studio

As we will be targeting .NET Framework 3.5, make sure you install ADO.NET Data Services Update for .NET Framework 3.5 SP1 in Windows 7 and Windows Server 2008 R2 at the following URL: `http://www.microsoft.com/downloads/details.aspx?familyid=79d7f6f8-d6e9-4b8c-8640-17f89452148e&displaylang=en`.

Create a Visual C# Console application using Visual Studio 2008. Herein, the application was called **OnSiteData,** as shown in the following screenshot. By default this application will target .NET Framework 3.5, as you may verify by looking at the properties of the application.

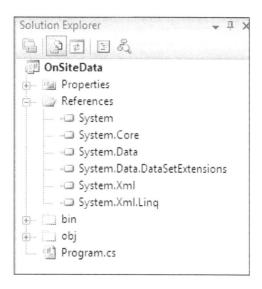

As we will be using the Entity Model and WCF, you may want to know how these and Data Access are connected. It will be helpful to review the following link to get the architectural background for what we will be doing in this section here: `http://msdn.microsoft.com/en-us/magazine/cc700340.aspx`.

In simple words, WCF will expose SQL Server data to the application via a certain model. For this purpose, we need to add a template of the Entity Model to the application and configure it to support our SQL Server's data access.

Add an Entity Model Template and bind it to the database

Right-clicking the project and choosing **Add | New Item...** opens the window as shown in the following screenshot:

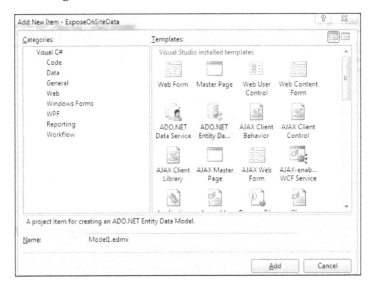

Highlighting the **ADO.NET Entity Data Model** under **Templates** and clicking **Add** adds the **Model1.edmx** file to the project. It is a good practice to change the name before adding the file (but here the default is accepted).

Adding this file wakes up the **Entity Data Model Wizard**, as shown in the next screenshot, where a choice will be made to generate the model from the database.

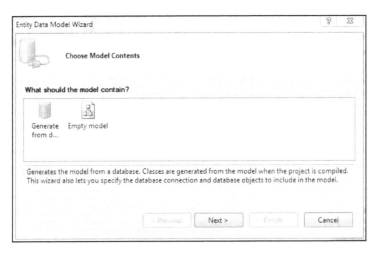

Clicking **Next >** after accepting the choice brings up the **Choose Your Data Connection** page of the wizard as shown in the following screenshot:

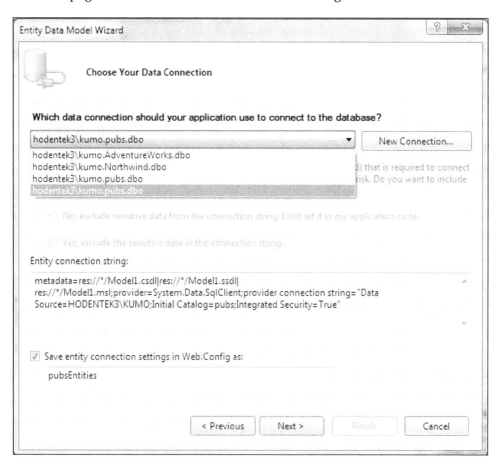

Here, you can choose an existing connection or create a new connection. As we have seen several times how this connection is made through the GUI interface, details are skipped here. We choose an existing connection, which is in this case that of the local SQL Server 2008 R2 with the **hodentek3/kumo.pubs.dbo** connection, shown in the next screenshot. The Entity connection string generated is shown and the default name for the entities, **pubsEntities**, is accepted. Adhering to the suggested best practices, the connection will be saved to the configuration, which adds the connection string to the **App.config** file.

Clicking **Next >** brings up the next page of the wizard, **Choose Your Database Objects**. After expanding the nodes, the displayed page appears as shown in the following screenshot:

To keep the discussion simple, only the `authors` table is chosen here. Clicking the **Finish** button adds the **pubModel** to the project, as shown in the next image, bringing with it the needed assemblies as shown in the **References** node. The **EntityType** is also shown in the same image as **pubsModel.authors**.

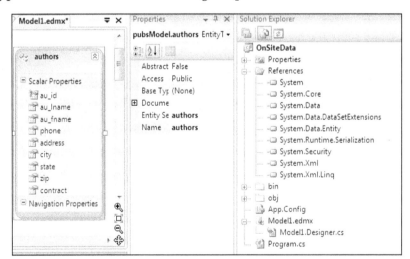

Configure the WCF Data Service

We follow along the suggested Microsoft sample (`http://cid-2fa13ebc6cc8e80f.`
`skydrive.live.com/browse.aspx/Public`) to create a WCF Data Service. To this
end, add a C# class file, called **PubService** (by right-clicking the project and choosing
New Item... followed by choosing the C# Class file). Since we are creating a service,
we need to add a reference to the project.

Right-click the project's **References** node and from the drop-down choose **Add
Reference....** This opens the **Add Reference** window where you scroll down and
add `System.Data.Services`.

Modify the default code as follows:

```
using System;
using System.Collections.Generic;
using System.Linq;
using System.Text;
using System.Data.Services;

namespace OnSiteData
{
  public class PubService: DataService<OnSiteData.pubsEntities>
  {
    //OnSiteData.pubsEntities is the data service we are creating
    //This method needs to be called only once to initialize
      service-wide policies.
    public static void InitializeService(IDataServiceConfiguration
      config)
      {
      // TODO: set rules to indicate which entity sets and service
        operations are visible, updatable, etc.
      // Examples:
        config.UseVerboseErrors = true;
        config.SetEntitySetAccessRule("*", EntitySetRights.All);
      // config.SetServiceOperationAccessRule("MyServiceOperation",
        ServiceOperationRights.All);
      }
  }
}
```

The policy, as implemented in the code, is very wide and should be used
with caution.

WCF Data Service to use Windows Azure AppFabric

As explained in *Chapter 1, Cloud Computing and Microsoft Azure Services Platform*, AppFabric is one of the components of the Windows Azure Platform that supports creating 'hybrid' applications that can access Windows Azure as well as on-site data. The readers should review the following link to understand how the present section works: http://msdn.microsoft.com/en-us/library/ee706713.aspx.

After having created the WCF Data Service, to create a REST-style data service that can be URL-accessed, we need to configure the service for hosting. While there are a number of hosting options for the service to be discoverable by a client, for using the relaying services of the Service Bus, the service endpoint needs to be hosted on the Windows Azure Service Bus. By doing so, the authentication is now on the Service Bus rather than at the origin of the data. The client accesses the service using the Service Bus as an intermediary.

Windows Azure AppFabric

Since we are using the Windows Azure AppFabric, we should have an account on Windows Azure, and the AppFabric can be accessed from the Windows Azure portal like the other services. The following screenshot shows the AppFabric project information (for a given account, which will expire by the time this book is published) in the portal. After creating the project, you can create **Service Namespace** using the **Add Service Namespace** button in the portal. For example, by clicking this button three different Service Namespaces have been added (You really need one for the demo, three were added just to show how easy it is to create a Service Namespace in the portal. Add only what you need as you will be paying for the services). You need to create a Service Namespace in order to access the service.

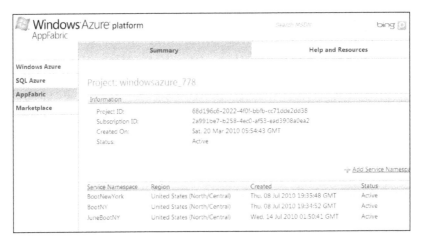

Clicking on **BootNY Service Namespace** in the previous screenshot, shows further details of this namespace, as shown in the next screenshot. There are two components of AppFabric, the **Service Bus** and the **Access Control Service**. The rest of the items shown are related to the number of connections and the pricing information for use of this service.

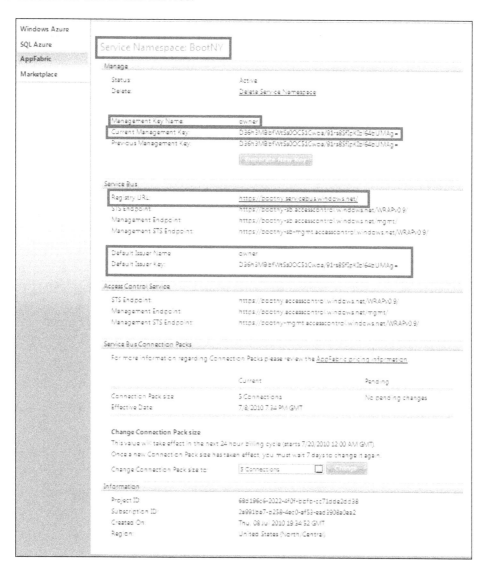

We will be using the Service Bus and the information that we need from the portal is as follows: **Service Namespace**, **RegistryURL**, **DefaultIssuerName**, and the **DefaultIssuerKey** (known as Shared Secret in the program code). These are the items that both the client and service share and these are on the portal of the authenticated user. These are the items we use in setting up code to host the WCF Data Service with a Service Bus endpoint.

Before we can host the service, we need to add the required references to use the WCF Services and the Service Bus libraries. These are the following:

- `System.ServiceModel` (see, `http://msdn.microsoft.com/en-us/library/system.servicemodel.aspx`)

- `System.ServiceModel.web` (see, `http://msdn.microsoft.com/en-us/library/system.servicemodel.web.aspx`)

- `Microsoft.ServiceBus` (see, `http://msdn.microsoft.com/en-us/library/microsoft.servicebus.aspx`)

The Service Bus assembly is not accessible in the **Add Reference** window and we need to browse the computer to find `Microsoft.ServiceBus` (this is in the case of Windows 7; the assemblies did not register correctly when installed). In the present installation, it was found in `C:\Windows\Assemblies`.

The following code is an adopted version of Microsoft sample, which hosts a Northwind database object on Windows Azure AppFabric Service Bus (`http://cid-2fa13ebc6cc8e80f.office.live.com/self.aspx/Public/ServiceBus%5EM DataService%5EMLocalSQLServer.zip`). The implemented changes are reflected to use the following:

Local database on the current computer and the current user's AppFabric service details, described in the previous section.

Replace the code in `Program.cs` with the following after adding the previous references from the **Add Reference** window.

```
using System;
using System.Collections.Generic;
using System.Linq;
using System.Text;

namespace OnSiteData
{
  using System;
  using System.Globalization;
  using System.ServiceModel;
  using Microsoft.ServiceBus;
```

```
using System.ServiceModel.Web;
using Microsoft.ServiceBus.Description;
using System.ServiceModel.Dispatcher;
using System.ServiceModel.Description;
using System.ServiceModel.Channels;
using System.IO;
using System.Xml;
using System.Text;

    internal sealed class Program
    {
      private static void Main()
      {
        Console.Write("Your Service Namespace Domain (ex.
          https://<DOMAIN>.servicebus.windows.net/): ");
        string serviceNamespaceDomain = Console.ReadLine();
// By setting EndToEndWebHttpSecurityMode.Transport we use //HTTPS.
// We are using HTTP and therefore  //EndToEndWebHttpSecurityMode.
None.
// We are not using the Access Control Service and therefore //
RelayClientAuthenticationType is set to none.
// WebHttpRelayBinding binding = new //WebHttpRelayBinding(EndTo
EndWebHttpSecurityMode.Transport, //RelayClientAuthenticationType.
RelayAccessToken);
//The A (address), B(Binding) and C (contract) are clearly defined in
//code
            WebHttpRelayBinding binding = new WebHttpRelayBinding
              (EndToEndWebHttpSecurityMode.Transport,
              RelayClientAuthenticationType.None);

        // Initialize ServiceHost using custom binding
        //Uri address = ServiceBusEnvironment.CreateServiceUri
          ("https", serviceNamespaceDomain, "DataService");
        Uri address = ServiceBusEnvironment.CreateServiceUri
          ("https", serviceNamespaceDomain, "PubService");
        WebServiceHost host = new WebServiceHost
          (typeof(PubService), address);
        host.AddServiceEndpoint("
          System.Data.Services.IRequestHandler", binding, address);
        var eb = new TransportClientEndpointBehavior() {
          CredentialType =
          TransportClientCredentialType.SharedSecret };
        eb.Credentials.SharedSecret.IssuerName = "owner";
        eb.Credentials.SharedSecret.IssuerSecret =
          "D36h3MBbfWtSs0OC51Cwoa/91rs8SfIpKIbl64bUMAg=";
        host.Description.Endpoints[0].Behaviors.Add(eb);
```

```csharp
        // The following behavior is used to work around exception
          caused by PUT/POST
        // requests when exposing via Service Bus
            MyBehavior mb = new MyBehavior();
            host.Description.Endpoints[0].Behaviors.Add(mb);

            // Start service
            host.Open();
            Console.WriteLine("Test the following URI in browser: ");
            Console.WriteLine(address + "authors");
            Console.WriteLine("Use the following URI if you want to
              generate client proxy for this service");
            Console.WriteLine(address);
            Console.WriteLine();
            Console.WriteLine("Press [Enter] to exit");
            Console.ReadLine();

            host.Close();
    }

    class MyInspector : IDispatchMessageInspector
    {

      #region IDispatchMessageInspector Members

      public object AfterReceiveRequest(ref
        System.ServiceModel.Channels.Message request,
        IClientChannel channel, InstanceContext instanceContext)
          {
            // Workaround for Service Bus scenario for PUT&POST
            MessageBuffer buffer =
              request.CreateBufferedCopy(int.MaxValue);
            Message copy = buffer.CreateMessage();
            MemoryStream ms = new MemoryStream();
            Encoding encoding = Encoding.UTF8;
            XmlWriterSettings writerSettings = new
              XmlWriterSettings { Encoding = encoding };
            XmlDictionaryWriter writer =
              XmlDictionaryWriter.CreateDictionaryWriter(
              XmlWriter.Create(ms));
            copy.WriteBodyContents(writer);
            writer.Flush();
            string messageBodyString =
              encoding.GetString(ms.ToArray());
            messageBodyString = @"<?xml version=""1.0""
              encoding=""utf-8""?><Binary>" +
            Convert.ToBase64String(Encoding.UTF8.GetBytes
              (messageBodyString)) + "</Binary>";
```

```
    ms = new
      MemoryStream(encoding.GetBytes(messageBodyString));
    XmlReader bodyReader = XmlReader.Create(ms);
    Message originalMessage = request;
    request = Message.CreateMessage(
      originalMessage.Version, null, bodyReader);
    request.Headers.CopyHeadersFrom(originalMessage);

    if
      (!request.Properties.ContainsKey
      (WebBodyFormatMessageProperty.Name))
      {
        request.Properties.Add(
          WebBodyFormatMessageProperty.Name,
          new WebBodyFormatMessageProperty(
          WebContentFormat.Raw));
      }

      return null;
    }

  public void BeforeSendReply(ref
    System.ServiceModel.Channels.Message reply, object
    correlationState)
    {
    }

  #endregion
}
  class MyBehavior : IEndpointBehavior
  {

    #region IEndpointBehavior Members

    public void AddBindingParameters(ServiceEndpoint endpoint,
      System.ServiceModel.Channels.BindingParameterCollection
      bindingParameters)
      {
      }

    public void ApplyClientBehavior(ServiceEndpoint endpoint,
ClientRuntime clientRuntime)
      {
      }

    public void ApplyDispatchBehavior(ServiceEndpoint endpoint,
EndpointDispatcher endpointDispatcher)
      {
      endpointDispatcher.DispatchRuntime.MessageInspectors.Add(
      new MyInspector());
```

```
            }
            public void Validate(ServiceEndpoint endpoint)
            {

            }

            #endregion
        }
    }
}
```

Parts of this code may not be needed for the present section as data updates or deletes are not made.

Build this project and run **Program.cs**. The console application runs and you get the following display as first line.

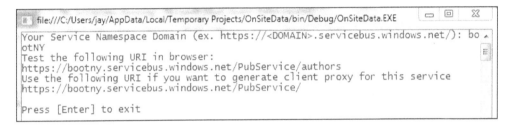

Type in **BootNY** for **Service Namespace Domain** as shown in the previous screenshot and press *Enter*. The rest of the information will be displayed. The authors table from the on-site pubs database can now be accessed at this URL: https://boodNY.servicebus.windows.net/PubService/authors and a proxy can be created using the other URL in the previous screenshot.

When you access the previous service on the Internet, you get the following display (only part of the displayed page is shown). Make sure the service is running (Run CloudToGround and don't close the DOS screen) before you access this page, otherwise, only some viewable information unrelated to the project will be shown. Also to see the display in the format shown in the following screenshot you need to turn off RSS feed in Internet Explorer (see for example, http://hodentekhelp. blogspot.com/2008/12/how-do-i-turn-off-atom-rss-feeds-in-ie.html):

Hosting a ASP.NET application client for the above service

The above service can be consumed by a client using an application that can be hosted on Windows Azure hosting service. The client can be an ASP.NET application; a RIA Silverlight project or some other suitable client application. While the details of the client application are not described here (to keep down the page count), the readers can find the project that consumes this service in the code bundle. As the present Service Bus details will no longer be valid when the book is published, the users should use Service Bus details from their own site.

Here is the display of the hosted client application consuming the above service (from the bundled project `DisplaySB`).

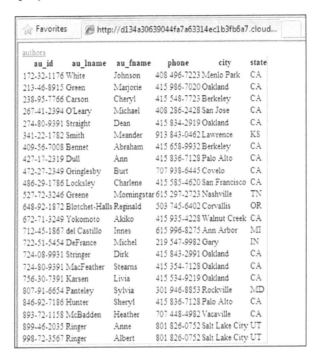

Summary

This chapter described applications that access SQL Server databases in the Cloud (SQL Azure) as well as on-site SQL Server databases. Three different scenarios: Ground-to-Cloud, Cloud-to-Cloud, and Cloud-to-Ground data access through ASP. NET applications were described.

In the next chapter, we consider how data can be synchronized between SQL Azure and SQL Servers using the SQL Azure Data Sync. SQL Data Sync allows easy information sharing with multiple SQL Azure data centers, mobile users, business partners, remote offices, and enterprise data sources.

Synchronizing SQL Azure

9

Synchronization of data between on-site data stores and data stored on data centers in the cloud, spanning geographically separated regions is essential for enterprises to run their applications efficiently. In SU4 (SQL Azure Update 4) the Copy Database feature was added, which addressed the backup support for SQL Azure and complemented the synchronization feature.

In the Microsoft ecosystem, data is stored on enterprise class SQL Servers; SQL Azure servers and SQL Server Compact to support the needs of diverse platform footprints. Microsoft Sync Framework addresses this general requirement with an extensible framework, the latest of which is SyncFramework 2.0 released in Oct 2009.

The Microsoft Sync Framework Power Pack for SQL Azure November CTP (2009) based on the general framework provides the necessary tools to synchronize with SQL Azure. The important tools in the power pack are the following:

- SQL Azure Provider for Microsoft Sync Framework
- A plug-in for Visual Studio 2008 SP1 (adds a new template, the `SqlAzureDataSync`)
- SQL Azure Data Sync Tool for SQL Server creating a Job to be executed by the SQL Server Agent

The new provider, the SQLSyncProvider, is the key to the synchronization. Targeted to DBAs, the SQL Azure Data Sync Tool provides a wizard-based interface to synchronize an SQL Azure database with an SQL Database. Since SQL Server Agent is needed to complete synchronization, SQL Express is excluded. With this tool the synchronization between an on-site SQL Server 2008 R2 database and a database on SQL Azure takes only a few clicks.

As data is accessed by clients of different footprints, from enterprise clients to mobile and hand-held clients, the power pack also provides an SQL Azure Data Sync client that helps caching data from SQL Azure so that the data can be accessed offline.

However, to work with this chapter you need some preparation.

Download and install the following:

Microsoft Sync Framework 2.0 Software Development Kit (SDK) (V2RTM Oct 2009). This provides the necessary interfaces to work with SQL Server 2008 R2, SQL Server CE, and SQL Server Express.

> Uninstall previous versions if any on the computer before installing the SDK and install only the 32-bit version (even if your computer is 64-bit) as the Power Pack supports only a 32-bit version.

```
http://www.microsoft.com/downloads/details.aspx?FamilyID=89adbb1e-
53ff-41b5-ba17-8e43a2e66254.
```

Download and install the MSI file Microsoft Sync Framework Power Pack for SQL Azure November CTP (32-bit) from here:

```
http://www.microsoft.com/downloads/details.aspx?FamilyID=bce4ad61-
5b76-4101-8311-e928e7250b9a&displaylang=en.
```

This installation consisting of the following elements and features supports most synchronization needs (Please read the previous link for more details):

- SqlAzureSyncProvider
- Sql Azure Offline Visual Studio Plug-In (adds `SqlAzureDataSyncClient`)
- SQL Azure Data Sync Tool for SQL Server
- New SQL Azure Events (events encountered during synchronization)
- Automated Provisioning (by way of SQL Azure provisioning classes)

In this chapter, we will learn the following:

- Using the SQL Azure Data Sync Tool to Synchronize SQL Azure with SQL Server
- Synchronizing SQL Azure with SQL Server Compact 3.5
- SQL Azure Data Sync Service

Using SQL Azure Data Sync Tool

In this section, we will be using the SQL Azure Data Sync Tool to provision a database that can be synchronized with a database on SQL Server 2008 R2. The process is driven by wizard and creates the necessary tables on both databases to support bi-directional synchronization and conflict resolution.

Provisioning the database

- Click open the highlighted tool from its short cut in **All Programs | Microsoft Sync Framework** as shown in the following screenshot:

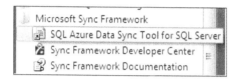

The **Introduction** page is displayed as shown in the following screenshot:

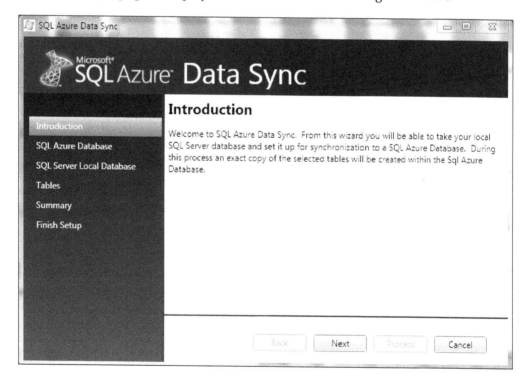

- Click **Next**. The window to insert SQL Azure database information is displayed as shown here:

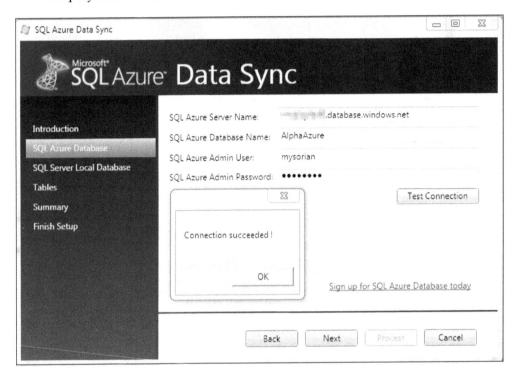

- Enter the credentials as shown in previous screenshot.

  The database **AlphaAzure** does not exist. This wizard creates a database **AlphaAzure**. This wizard therefore provisions a database on SQL Azure. Make sure you have configured firewall information in the portal as described in *Chapter 2, SQL Azure Services*. If the database already exists before synchronization, the database will be dropped and a new database with that name will be created.

- Click **OK** and Click **Next**.

  The **SQL Server Local Database** related entry page is displayed as shown.

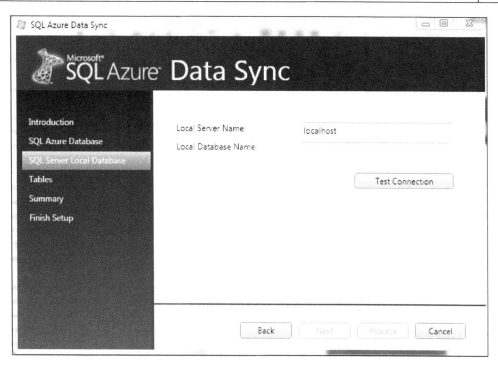

We will be connecting to a named instance of SQL Server 2008 R2, namely
Hodentek3\KUMO. We will synchronize with the Alpha database (which has three
user tables) on Hodentek3\KUMO shown here:

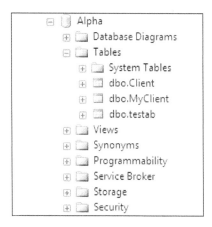

With the correct server name and the table for which the user has permissions, (in this case the administrator) the entries are accepted as shown here:

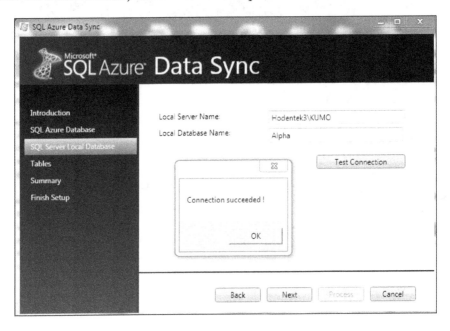

- Click **OK** and Click **Next**. The **Tables** page of the wizard is displayed as shown here:

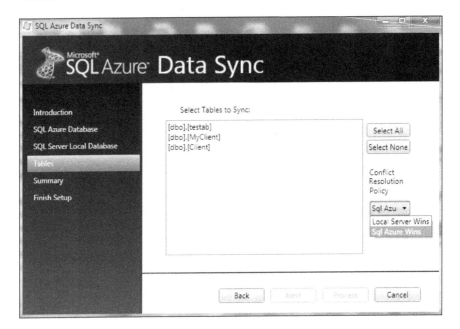

These are all the tables on the local server (Hodentek3\KUMO). The interface also provides a setting for conflict resolution.

- · Accept the default, **SQL Azure Wins** and click **Select All button**.

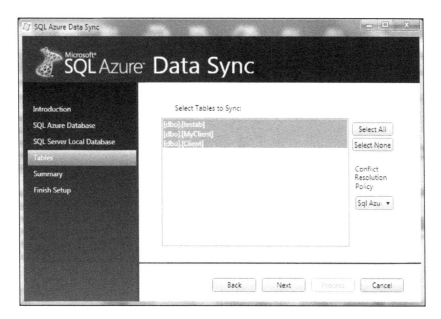

- Click **Next**.

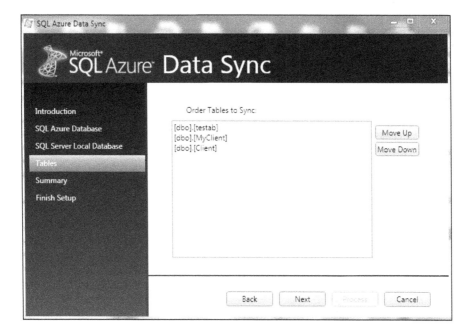

In the Order Tables to Sync window you can **Move Up** or **Move Down** the tables as per your requirements. Default was accepted since these tables are in no way related. If these tables are related to each other by Primary Key/ Foreign Key relationships then you must order the sequence in which the synchronization takes place so as not to violate the referential constraints.

- Click **Next.**

The **Summary** page is displayed as shown here:

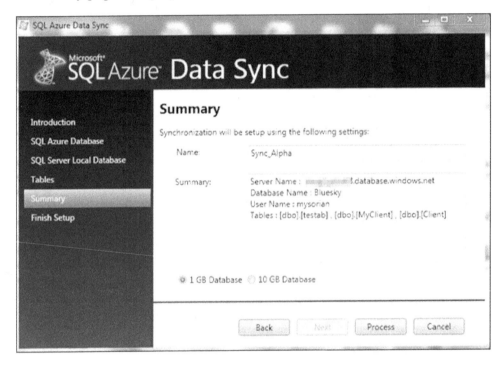

Here, depending on the size of the database tables you can provision a 1GB or a 10GB database (at the point in time the CTP came out, 50GB databases were not supported). Here, the **1GB Database** default is accepted. Also the default name **Sync_Alpha** for synchronization is accepted.

- Click **Process.**

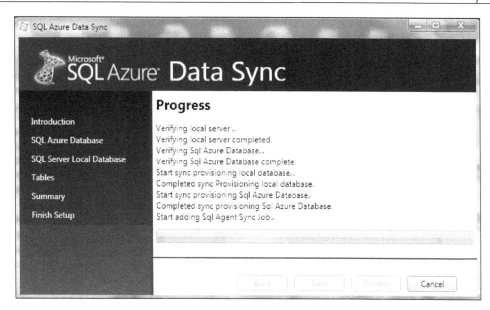

Initially this shows a **Progress** page showing the details of synchronization and finally displays the following screenshot:

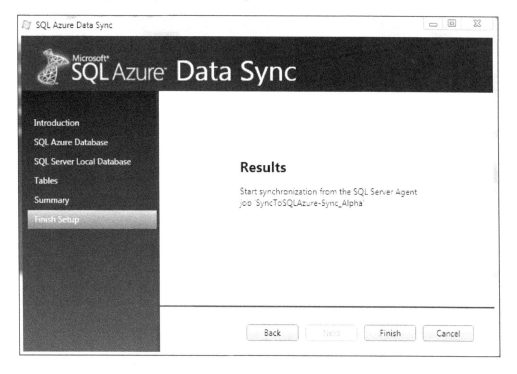

- Click **Finish**.

    This will have created a database `AlphaAzure` in SQL Azure with all the Meta data for the tables on the on-site server database `Alpha`.

Running SQL Server Agent in SSMS

By default, SQL Server Agent may not be running. As the administrator of the computer you have the credentials of the SQL Server Agent's service (credentials assumed during installation of SQL Server 2008 R2) and hence, you can start and stop this service. You can start/stop from the Control Panel through **Administrative Tools | Services**. Run the SQL Server Agent by following these steps:

1. Start the SQL Server Agent if it has stopped in the SQL Server Management Studio.
2. Expand the **Jobs** node in the SQL Server Agent in `Hodentek3\KUMO` as shown.

For minimum permissions to work with synchronization, refer to the following link: `http://msdn.microsoft.com/en-us/library/ee845032?v=SQL.10.aspx`.

The job **SyncToSQLAzure-Sync_Alpha** accomplishes the following task:

```
ConflictResolutionPolicy SqlAzureWins',
    @flags=0
IF (@@ERROR <> 0 OR @ReturnCode <> 0) GOTO QuitWithRollback
EXEC @ReturnCode = msdb.dbo.sp_update_job @job_id = @jobId, @start_
step_id = 1
IF (@@ERROR <> 0 OR @ReturnCode <> 0) GOTO QuitWithRollback
EXEC @ReturnCode = msdb.dbo.sp_add_jobschedule @job_id=@jobId, @
name=N'Happen once a day',
    @enabled=1,
    @freq_type=4,
    @freq_interval=1,
    @freq_subday_type=1,
    @freq_subday_interval=0,
    @freq_relative_interval=0,
```

```
    @freq_recurrence_factor=0,
    @active_start_date=20090722,
    @active_end_date=99991231,
    @active_start_time=0,
    @active_end_time=235959,
    @schedule_uid=N'b148181f-8358-45e7-8a77-092f6b084147'
IF (@@ERROR <> 0 OR @ReturnCode <> 0) GOTO QuitWithRollback
EXEC @ReturnCode = msdb.dbo.sp_add_jobserver @job_id = @jobId, @
server_name = N'(local)'
IF (@@ERROR <> 0 OR @ReturnCode <> 0) GOTO QuitWithRollback
COMMIT TRANSACTION
GOTO EndSave
QuitWithRollback:
    IF (@@TRANCOUNT > 0) ROLLBACK TRANSACTION
EndSave:
GO
```

1. Right-click the job and choose the menu item **Start Job at Step....**

    The job starts and a progress window pops up and after completion displays
    the following:

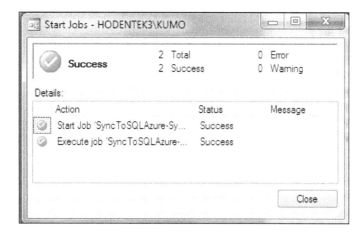

2. Close the window. Connect to SQL Azure and sure enough you will find **the AlphaAzure** database as shown here:

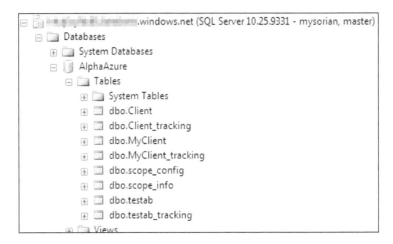

Note that in addition to the three tables a few more tables related to scope and tracking will be created in SQL Azure.

The Client_tracking table keeps track of the Client table during synchronization. This is needed to take care of incremental changes to the table in subsequent synchronizations.

```
SET QUOTED_IDENTIFIER ON
GO
CREATE TABLE [dbo].[Client_tracking](
  [ID] [int] NOT NULL,
  [update_scope_local_id] [int] NULL,
  [scope_update_peer_key] [int] NULL,
  [scope_update_peer_timestamp] [bigint] NULL,
  [local_update_peer_key] [int] NOT NULL,
  [local_update_peer_timestamp] [bigint] NOT NULL,
  [create_scope_local_id] [int] NULL,
  [scope_create_peer_key] [int] NULL,
  [scope_create_peer_timestamp] [bigint] NULL,
  [local_create_peer_key] [int] NOT NULL,
  [local_create_peer_timestamp] [bigint] NOT NULL,
  [sync_row_is_tombstone] [int] NOT NULL,
  [restore_timestamp] [bigint] NULL,
  [last_change_datetime] [datetime] NULL,
 CONSTRAINT [PK_dbo.Client_tracking] PRIMARY KEY CLUSTERED
 (
```

```
    [ID] ASC
)WITH (PAD_INDEX   = OFF, STATISTICS_NORECOMPUTE   = OFF,
   IGNORE_DUP_KEY = OFF, ALLOW_ROW_LOCKS   = ON, ALLOW_PAGE_LOCKS   =
   ON)
)


GO
```

The Client table in the server `Hodentek3\KUMO` is as shown here, which is synchronized with the SQL Azure database AlphaAzure.

HODENTEK3\KUMO.Alpha - dbo.Client		SQLQuery2.sql - hh... (mysorian (159))	
ID	name	city	age
1	Joe Hard	Los Angeles	35
2	Tom Soft	Los Angeles	43
3	Mary Nice	Los Angeles	25
4	Jay Kris	Princeton	45
5	John Depuis	Paris	38
6	Lora Smith	Denver	72
* NULL	NULL	NULL	NULL

Verifying bi-directional synchronization

The wizard updates both the databases at the same time and this is called bi-directional synchronization. In order to see how this works: follow the procedure as indicated.

1. Add an extra row with the following data to the `Client` table of `Alpha` database in `Hodentek3\KUMO`:

    ```
    Name=James Bond, city= London, age=50
    ```

2. In the SQL Azure's `Client` table change the name 'Joe Hard' to 'Joh Howard Junior' with the following update query:

    ```
    Update client
    set name='Joh Howard Junior'
    where name='Joe Hard'
    ```

    By running the previous code we have made changes to both the on-site data in the Alpha table and the data in SQL Azure.

3. Now run the `Job` in SSMS (`Hodentek3\KUMO`).

Again, you will have a successful run.

You can verify by querying the databases in the on-site server and the SQL Azure that the changes are synchronized demonstrating bi-directional synchronization. SELECT query against Alpha database in Hodentek3\KUMO and the result set returned is shown in the following screenshot:

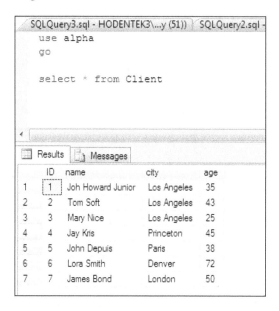

SELECT query run in the AlphaAzure database on SQL Azure and the result set returned is shown in the following screenshot:

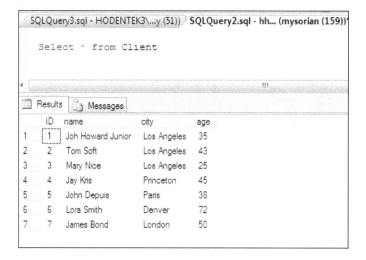

Conflict resolution

While synchronizing the on-site data with SQL Azure the conflict resolution was set so that SQL Azure wins. This means that if changes were made to the same row element in both SQL Azure and SQL Server, the changes made to the SQL Azure will be the one that is synchronized.

In order to test, follow the indicated steps:

1. Modify the client table in the databases as follows:

   On SQL Azure run the following query:

   ```
   update client
   set name='James Joyce'
   where name='Tom Soft'
   ```

2. On Hodentek3\KUMO's Alpha database, run the following query:

   ```
   Use Alpha
   Go
   update Client
   set name='Marie Curie'
   where name='Tom Soft'
   ```

   Now by running the previous queries we have created a conflict for the name=**'Tom Soft'**. On SQL server we have 'Marie Curie' and on SQL Azure we have 'James Joyce'.

3. Run the synchronization job again and verify that SQL Azure wins, that is, both SQL Azure `AlphaAzure` databases' `Client` table and the table `Client` in Hodentek3\KUMO's `Alpha` database will have 'Tom Soft' replaced by 'James Joyce' , the update made to SQL Azure.

Once the synchronization is run you could run the SQL Server Agent job again, however if you make schema changes to the tables you need to run the tool again. It is also possible to run the synchronization programmatically as you may find in this link assuming you have run synchronization once as described previously.

```
http://msdn.microsoft.com/en-us/windowsazure/ee960244.aspx.
```

Synchronizing SQL Azure data with SQL Server Compact

There are many problems encountered by both users and enterprises when users try to connect to the corporate database remotely. These are usually due to network problems, data access speeds, single point of failure like server going down, and scalability (many users trying to connect). Occasionally Connected Application (OCA) overcomes these by providing not all but just the needed data that is cached on a local, small footprint database that can be synchronized with the corporate database when conditions are favorable. A prime candidate for this kind of application is Microsoft SQL Server Compact edition (SQLCE). It is an embedded database that allows integration of desktop and mobile applications. Its importance can only grow as more applications move into cloud and mobile platforms. It can be used in several ways such as:

- Single user use
- Local cache of remote SQL Server database
- Occasionally connected clients

A typical example is a travelling salesman who takes orders and uploads some order or receives some new catalog. In extending this to SQL Azure, the SQL Azure data is cached offline to SQL Server Compact, which is a small footprint database.

In this section, we will look at synchronizing data on SQL Azure with data on SQL Server Compact. Synchronizing with SQL Server Compact is greatly simplified by the Visual Studio plug-in described earlier. In this post, you can access two of the key articles on using this database from two perspectives: `http://hodentekmsss.blogspot.com/2010/07/sql-server-compact-35-basics-you-must.html`. As working with SQL Server Compact in SSMS is not very intuitive, the author strongly recommends reading these articles.

The Visual Studio plug-in available with the Power Tools SDK provides the template files only in C#.

Provisioning SQL Azure Data cache

It is assumed that the Power Tools SDK has been installed.

1. Create a Windows Console application in C#.

   Herein called `SyncCache`.

2. Add the plug-in by right-clicking on **SyncCache** and choose to add a new item from the drop-down list. Choose the item shown in the following screenshot of the **Add New Item** window:

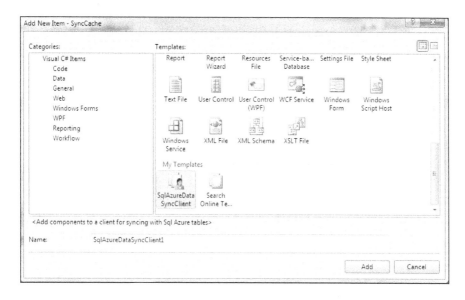

If you are creating a number of **SqlAzureDataSync Clients** it may be better to provide an appropriate name. Herein, the default name is accepted.

1. Click **Add**.

   You should see the following screenshot displayed:

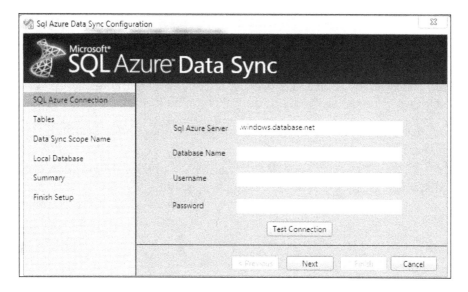

This is the **SQL Azure Connection** page that you have seen in the other chapters.

1. Insert the required items and test if the connection is OK.

   Make sure that there are no connectivity problems such as network connection problems, firewall configuration, and so on. The **Test Connection** button when clicked should succeed.

2. Click **Next** in the previous page after inserting all required items.

   The following image is displayed. This is presently displaying all the tables on the `Bluesky` database on the SQL Azure server as we have seen in other chapters.

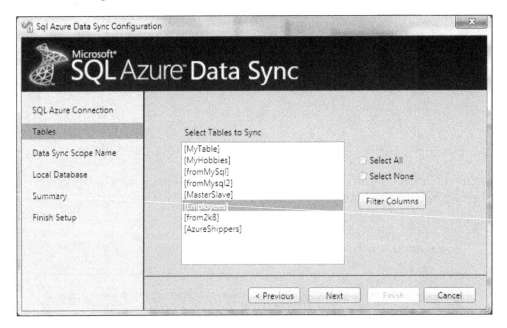

You could choose all or you can choose just the one you are interested in. Let us assume that we are interested only in certain columns from the `Employees` table.

1. Choose Employees as shown in the previous image and click the **Filter Columns** button.

2. Click **Next**. The **Data Sync Scope Name** page of the configuration wizard is displayed as shown in the following screenshot.

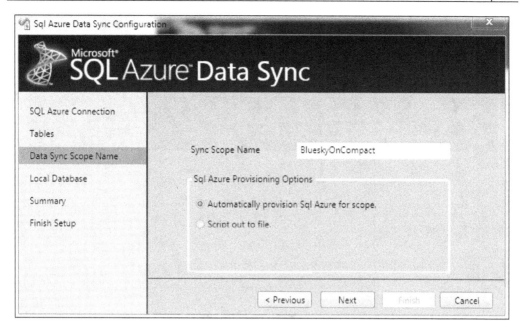

The Filter Column button does not seem to function as expected. It was confirmed that the CTP was released with the button left on the wizard screen by oversight (`http://social.msdn.microsoft.com/Forums/en-US/ssdsgetstarted/thread/72dee40f-22b1-4bb4-b2ec-3d24324eb836`). It is therefore expected that it won't work. However, this does not affect the ensuing details.

You can script the provisioning options to a file or let it go automatically.

1. Choose automatic option.

    You may also change the **Sync Scope Name**, herein the default is changed to **BlueskyOnCompact**.

2. Click **Next** to display the following page where the file location of the Compact database to be provisioned is displayed when this process is completed. This could be an existing database location.

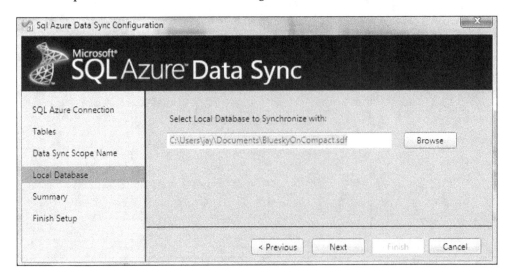

3. Clicking **Next** will take you to the **Summary** page where the name of the SQL Azure server, the scope name, and the Local CE database are recorded.

4. Click **Next**. The processing starts and the following image is displayed when completed.

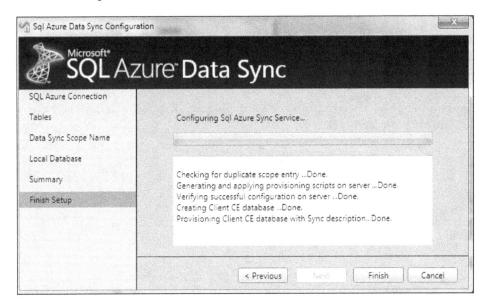

5. Click **Finish**.

6. You have completed creating a cached data on a Compact database, which is capable of being synchronized with SQL Azure.

   At this point only the Metadata of the table and the other necessary tables for incremental updates are created.

The project folder gets modified and the wizard also adds all the required library references to the project (shown enclosed in a blue rectangle) as well as creating the file used during synchronization as shown in the following screenshot:

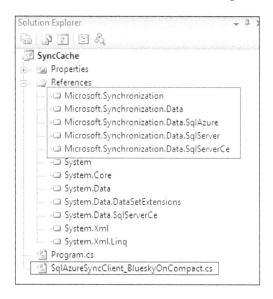

It is instructive to review the file SQLAzureSyncClient_BlueskyOnCompact.cs as it shows how the SyncOrchestrator establishes connections to the two databases; establishes the direction of synchronization; and how the databases get changed during upload and download sync operations of this bi-directional process.

We can now go to the SQL Server Management Studio and bring up the database file that was created by the wizard. By default the connection to SQL Server Compact through Connect to database wizard is not displayed (please refer to the articles in link regarding use of SSMS for SQL Server Compact: http://hodentekmsss. blogspot.com/2010/07/sql-server-compact-35-basics-you-must.html).

Reviewing SQL Server Compact database

As described in the previous link, you can browse for files with extension `.sdf`, which are SQL Server Compact files as shown in the following screenshot:

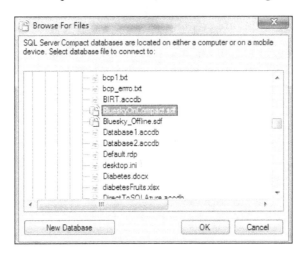

You need to expand the nodes and select the file created by the wizard, namely, `BlueskyOnCompact.sdf`. There is yet another database file `Bluesky_offline.sdf` from another run of the wizard.

Choosing the one highlighted and clicking **OK** opens up the SQL Azure Compact database whose tree view structure is as shown in the following image. If you have problems with the SSMS, reviewing the article link suggested will help.

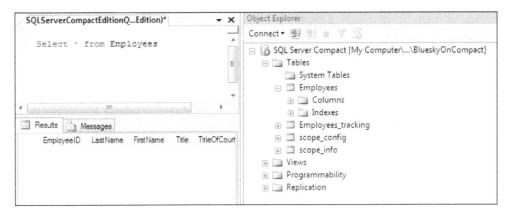

Build and run synchronization

This shows only the meta data of the table. In order to populate the table, you need to run the wizard created file in Visual Studio.

1. Now add the following code to the `Program.cs` file as shown here.

    ```
    using System;
    using System.Collections.Generic;
    using System.Linq;
    using System.Text;

    namespace SyncCache
    {
    classProgram
        {
    staticvoid Main(string[] args)
            {
    SqlAzureSyncClient_BlueskyOnCompact.Synchronize();
            }
        }
    }
    ```

2. **Build** the project and hit the **Start Debugging** (*F5*) menu item.

    The program writes to the console the result of synchronization and now you can run the query you ran earlier in SSMS. You will see the data in the compact database's `Employees` table.

The wizard makes it very easy to synchronize. As tested in the previous section, you can test for both bi-directionality of synchronization as well as incremental changes made to the data on both databases.

It is also highly recommended that you review the new tracking tables created and their structure in the SQL Azure and SQL Compact.

Also remember that once the scope is established you cannot make changes to the schema to be synchronized. If the schema changes a fresh run of the wizard would be necessary.

SQL Azure Data Sync Service

SQL Azure Data Sync Service is not in production but only in preview, accessible from the SQL Azure Labs portal at the following URL:

```
http://www.sqlazurelabs.com/default.aspx
```

The web page accessing this URL is shown here:

When you click SQL Azure Data Sync the following window is displayed where you create SQL Server Data Sync services. In the following screenshot there are two such services created.

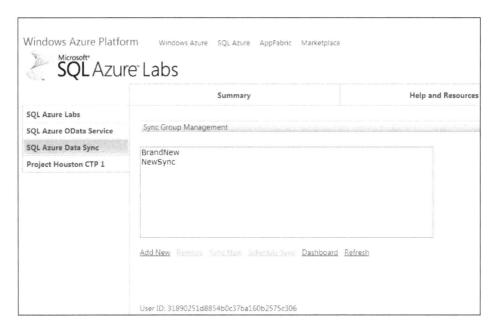

This service, when it goes into production will support creating 'Sync Groups'; groups of geographically separated SQL Azure servers (two or more) that participate in bi-directionally synchronizing data (hub and spoke model of hierarchy) with one of its members designated as a 'hub' so that enterprise data can be served, or utilized from a source closest to the end user.

The purported activities supported by SQL Azure Data Sync Service are:

- Specify tables from a 'hub' database to be shared with other SQL Azure databases
- Add databases to Sync Groups, so that data changes can be bi-directionally synchronized between member databases
- Automatically create tables and schema in the member databases based on the tables being shared from the SQL Azure "Hub"
- Create synchronization schedules that define when synchronization tasks are to be executed by the service
- View the status of pending, in-process, and completed jobs

A complete walkthrough of creating and using the service is available here:

```
https://datasync.sqlazurelabs.com/helpandresources.aspx
```

Summary

In this chapter, the main features of Microsoft Synchronization technology as applied to SQL Azure-related modifications were described. Specifically, the usage of SQL Azure Data Sync Tool — which provisions a database on SQL Azure — that can be synchronized with a database on the on-site SQL Server 2008 R2, which supports bi-directional synchronization that can be configured to address conflict resolution is described. The Visual Studio plug-in that helps to create a cache on a SQL Server Compact database is also described, this again supports bi-directional synchronization and conflict resolution. Further, the new SQL Azure Data Sync Service and its possible future role in SQL Azure Service are described.

This book is being written during a period in which many new features have been added and therefore the topics that did not fit into the earlier chapters are described in the next chapter.

10
Recent Developments

From August 2009 CTP until now (October 2010), SQL Azure has gone through a lot of changes; modifications have been made and new features have been added and it remains a continuously evolving project. Its growth has been driven by a variety of forces, including those from third parties. Customer's wish lists and the changing perception of businesses as to how best the cost can be justified while keeping the security in focus are some of the other drivers.

In this chapter, a miscellany of topics are discussed. While some of the topics did not fit the focus of the existing chapters and were therefore added here, others were added as they started debuting during the period the book was written. In order to make this book as current as possible, the following topics are described (only succinctly):

- SQL Azure updates
- SQL Azure security
- Using SQL Azure Firewall API
- SQL Azure with MS Access 2010 and MS Excel
- OpenOffice Access to SQL Azure
- Accessing SQL Azure with non-.NET Framework Languages
- OData Service for SQL Azure
- Consuming SQL Azure data with PowerPivot
- SQL Azure with WebMatrix
- More third-party tools to SQL Azure
- Managing SQL Azure databases with the Houston Project (CTP1)
- Data Application Component and SQL Azure
- References

SQL Azure updates

The following are the five updates introduced from the beginning of the year 2010:

1. Service Update SU1 may be accessed here: `http://blogs.msdn.com/b/` `sqlazure/archive/2010/02/17/9965464.aspx`

   Features added are the following:

   - Troubleshooting and Support for DMVs

     DMVs supported: sys.dm_exec_connections, sys.dm_exec_requests, sys.dm_exec_sessions, sys.dm_tran_database_transactions, sys.dm_tran_active_transactions, sys.dm_db_partition_stats

   - Modifying database size 1GB <-> 10GB with alter database statement
   - Idle session timeouts increased to 30 minutes from 5 minutes
   - Improved algorithm to terminate long running transactions

2. Service Update SU2 may be accessed from here: `http://blogs.msdn.` `com/b/sqlazure/archive/2010/04/16/9997517.aspx`

   Service enhancements and features added are the following:

   - SQL Azure became available in 20 more countries
   - Support for Multiple active record sets (MARS)
   - Alter database name with rename (right-click and change name)
   - Application and Multi-server management with Data-tier supported in SSMS as well as via Visual Studio 2008 SP1 and Visual Studio 2010 providing the ultimate experience in database deployment

3. Service Update SU3 may be accessed from here: `http://blogs.msdn.` `com/b/sqlazure/archive/2010/06/25/10030461.aspx`

   Service enhancements and features added are the following:

   - SQL Azure became available in two more data centers (East Asia and Western Europe)
   - 50GB databases were introduced
   - Support for Spatial and hierarchical data types

4. SQL Azure—SU4 may be accessed from here: `http://blogs.msdn.com/b/` `zaneadam/archive/2010/08/24/new-features-in-sql-azure-august-` `update.aspx`

   This appeared at the end of August 2010 and some new features were added. The features that were added are:

◦ Database Copy – You can make a snapshot copy of your database and place it on another server. This is deemed to be the first step in backup support for SQL Azure and it also happens to be the top item on the wish list. It may, however, be noted that even without this the copies are automatically replicated at the data center.

Review this example of copying a database here: `http://hodentek.blogspot.com/2010/08/here-comes-update-su4-to-sql-azure.html`

◦ Documentation beefed up to include a how-to section for common tasks as seen at this link here: `http://hodentek.blogspot.com/2010/08/here-comes-update-su4-to-sql-azure.html`

◦ Update to the Houston Project. Please refer to this link to see how one can leverage SQL Azure Management using a browser: `http://hodentek.blogspot.com/2010/09/who-said-you-cannot-have-design-view-of.html`

5. SQL Azure Update SU5 (Oct 2010) can be accessed here: `http://blogs.msdn.com/b/sqlazure/archive/2010/10/22/10079540.aspx`

This update, as well as the previous updates, is available at all data centers. The focus, according to the previous link, was internal operational improvements that will allow for future additions. It now supports sp_tableoption stored procedure.

Further enhancements were made to MSDN Documentation. Now these are added:

- Hints
- Error Messages
- Microsoft Sync Framework 2.1

SQL Azure security

Security is at the top of users' concerns and it is a vast topic in itself. The best source to learn about Windows Azure security is here: `http://azuresecurity.codeplex.com/` and it is summarized here: `http://blogs.msdn.com/b/jmeier/archive/2010/08/03/now-available-azure-security-notes-pdf.aspx`

For details about SQL Azure application security, follow this link: `http://azuresecurity.codeplex.com/wikipage?title=ASP.NET%20Forms%20Auth%20to%20SQL%20Azure&referringTitle=Web%20Application%20Scenarios`

SQL Azure security is based on IP screening (Firewalls), user credentials during connection over the wire by SSL, authentication to applications using Forms, and authorization based on roles coded in applications.

Using SQL Azure Firewall API

As we learnt from *Chapters 2, SQL Azure Services* and *Chapter 3, Working with SQL Azure Databases from Visual Studio 2008*, SQL Azure Firewall is the main line of defense and mandatory for SQL Azure. The firewall is defined by a name, a start IP Address, and an End IP Address. These are stored in the `master` database of the SQL Server in the table `sys.firewall_rules`. In order to retrieve the firewall rules we need to connect to SQL Azure and retrieve the columns of the table `sys.firewall_rules`. These can be retrieved programmatically as shown in this `Program.cs` file of a C# console project:

```
using System;
using System.Collections.Generic;
using System.Linq;
using System.Text;
using System.Data.SqlClient;

namespace GetFirewallRules
{
    class Program
    {
        static void Main(string[] args)
        {
            String conStr="Data Source=<your server
              name>.database.windows.net;Initial Catalog=master;User
              ID=<your usrename>;Password=<your password>";

            SqlConnection conn = new SqlConnection();
            conn.ConnectionString = conStr;
            conn.Open();
            SqlCommand cmd = new SqlCommand("SELECT name,
              start_ip_address, end_ip_address FROM
              sys.firewall_rules", conn);
            using (SqlDataReader reader = cmd.ExecuteReader())
            while (reader.Read())
            {
                Console.WriteLine(reader.GetValue(0)+",    "+"Start IP:
                  "+ reader.GetValue(1)+",    "+"End IP:
                  "+reader.GetValue(2));
                Console.WriteLine("");
            }
        }
    }
}
```

The result of running this program is shown in the following screenshot and displays the firewall rules presently configured:

Using similar logic, new rules can be added and existing rules can be programmatically deleted.

SQL Azure with MS Access 2010

There is a great deal of interest among small businesses regarding the ability to access data on SQL Azure using MS Access. During the early days of SQL Azure, it was not possible to connect to SQL Azure using an ODBC connection as certain procedures were not supported on SQL Azure, although ODBC was one of the connection methods. The problem was resolved when SQL Azure was updated so that MS Access could access the databases (see `http://social.msdn.microsoft.com/Forums/en-US/ssdsgetstarted/thread/05dd7620-f209-43d2-8c41-63b251c62970/#426310be-7a88-4933-ac9c-0772ccb833be`).

Import a SQL Azure table into MS Access

This section looks at connecting to SQL Azure with MS Access from the Microsoft Office Professional Plus 2010 (x32 bit and in beta). First we create an ODBC DSN on the computer and then use MS Access 2010 to connect to it.

1. Create a new Microsoft Access database on your computer **FromSQLAzure.accdb**.

2. Under the **External Data** tab in the 'ribbon', click the **ODBC Database** icon.

3. In the **Get External Data – ODBC Database** window accept the first option, namely, **Import the source data into a new table in the current database**. Click **OK**.

4. In the **Select Data Source** window click **New....**

5. In the **Create New Data Source** window scroll-down and choose **SQL Server Native client10.0**. Click **Next >**.

6. In the window displayed, enter a name for the data source. Herein, SQLAzureDSN. Click **Next >**.

7. In the information window that follows click **Finish**.

8. In the **Create a New Data Source to SQL Server**, enter an optional description (**Import from SQL Azure**). For the **Server:** enter the full name of the SQL Azure server instance you created in the SQL Azure portal. Click **Next >**.

9. In the authentication window that follows, choose the second option, namely, **With SQL Server authentication using a loginID and password entered by the user**. For **LoginID** use your **UserID** (actually in the format **UserID @ servername**) for the SQL Azure database and for password use your password. Click **Next >**.

10. In the next wizard screen you can keep the default master or browse for a database by clicking the handle. Herein, the Bluesky database was chosen after clicking the drop-down handle. Accept other defaults and click **Next >**.

11. In the next page, accept all defaults and click **Finish**. The summary page (**ODBC SQL Server Setup**), which can be tested, is displayed:

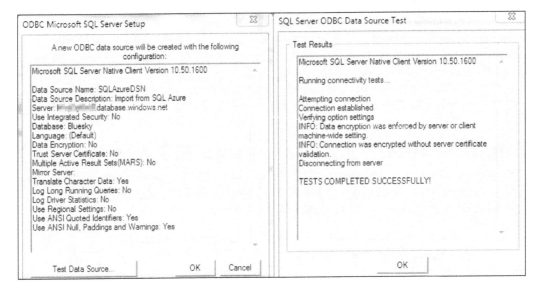

12. Click **OK** after testing (Close the test screen and the wizard screen).

13. This brings you back to the **Select Data Source** window displaying your DSN. Click **OK**.

14. The **SQL Server Login** page is displayed. Enter the password and click **OK**.

15. The **Import Objects** window is displayed:

16. Highlight the objects you want to import. Herein, only one of the tables (fromMySql2) is highlighted. Click **OK**.

17. The **Get External Data — ODBC** window is displayed with the note that **All Objects were imported successfully**. You need not save the steps of this import. Click **Close**.

18. The table is imported into the FromSqlAzure database as shown in the following screenshot:

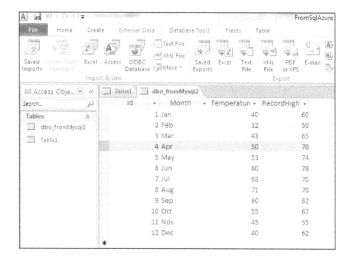

Creating a table in MS Access linked to SQL Azure

By choosing the second option in the third step and using the DSN created in the previous subsection, you can create a linked table to a SQL Azure database table in MS Access.

1. Choose the second option in the third step and click **OK**.

2. In the Select Data Source window scroll and choose the previously created DSN, the **SQLAzureDSN** as shown in the following screenshot. Click **OK**:

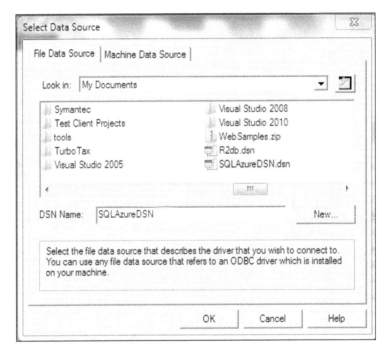

3. In the **SQL Server Login** page enter credentials and click **OK**.

4. In the Link Tables window, choose the table(s) and click **OK**. Herein, only the Employees table is chosen as shown in the following screenshot:

5. The linked table **dbo_Employees** gets created as shown in the following screenshot (only some columns are shown):

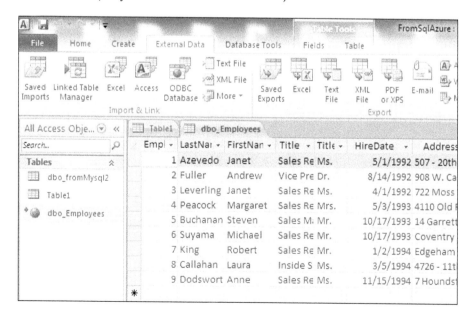

6. The following screenshot shows the database structure in SQL Azure:

7. The next screenshot shows the structure of the linked table in MS Access:

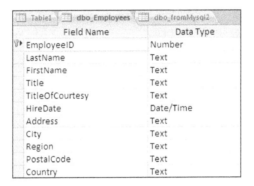

Connecting to SQL Azure from MS Excel 2010

We saw how easy it was to access SQL Azure from MS Access and it is even easier to connect from Microsoft Excel 2010.

From the main menu in MS Excel click **Data** and then click **From Other Sources** icon in **Get External Data**, which displays a drop-down list from which you select **From SQL Server**.

The **Data Center Wizard** screen is displayed. You provide the name of the SQL Azure server for the Server name textbox and insert your log on credentials (remember it is username- and password-based authentication) and click to go to the next step of the wizard.

The Select Database and Table page of the wizard is displayed. From here on you can work with the database and tables. It cannot be any easier than this.

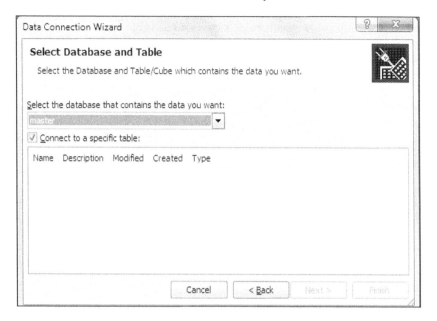

OpenOffice Access to SQL Azure

SQL Azure can not only be accessed via Microsoft products, it can also be accessed by open source software. This section describes how one may access SQL Azure with OpenOffice.

OpenOffice — as the name implies — is the Open Source Office suite of programs that can be freely downloaded and distributed. General information about OpenOffice. org can be found here: `http://www.openoffice.org/about_us/introduction. html`. By following the indicated steps it is quite easy to connect to SQL Azure:

1. Download the latest version of the software here (in the Download tab): `http://download.openoffice.org/index.html`. Present (August 2010) version is 3.2.1 and File name:`OOo_3.2.1_Win_x86_install-wJRE_en-US. exe` (~152 MB).

2. Double-click the executable to open and install OpenOffice 3.2.1. It is a relatively fast install. The program, by default, will be in the `Program Files\OpenOffice.org 3` folder. You will find a number of executable programs in the program folder such as `sbase.exe` (Database program similar to MS Access), `scalc.exe` (similar to MS Excel), and so on. Shortcuts are added to the `All Programs` as shown in the following screenshot:

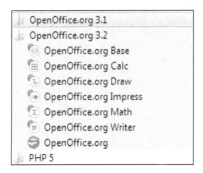

3. Click and run `OpenOffice.org Base` as an administrator. The user interface of the database program opens as shown in the next screenshot:

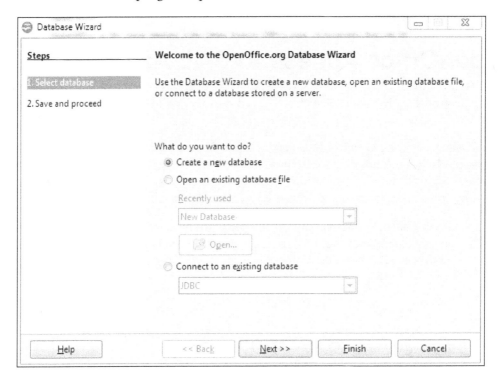

4. Choose the **Connecting to an existing database** option and from the drop-down, shown in the following screenshot, choose **ODBC**:

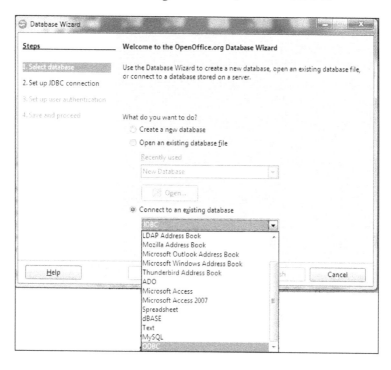

5. Clicking **Next >>** opens the **Set up ODBC connection** page as shown in the next screenshot:

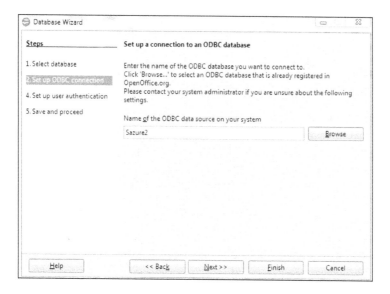

6. **Browse** and find an ODBC file, such as `Sazure2` in the **Data Source** window displayed (this should show all ODBC files on your machine).

7. Clicking **Next >>** will open up the **Set up user authentication** page, where you need to provide the **User name**. Provide the username in the format <SQL Azure username>@<SQL Azure server name> and place a check mark for the checkbox **Password required**. You may test and verify that the connection information is valid. Here, the Sql Azure server name is the first part of the 4 part server name.

8. Clicking **Next >>** will bring up the final step of the wizard as shown in the next screenshot:

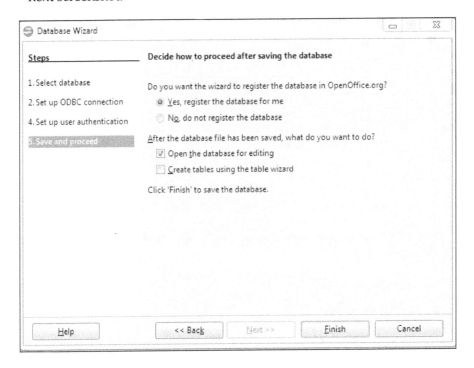

9. Registering is not mandatory, but it is recommended. Accept the default, **Open the database for editing**. Click **Finish**. You may need to save the database with a name of your choice. Herein, it is `AugSqlAzure.odp`. Odp is the extension used by OpenOffice. After it is saved, the database user interface opens as shown in the next screenshot:

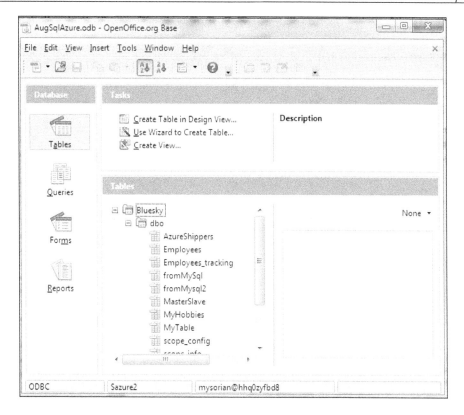

This UI can be used for creating Reports, running SQL queries, Interactive forms, and many more. The next screenshot shows a Report created using a few columns from the Employee table in the Bluesky database:

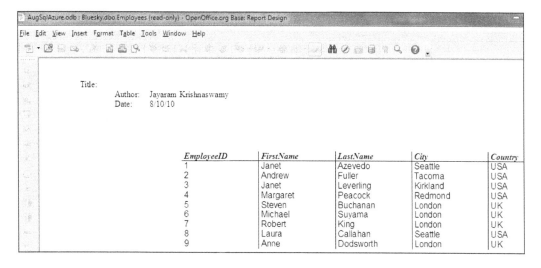

There appears to be one problem with this software. If you try to enable the `*.odb` file, sometimes it takes a while to get the data in. This is probably due to connectivity with the database, rather than the OpenOffice program.

Accessing SQL Azure with non-.NET Framework languages

In order to appeal to a larger user base, Microsoft has extended its support to non-.NET Framework languages. With this support, developers can connect to SQL Azure with languages such Java, PHP, and Ruby. In this section, these access methods are described with some examples.

Accessing SQL Azure with Java

Even before the advent of SQL Azure, Microsoft provided various JDBC drivers to connect to SQL Server Databases, so that applications can be developed. Additionally, JDBC-ODBC bridges could also be used to connect to Microsoft SQL Servers.

In order to connect to SQL Azure, you need to install the following components:

- Java compiler *Java SE Development Kit 6u21* from the following site: `http://www.oracle.com/technetwork/java/javase/downloads/jdk6-jsp-136632.html`. Make sure you have the correct JVM from here by clicking the link **"Do I have Java?"** `http://java.com/en/download/index.jsp`. If the version is correct, you should see the following display after some processing of request:

- You need to install the appropriate version of JDBC. The correct version to use is JDBC 3.0 and this can be downloaded from here: `http://www.microsoft.com/downloads/details.aspx?FamilyID=a737000d-68d0-4531-b65d-da0f2a735707&displaylang=en`. The file to download is: `1033\sqljdbc_3.0.1301.101_enu.exe`.

- The JDBC zip download should be unzipped to a folder that has no white spaces in its name. Herein, it was downloaded and files reordered such that the needed `sqljdbc_3.0` folder that contains the `sqljdbc4.jar` file is in the following directory: `C:\JTDS\sqljdbc_3.0\enu`. The reason for this is that the `CLASSPATH` setting should adhere to the 8.3 file name convention.

  Make sure that you can run `javac` from any location by configuring the Environmental variable `PATH`. If you need to know how, follow this link: `http://hodentekhelp.blogspot.com/2010/08/compiling-java-in-Windows-7.html`.

- Using the following java file, the `MyTable` table in SQL Azure's `Bluesky` database will be accessed. The contents of `MyTable` are shown in the following Select query:

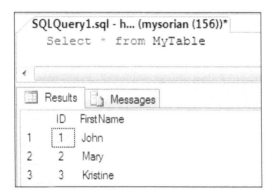

- Create a file `ConnectToSqlAzure.java` as follows:

```java
import java.sql.*;

public class ConnectToSqlAzure
{
    public static void main(String[] args)
    {
        try
        {
            java.lang.Class.forName(
                "com.microsoft.sqlserver.jdbc.SQLServerDriver" );
```

```
        Connection c = java.sql.DriverManager.getConnection(
            "jdbc:sqlserver://<server_name>.database.windows.net;"
            +"database=Bluesky;user=<user_name>@<server_name>;<Your
            SQL Azure password>");

        Statement s  = c.createStatement();
        ResultSet  r =s.executeQuery("select * from MyTable");
        while(r.next())
        {
           System.out.println(r.getString(2));
        }
           System.out.println( "Connected!" );
      }
      catch( Exception ex )
      {
         ex.printStackTrace();
      }
    }
 }
```

If you are not copying the code, make sure the java filename and the classname in the code are identical. Save this file to a suitable location.

- Compile the file using the following command line statement:

```
C:\Users\jay>javac ConnectToSqlAzure.java
```

This creates the class file ConnectToSqlAzure.class in the same directory.

- Next we have to set the correct CLASSPATH to the JDBC file.

Run the following command line statement exactly as shown next:

```
C:\Users\jay>set classpath=.;C:\JTDS\sqljdbc_3.0\enu\sqljdbc4.jar
```

- Now run the java program as shown in the next screenshot (the result is also shown in the next screenshot):

```
C:\Users\jay>java ConnectToSqlAzure
John
Mary
Kristine
Connected!
```

The problematic steps are mostly syntax-related, or in the setting of the CLASSPATH. If you are using the Microsoft documentation for the java sample in the Windows Azure SDK (IntroToSQLAzureVS2010, Hands-On Labs: Task 6) make sure you remove the Encrypt attribute in the connection string.

Accessing SQL Azure with PHP

The worldwide adoption of PHP, prompted Microsoft to support PHP extensively, not only on enterprise applications, but also on the cloud. For developing PHP applications that can be hosted on the cloud platform Microsoft provided the FastCGI web role, which overcomes the limitations of CGI. In order to connect to SQL Azure, Microsoft provided the needed SQL Server drivers, which were recently extended to support PHP Data Objects (PDO). For details of the latest version of SQL Drivers follow this link: `http://blogs.msdn.com/b/sqlphp/ archive/2010/08/04/microsoft-drivers-for-php-for-sql-server-2-0- released.aspx`.

For the purposes of following this section you need the following:

- Most recent OS including Windows 7 and Windows XP with SP3.
- PHP 5 (You need PHP 5.2.4 or later. PHP 5.2.13 is used in this section).
- Web server must be configured to run PHP. Using FastCGI, PHP applications can be hosted on IIS.
- Microsoft SQL Server 2008 R2 Native Client should be present on the same computer as the drivers.

For more detailed information follow this link: `http://msdn.microsoft.com/en- us/library/cc296170%28v=SQL.90%29.aspx`.

If you are starting from scratch you should go through the following list.

- Download and install PHP from here: `http://php.net`
- Follow this link to configure IIS7 for FastCGI `http://learn.iis.net/page. aspx/246/using-fastcgi-to-host-php-applications-on-iis-7/`.

- After doing this, your website should be able to process PHP scripts. Here is a screenshot of the website on this computer for this section:

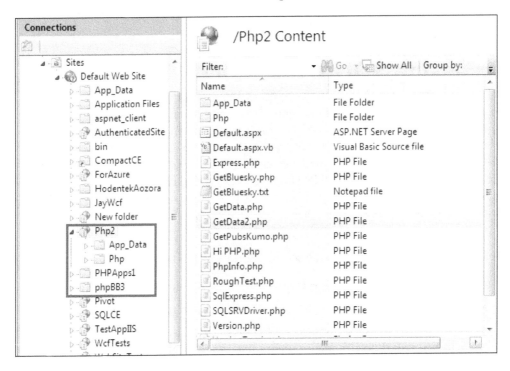

- Test the site with a file, such as `PhpInfo.php` shown here by placing it in the site directory's root folder:

```
<?php phpinfo(); ?>
```

- Download and install the SQL Server drivers `SQLServerDriverForPHP11.EXE` for PHP from (version 1.1 was used) here: `http://www.microsoft.com/downloads/details.aspx?displaylang=en&FamilyID=ccdf728b-1ea0-48a8-a84a-5052214caad9`.

- Load the Microsoft Drivers for PHP.

- Open the folder where PHP 5.2.13 is installed. The folder structure of this is shown in the following screenshot. The folder `ext` contains all the dynamic link library files (`dlls`). The file `php-cgi.exe` is used to run PHP scripts from the command line, a useful tool to troubleshoot applications. The `php_manual_en.chm` is invaluable. This folder's `php.ini` file is where you make modifications so that PHP can find the driver file. The SQL Server driver is installed in the `ext` folder:

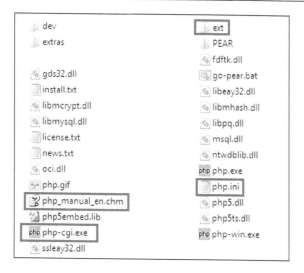

- Download and install SQL Server drivers for PHP from here: File SQLServerDriverForPHP11.exe at http://www.microsoft.com/downloads/details.aspx?displaylang=en&FamilyID=ccdf728b-1ea0-48a8-a84a-5052214caad9 (for version 1.1) and File sqlsrv20.exe at http://www.microsoft.com/downloads/details.aspx?displaylang=en&FamilyID=80e44913-24b4-4113-8807-caae6cf2ca05 (for version 2.0).

- Load the drivers so that the program can find the driver files.

- Modify php.ini file by adding the following as shown in the next screenshot:

```
[PHP_MING]
extension=php_ming.dll
[PHP_MSQL]
extension=php_msql.dll
[PHP_MSSQL]
extension=php_mssql.dll
extension = php_sqlsrv_52_nts_vc6.dll

[PHP_MYSQL]
extension=php_mysql.dll
```

- Copy the file php_sqlsrv_52_nts-vc6.dll from the download location of the 1.1 driver to the ext directory.

With these taken care of, you could run PHP programs off the local IIS 7 web server to access data on the SQL Servers. You can use a script such as the one shown here to access data on the SQL Azure database. The following PHP (GetData2.php) program accesses the Employee table in the Bluesky database. This is a simple program displaying all the columns from the table in an array format. For more information on using the SQL Drivers, read the following MSDN documentation: http://msdn.microsoft.com/en-us/library/ee229551(v=SQL.10).aspx.

```php
<?php
  $serverName = "tcp:<SERVER_NAME>.database.windows.net,1433";
   $userName = '<USER_NAME>@<SERVER-NAME>';
   $userPassword = '<PASSWORD>';
   $dbName = "Bluesky";


   $connectionInfo = array("Database"=>$dbName, "UID"=>$userName,

"PWD"=>$userPassword, "MultipleActiveResultSets"=>true);

   sqlsrv_configure('WarningsReturnAsErrors', 0);
   $conn = sqlsrv_connect( $serverName, $connectionInfo);
   if($conn === false)
   {
      FatalError("Failed to connect...");
   }


// Select some data from our database

$tsql="SELECT * from Employees";
$getItems=sqlsrv_query($conn,$tsql);
while( $row = sqlsrv_fetch_array( $getItems, SQLSRV_FETCH_ASSOC ) )
   {
      print_r( $row );
   }
sqlsrv_free_stmt( $getItems );
   sqlsrv_close( $conn );
?>
```

When the previously mentioned file is browsed, the following is displayed (only part of it is shown):

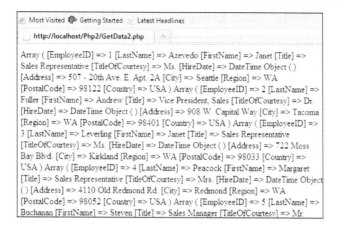

OData Service for SQL Azure

Accessing data on any source (relational, XML, file system), from anywhere using a variety of languages (ASP.NET, PHP, Java) via a platform of any size (mobile to enterprise), has become a necessity in modern business operations. The Open Data Protocol, (OData) an emerging standard for querying data (and updating) over the Web, will assume a central role.

In relation to this, Microsoft has made available OData service on its SQL Azure Labs (a developer preview) portal for accessing data on SQL Azure over the Web. This service is REST-based. In this section, data on a SQL Azure database will be accessed using this service. You need to have a SQL Azure account to work with this section.

- Browse to the portal using this URL: `https://www.sqlazurelabs.com/`.

- The portal will open as shown in the following image:

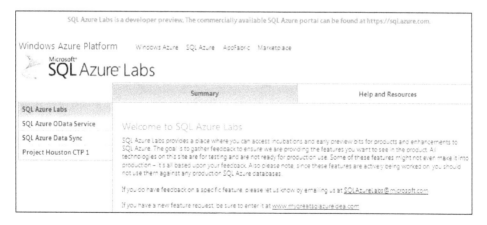

- Click **SQL Azure OData Service**.
- You may need to sign-in to your Windows Live ID account.
- Once you do that the portal opens as shown in the next screenshot:

- The **Server Name** and the **User Name** are already recognized. It is also possible to create a new server (not explored here).
- Enter password and click **Connect**.
- You get connected to the database and the service end point, shown at the bottom, is displayed as shown in the following screenshot:

Summary	Help and Resources

The Open Data Protocol (OData) is an emerging standard for querying and updating data over the Web. OData is a REST-based protocol whose core focus is to maximize the interoperability between data services and clients that wish to access that data. It is thus being used to expose data from a variety of sources, from relational databases and file systems to content management systems and traditional websites. In addition, clients across many platforms, ranging from ASP.NET, PHP, and Java websites to Microsoft Excel and applications on mobile devices, are finding it easy to access those vast data stores through OData as well.

Full information about OData can be found on its dedicated website www.odata.org

Configure OData Service

Connection Information

Server Name: ▓ ▓ ▓ ▓.database.windows.net   Create a New Server

User Name: mysorian

Password: [   ] Disconnect

Database Information

Database: Bluesky ▼

Enable OData ☑

User Mapping

The OData interface to SQL Azure allows you to map both specific users to ACS access keys or to allow anonymous access through a single SQL Azure user. Whichever options you chose, please keep in mind that the interface will impersonate the SQL Azure user you choose. Please ensure you configure these user's security access accordingly.

Anonymous Access User: dbo ▼

+ Add User

https://odata.sqlazurelabs.com/OData.svc/v0.1/▓▓▓▓/Bluesky

- Here, you can change the database (we have just one database `Bluesky`), as well as enable/disable data. If you have setup users you can change it as well. Here, the default is anonymous access.

- Click on the URL `https://odata.sqlazurelabs.com/OData.svc/v0.1/<your four part server name>/Bluesky`.

- You will see the data displayed in an ATOM Format as shown in IE 8.0 (some nodes expanded).

```
<?xml version="1.0" encoding="utf-8" standalone="yes" ?>
- <service
    xml:base="https://odata.sqlazurelabs.com/OData.svc/v0.1/hhq0zyfbd8/Bluesky/"
    xmlns:atom="http://www.w3.org/2005/Atom"
    xmlns:app="http://www.w3.org/2007/app"
    xmlns="http://www.w3.org/2007/app">
  - <workspace>
      <atom:title>Default</atom:title>
    - <collection href="MyTables">
        <atom:title>MyTables</atom:title>
      </collection>
    - <collection href="scope_info">                    Bluesky database tables
        <atom:title>scope_info</atom:title>
      </collection>
    + <collection href="fromMysql2">
    + <collection href="scope_config">
    + <collection href="Employees_tracking">
    + <collection href="MasterSlaves">
    + <collection href="Employees">
    + <collection href="from2k8">
    + <collection href="AzureShippers">
    </workspace>
</service>
```

The previous screenshot shows all the tables in the Bluesky database.

Now append /MyTables to the URL on the web page https://odata.sqlazurelabs.com/OData.svc/v0.1/<your four part server name>/Bluesky/MyTables. The web page displays data for only the MyTables, as shown in the following screenshot:

```
<?xml version="1.0" encoding="utf-8" standalone="yes" ?>
- <feed xml:base="https://odata.sqlazurelabs.com/OData.svc/v0.1/hhq0zyfbd8/Bluesky/"
    xmlns:d="http://schemas.microsoft.com/ado/2007/08/dataservices"
    xmlns:m="http://schemas.microsoft.com/ado/2007/08/dataservices/metadata"
    xmlns="http://www.w3.org/2005/Atom">
    <title type="text">MyTables</title>

    <id>https://odata.sqlazurelabs.com/OData.svc/v0.1/hhq0zyfbd8/Bluesky/MyTables/</id>
    <updated>2010-08-06T12:50:41Z</updated>
    <link rel="self" title="MyTables" href="MyTables" />
  - <entry>
      <id>https://odata.sqlazurelabs.com/OData.svc/v0.1/hhq0zyfbd8/Bluesky/MyTables
        (1)</id>
      <title type="text" />
      <updated>2010-08-06T12:50:41Z</updated>
    + <author>
      <link rel="edit" title="MyTable" href="MyTables(1)" />
      <category term="Bluesky.MyTable"
        scheme="http://schemas.microsoft.com/ado/2007/08/dataservices/scheme" />
    - <content type="application/xml">
      - <m:properties>
          <d:FirstName>John</d:FirstName>
          <d:ID m:type="Edm.Int32">1</d:ID>
        </m:properties>
      </content>
    </entry>
  + <entry>
  + <entry>
  </feed>
```

All the columns in the `MyTables` table are displayed.

- To get the FirstName of the first row append to the service URL `MyTables (1)/FirstName`. The display will be as shown in the following screenshot:

```
<?xml version="1.0" encoding="utf-8" standalone="yes" ?>
<FirstName
   xmlns="http://schemas.microsoft.com/ado/2007/08/dataservices">John</FirstName>
```

Follow this link to learn more about OData, OData URI conventions, Operations, and the various supported formats here:

http://www.odata.org/developers/protocols/uri-conventions.

The display is in an ATOM format and if you want to display on a web page you could do it in a number of ways. This is outside the scope of this book. Please refer to other resources such as, http://www.asp.net/ajaxlibrary/Ajax%20 and%20ADO%20NET%20Data%20Services.ashx and for JSON format, http:// www.packtpub.com/article/twitter-newyork-times-api-aspdotnet-ajax- microsoft-cdn.

Consuming SQL Azure data with PowerPivot

PowerPivot with SQL Azure gives an enormous amount of power to SQL Azure. The reason for this, is that PowerPivot can work with massive amounts of data in reasonable time compared to other methods. PowerPivot teaming with SQL Azure is the best way for business intelligence to achieve excellent performance. PowerPivot is an add-in for Excel2010, which means you need to have Excel2010 on your computer. The data that PowerPivot extracts from the database will be stored in a local OLAP database engine in memory, which provides the analytic capability to Excel2010. Call it a combo Excel + Analysis services in one package.

In this short section, we will not look at any of the exotic things you can do with PowerPivot, but show you how easy it is to connect and extract data from SQL Azure. We assume you have Excel2010 (in here a Beta version of *Microsoft Office Professional Plus* is installed). You can explore PowerPivot further at http://www. powerpivot.com/.

When you install PowerPivot (follow this link: `http://hodentek.blogspot.com/2010/05/deliver-knock-out-punch-with-powerpivot.html`) you would be adding a PowerPivot menu item to Excel2010. This is your starting point to connect to SQL Azure.

When you click on the PowerPivot menu item in Excel2010, you will display the PowerPivot toolbar item as shown in the following screenshot:

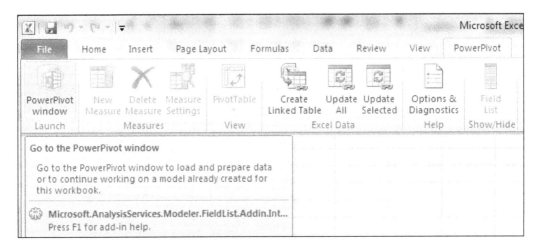

Click the toolbar item **PowerPivot window**. This opens another window as shown in the following screenshot. Make sure your computer has enough resources for this to happen; otherwise it may take considerable time:

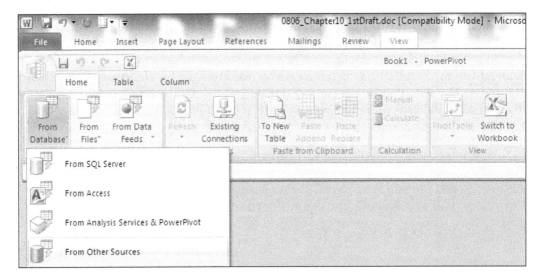

Click on the **From Other Sources** icon, shown in the previous screenshot. The **Table Import Wizard** is displayed as shown in the following screenshot. You can see different sources from which PowerPivot can extract data:

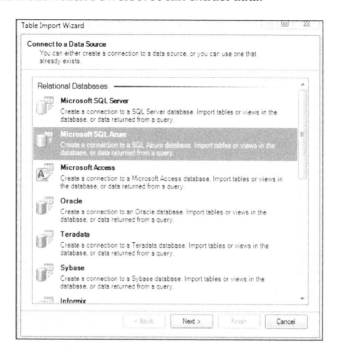

Highlight **Microsoft SQL Azure** and click **Next >**. You then get the **Connect to a Microsoft SQL Azure Database** page of the wizard as shown in the following screenshot:

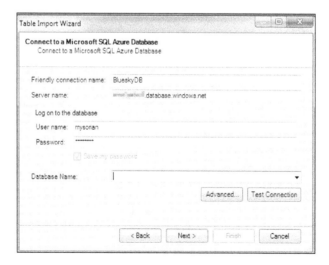

After you enter the required information you can browse for the databases on the server with the drop-down handle. In the present case, two databases Bluesky and master were displayed. You can test the connection.

Click **Next >** and you get a page displayed where you can select table(s) to retrieve data (image not shown).

When you click **Next >** you will see all the tables in the database. Now you can make your selection. Here, only a single table has been selected.

Click **Finish** and you will get a screen, which shows that the operation was successful (image not shown).

When you close the Importing page of the wizard, the imported information will be displayed in the Excel spreadsheet as shown in the next screenshot:

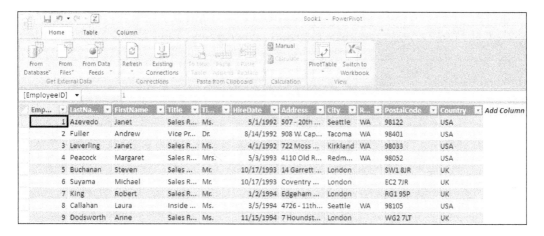

It cannot be any simpler than this, can it? After you retrieve data you can slice it and dice it using the powerful analytic engine with which it is built. This is outside the scope of this section.

SQL Azure with WebMatrix

WebMatrix is a recently released free tool, which is best described by Microsoft as:

> *"Everything you need to build Web sites using Windows. Small, simple, and seamless".*

You can start learning about WebMatrix from this link here (a brief description): `http://hodentek.blogspot.com/2010/07/webmatrix-reloaded.html` and here for a more detailed description and to download the program, which is presently in Beta: `http://www.microsoft.com/web/webmatrix/`.

In this section we look at the connectivity of WebMatrix with SQL Azure. A WebMatrix Web site has content section for site files; support for databases as well as creating reports.

In order to explore connectivity with databases we start off by creating a website such as the one in the following screenshot, which shows some details of this tool:

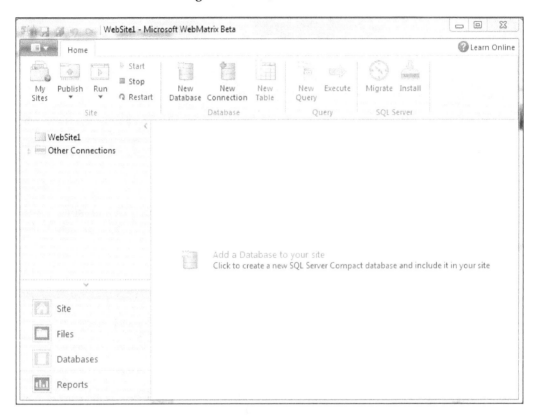

We now add the SQL Azure database to this tool. You need to provide the connection information like you did in other connectivity tools and you can store the password. This tool can also be used for both DDL and DML. Here is the SQL Azure data on this interface:

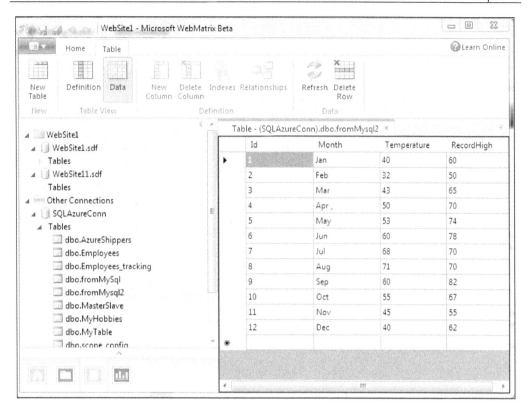

More third-party tools to SQL Azure

Driven by opportunities that may open up, more and more third-party vendors are developing tools for the Azure Platform. Gem Query is one such tool.

Gem Query for SQL Azure developers

Microguru, a third-party vendor has developed another Free SQL Azure development tool named Gem Query. This tool can be downloaded freely from the following URL: `http://www.download3000.com/download-gem-query-for-sql-azure-count-reg-56128.html`. You must install Microsoft .NET Framework 3.5 SP1 to use this tool. This tool supports both DDL and DML SQL queries and you can execute on top of your SQL Azure database. Using this tool you can directly connect with your SQL Azure database; developers don't need to maintain any local databases for synchronization.

Managing SQL Azure databases with the Houston Project (CTP1)

This web-based management tool is supposed to take the pain out of working and managing SQL databases. Details are found here: `http://www.davidaiken.com/2010/07/21/manage-your-sql-azure-databases-with-project-houston/`. The project can be accessed from the SQL Azure Labs portal—`https://www.sqlazurelabs.com/`—we saw earlier, which you can access after signing in with your Windows Live ID. The next screenshot shows the opening page of this project in the SQL Azure Labs portal:

Summary	Help and Resources

Microsoft Project Code-Named "Houston" CTP 1

Microsoft® Project Code-Named "Houston" is a lightweight and easy to use database management tool for SQL Azure databases. It is designed specifically for Web developers and other technology professionals seeking a straightforward solution to quickly develop, deploy, and manage their data-driven applications in the cloud. Project "Houston" provides a web-based database management tool for basic database management tasks like authoring and executing queries, designing and editing a database schema, and editing table data.

This CTP release is deployed to the North Central US data center. For best results, use this tool for managing your databases located in the same data center. Additional data centers will be added in the future.

Documentation for this release is provided at the SQL Azure Team Blog. Documentation for this release includes a description of supported scenarios, links to instructional videos and other project resources, a list of known issues and workarounds, and instructions for providing feedback about this release.

This release of Project "Houston" is not supported by standard Microsoft support services. For community-based support, post a question to the SQL Azure Labs MSDN forums. The product team will do its best to answer any questions posted there.

Launch Houston

The Microsoft® Project Code-Named "Houston" privacy statement can be viewed by clicking here.

You need to enter your server information before you can use this project. Provide all the necessary information on this page shown in the next screenshot (site URL: `https://manage.sqlazurelabs.com/`):

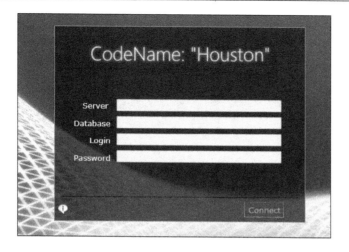

When you click **Connect** after providing the information, you get to this rather nice looking (departure from the bland SSMS) web page shown in the next screenshot. This interface also provides all the necessary hooks to work with SQL Azure Databases:

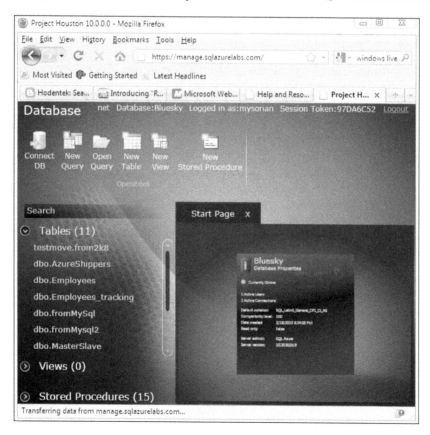

Here is a table Houston Publishers created in this interface. It can be saved (committed) on SQL Azure.

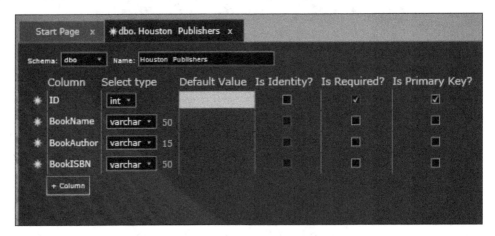

Data Application Component and SQL Azure

A Data Application Component is an entity that integrates all data-tier-related objects used in authoring, deploying, and managing them into a single unit instead of having to work with them separately. Programmatically DACs belong to classes that are found in The Microsoft.SqlServer.Management.Dac namespace. DACs are stored in a DacStore and managed centrally. DACs can be authored and built using SQL Server Data-Tier Application templates in VS2010 (now in Beta 2) or using SQL Server Management Studio. More detailed information using SSMS and VS 2008 or VS2010 may be found in this post: http://hodentekmsss.blogspot.com/2010/07/sql-server-2008-r2-and-data-tier.html.

As explained in the Service updates section of this chapter, data-tier applications are supported in SQL Azure. That means it is possible to extract a data-tier application and deploy to another SQL Azure server.

In this section, a data-tier application is extracted from the Bluesky database in North America and deployed to a SQL Azure server in Southeast Asia. The following screenshot shows the two servers in juxtaposition:

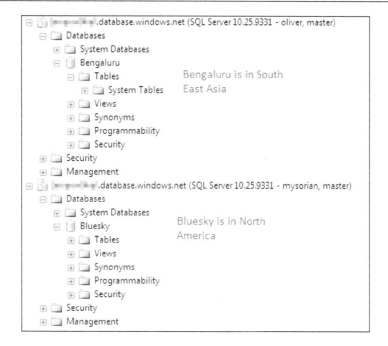

This next screenshot shows how you begin the extraction from the Bluesky database. This is wizard-driven and you just need to follow the steps. Finally, you will be saving a file with the extension datpac to a known location on your local machine:

The deployment to the server in Southeast Asia is shown in the next screenshot. Follow the wizard to complete. During this time, you need to browse and find the saved file from the extraction process:

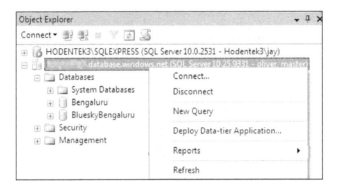

When the process is completed, you will have deployed a new database to the server, which has all the objects of the Bluesky database as shown in the following screenshot:

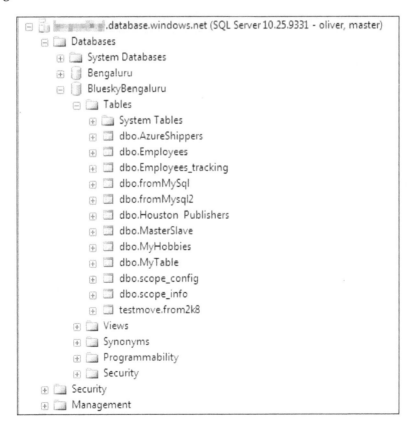

SQL Azure with Microsoft LightSwitch

Microsoft Visual Studio LightSwitch (VSLS) is the most recent Visual Studio suite of products, which provides a fast and easy means to create professional quality line-of-business applications for the three important application genres, desktop, web, and the cloud.

One of the data sources to which Microsoft LightSwitch can connect to out-of-the-box is SQL Azure and it is really very easy to do. Check out the following full-length article to see how you can display data on your SQL Azure with a .NET 4.0 web tool (`http://www.packtpub.com/article/microsoft-lightswitch-application-using-sql-azure-database`).

References

The most important source of information is Microsoft. The following are the most essential links as they provide links to other related sources:

1. `http://www.microsoft.com/windowsazure/`

    This is where you start learning to use Windows Azure. This is where you sign up for the services.

2. `https://accountservices.passport.net/ppnetworkhome.srf?lc=1033&mkt=EN-US`

    This is the place to sign up for Windows Live ID

3. `https://windows.azure.com/Cloud/Provisioning/Default.aspx`

    This is the portal (Gateway) to Windows Azure. You can come here and provision the service after you get your Windows Live ID and create an account to access the services. Don't overlook the 'Help and Resources' tab on this page.

4. The following site has a comprehensive blog on everything related to Windows Azure.

    `http://oakleafblog.blogspot.com/`

5. The SQL Azure Labs site is an incubation site for future Windows Azure Projects

    `http://www.sqlazurelabs.com`

6. References to links in the book.

    The links referenced in the book are collected and arranged in the `BookLinks.doc` available as a download from the Packt site. This makes it easy to read the book and access the links.

Summary

This chapter described a miscellany of topics related to SQL Azure, which made their debut during the time the book was written. Some of the topics discussed did not fit into the focus of the other chapters. Some of the topics such as WebMatrix, the Houston project, and Microsoft LightSwitch are still in their early stages of development, but are sure to impact on the future of SQL Azure while others such as OData Service and PowerPivot may undergo changes. Of the non-Microsoft languages, only Java and PHP are described but one could also use Ruby. The next phase of development may very well include support for OLE DB and the hosting of Reporting Services on the Azure platform.

Index

A

B

C

Thank you for buying
Microsoft SQL Azure: Enterprise
Application Development

About Packt Publishing

Packt, pronounced 'packed', published its first book "Mastering phpMyAdmin for Effective MySQL Management" in April 2004 and subsequently continued to specialize in publishing highly focused books on specific technologies and solutions.

Our books and publications share the experiences of your fellow IT professionals in adapting and customizing today's systems, applications, and frameworks. Our solution based books give you the knowledge and power to customize the software and technologies you're using to get the job done. Packt books are more specific and less general than the IT books you have seen in the past. Our unique business model allows us to bring you more focused information, giving you more of what you need to know, and less of what you don't.

Packt is a modern, yet unique publishing company, which focuses on producing quality, cutting-edge books for communities of developers, administrators, and newbies alike. For more information, please visit our website: www.packtpub.com.

About Packt Enterprise

In 2010, Packt launched two new brands, Packt Enterprise and Packt Open Source, in order to continue its focus on specialization. This book is part of the Packt Enterprise brand, home to books published on enterprise software – software created by major vendors, including (but not limited to) IBM, Microsoft and Oracle, often for use in other corporations. Its titles will offer information relevant to a range of users of this software, including administrators, developers, architects, and end users.

Writing for Packt

We welcome all inquiries from people who are interested in authoring. Book proposals should be sent to author@packtpub.com. If your book idea is still at an early stage and you would like to discuss it first before writing a formal book proposal, contact us; one of our commissioning editors will get in touch with you.

We're not just looking for published authors; if you have strong technical skills but no writing experience, our experienced editors can help you develop a writing career, or simply get some additional reward for your expertise.

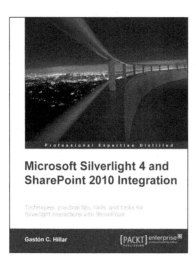

Microsoft Silverlight 4 and SharePoint 2010 Integration

ISBN: 978-1-849680-06-6   Paperback: 336 pages

Techniques, practical tips, hints, and tricks for Silverlight interactions with SharePoint

1. Develop Silverlight RIAs that interact with SharePoint 2010 data and services

2. Explore the diverse alternatives for hosting a Silverlight RIA in a SharePoint 2010 Page

3. Work with the new SharePoint Silverlight Client Object Model to interact with elements in a SharePoint Site

4. Access and interact with external data sources and WCF Data Services

Microsoft Silverlight 4 Data and Services Cookbook

ISBN: 978-1-847199-84-3   Paperback: 476 pages

Over 80 practical recipes for creating rich, data-driven business applications in Silverlight

1. Design and develop rich data-driven business applications in Silverlight

2. Rapidly interact with and handle multiple sources of data and services within Silverlight business applications

3. Packed with practical, hands-on cookbook recipes, illustrating the techniques to solve particular data problems effectively within your Silverlight business applications

Please check **www.PacktPub.com** for information on our titles

Learning SQL Server 2008 Reporting Services

ISBN: 978-1-847196-18-7   Paperback: 512 pages

A step-by-step guide to getting the most of Microsoft SQL Server Reporting Services 2008

1. Everything you need to create and deliver data-rich reports with SQL Server 2008 Reporting Services as quickly as possible

2. Packed with hands-on-examples to learn and improve your skills

3. Connect and report from databases, spreadsheets, XML Data, and more

4. No experience of SQL Server Reporting Services required

Entity Framework Tutorial

ISBN: 978-1-847195-22-7   Paperback: 228 pages

Learn to build a better data access layer with the ADO.NET Entity Framework and ADO.NET Data Services

1. Clear and concise guide to the ADO.NET Entity Framework with plentiful code examples

2. Create Entity Data Models from your database and use them in your applications

3. Learn about the Entity Client data provider and create statements in Entity SQL

4. Learn about ADO.NET Data Services and how they work with the Entity Framework

Please check **www.PacktPub.com** for information on our titles